D0913486

ISBN: 978129003514

Published by:
HardPress Publishing
8345 NW 66TH ST #2561
MIAMI FL 33166-2626

Email: info@hardpress.net
Web: http://www.hardpress.net

Mrs Frank Dinkelspiel
1425 East South Temple
Salt Lake City, Utah
Hyland 6286 -
So.

Isabelle Brisacher
Fillmore 9908

PLUM BUN

PLUM BUN

JESSIE REDMON FAUSET

(*Author of* "THERE IS CONFUSION")

"*To Market, to Market
To buy a Plum Bun;
Home again, Home again,
Market is done.*"

NEW YORK
FREDERICK A. STOKES COMPANY
PUBLISHERS

MADE AND PRINTED IN GREAT BRITAIN BY PURNELL AND SONS
PAULTON (SOMERSET) AND LONDON

To

MY FATHER AND MOTHER

REDMON AND ANNA FAUSET

PLUM BUN

A Novel Without a Moral

CONTENTS

	PAGE
HOME	9
MARKET	85
PLUM BUN	175
HOME AGAIN	239
MARKET IS DONE	331

HOME

CHAPTER I

OPAL STREET, as streets go, is no jewel of the first
water. It is merely an imitation, and none too
good at that. Narrow, unsparkling, uninviting, it
stretches meekly off from dull Jefferson Street to the
dingy, drab market which forms the north side of
Oxford Street. It has no mystery, no allure, either
of exclusiveness or of downright depravity; its usages
are plainly significant,—an unpretentious little street
lined with unpretentious little houses, inhabited for
the most part by unpretentious little people.

The dwellings are three stories high, and contain
six boxes called by courtesy, rooms—a "parlour",
a midget of a dining-room, a larger kitchen and,
above, a front bedroom seemingly large only because
it extends for the full width of the house, a mere
shadow of a bathroom, and another back bedroom
with windows whose possibilities are spoiled by their
outlook on sad and diminutive back-yards. And
above these two, still two others built in similar wise.

In one of these houses dwelt a father, a mother
and two daughters. Here, as often happens in a
home sheltering two generations, opposite, unevenly matched emotions faced each other. In
the houses of the rich the satisfied ambition of the
older generation is faced by the overwhelming ambition of the younger. Or the elders may find
themselves brought in opposition to the blank

indifference and ennui of youth engendered by the realization that there remain no more worlds to conquer; their fathers having already taken all. In houses on Opal Street these niceties of distinction are hardly to be found; there is a more direct and concrete contrast. The satisfied ambition of maturity is a foil for the restless despair of youth.
, Affairs in the Murray household were advancing towards this stage; yet not a soul in that family of four could have foretold its coming. To Junius and Mattie Murray, who had known poverty and homelessness, the little house on Opal Street represented the *ne plus ultra* of ambition; to their daughter Angela it seemed the dingiest, drabbest chrysalis that had ever fettered the wings of a brilliant butterfly. The stories which Junius and Mattie told of difficulties overcome, of the arduous learning of trades, of the pitiful scraping together of infinitesimal savings, would have made a latter-day Iliad, but to Angela they were merely a description of a life which she at any cost would avoid living. Somewhere in the world were paths which lead to broad thoroughfares, large, bright houses, delicate niceties of existence. Those paths Angela meant to find and frequent. At a very early age she had observed that the good things of life are unevenly distributed; merit is not always rewarded; hard labour does not necessarily entail adequate recompense. Certain fortuitous endowments, great physical beauty, unusual strength, a certain unswerving singleness of mind,—gifts bestowed quite blindly and disproportionately by the forces which control life,—these were the qualities which contributed toward a glowing and pleasant existence.

Angela had no high purpose in life; unlike her sister Virginia, who meant some day to invent a marvellous method for teaching the pianoforte, Angela felt no impulse to discover, or to perfect. True she thought she might become eventually a distinguished painter, but that was because she felt within herself an ability to depict which as far as it went was correct and promising. Her eye for line and for expression was already good and she had a nice feeling for colour. Moreover she possessed the instinct for self-appraisal which taught her that she had much to learn. And she was sure that the knowledge once gained would flower in her case to perfection. But her gift was not for her the end of existence; rather it was an adjunct to a life which was to know light, pleasure, gaiety and freedom.

Freedom! That was the note which Angela heard oftenest in the melody of living which was to be hers. With a wildness that fell just short of unreasonableness she hated restraint. Her father's earlier days as coachman in a private family, his later successful, independent years as boss carpenter, her mother's youth spent as maid to a famous actress, all this was to Angela a manifestation of the sort of thing which happens to those enchained it might be by duty, by poverty, by weakness or by colour.

Colour or rather the lack of it seemed to the child the one absolute prerequisite to the life of which she was always dreaming. One might break loose from a too hampering sense of duty; poverty could be overcome; physicians conquered weakness; but colour, the mere possession of a black or a white skin, that was clearly one of those fortuitous endowments of the gods. Gratitude was no strong ingredient in this girl's nature, yet very often early she began thanking Fate for the chance which in that household of four had bestowed on her the heritage of her mother's fair skin. She might so easily have been, like her father, black, or have received the melange which had resulted in Virginia's rosy bronzeness and her deeply waving black hair. But Angela had received not only her mother's creamy complexion and her soft cloudy, chestnut hair, but she had taken from Junius the aquiline nose, the gift of some remote Indian ancestor which gave to his face and his eldest daughter's that touch of chiselled immobility.

.   .   .   .   .

It was from her mother that Angela learned the possibilities for joy and freedom which seemed to her inherent in mere whiteness. No one would have been more amazed than that same mother if she could have guessed how her daughter interpreted her actions. Certainly Mrs. Murray did not attribute what she considered her happy, busy, sheltered life on tiny Opal Street to the accident of her colour; she attributed it to her black husband whom she had been glad and proud to marry. It is equally certain that that white skin of hers had not saved her from occasional contumely and insult. The famous actress for whom she had worked was aware of Mattie's mixed blood and, boasting temperament rather than refinement, had often dubbed her " white nigger ".

Angela's mother employed her colour very much as she practised certain winning usages of smile and voice to obtain indulgences which meant much to her and which took nothing from anyone else. Then, too, she was possessed of a keener sense of humour than her daughter; it amused her when by herself to take lunch at an exclusive restaurant whose patrons would have been panic-stricken if they had divined the presence of a " coloured " woman no matter how little her appearance differed from theirs. It was with no idea of disclaiming her own that she sat in orchestra seats which Philadelphia denied to coloured patrons. But when Junius or indeed any other dark friend accompanied her she was the first to announce that she liked to sit in the balcony or gallery, as indeed she did; her infrequent occupation of orchestra seats was due merely to a mischievous determination to flout a silly and unjust law.

Her years with the actress had left their mark, a perfectly harmless and rather charming one. At least so it seemed to Junius, whose weakness was for the qualities known as " essentially feminine ". Mrs. Murray loved pretty clothes, she liked shops devoted to the service of women; she enjoyed being even on the fringe of a fashionable gathering. A satisfaction that was almost ecstatic seized her when she drank tea in the midst of modishly gowned women in a stylish tea-room. It pleased her to stand in the foyer of a great hotel or of the Academy of Music and to be part of the whirling, humming, palpitating gaiety. She had no desire to be of these people, but she liked to look on; it amused and thrilled and kept alive some unquenchable instinct for life which thrived within her. To walk through Wanamaker's on Saturday, to stroll from Fifteenth to Ninth Street on Chestnut, to have her tea in the Bellevue Stratford, to stand in the lobby of the St. James' fitting on immaculate gloves; all innocent, childish pleasures pursued without malice or envy contrived to cast a glamour over Monday's washing and Tuesday's ironing, the scrubbing of kitchen and bathroom and the fashioning of children's clothes. She was endowed with a humorous and pungent method of presentation; Junius, who had had the wit not to interfere with these little excursions and the sympathy to take them at their face value, preferred one of his wife's sparkling accounts of a Saturday's adventure in " passing " to all the tall stories told by cronies at his lodge.

Much of this pleasure, harmless and charming though it was, would have been impossible with a dark skin.

In these first years of marriage, Mattie, busied with the house and the two babies had given up those excursions. Later, when the children had grown and Junius had reached the stage where he could afford to give himself a half-holiday on Saturdays, the two parents inaugurated a plan of action which eventually became a fixed programme. Each took a child, and Junius went off to a beloved but long since suspended pastime of exploring old Philadelphia, whereas Mattie embarked once more on her social adventures. It is true that Mattie accompanied by brown Virginia could not move quite as freely as when with Angela. But her maternal instincts were sound; her children, their feelings and their faith in her meant much more than the pleasure which she would have been first to call unnecessary and silly. As it happened the children themselves quite unconsciously solved the dilemma; Virginia found shopping tiring and stupid, Angela returned from her father's adventuring worn and bored. Gradually the rule was formed that Angela accompanied her mother and Virginia her father.

.   .   .   .   .

On such fortuities does life depend. Little Angela Murray, hurrying through Saturday morning's scrubbing of steps in order that she might have her bath at one and be with her mother on Chestnut Street at two, never realized that her mother took her pleasure among all these pale people because it was there that she happened to find it. It never occurred to her that the delight which her mother obviously showed in meeting friends on Sunday morning when the whole united Murray family came out of church was the same as she showed on Chestnut Street the previous Saturday, because she was finding the qualities which her heart craved, bustle, excitement and fashion. The daughter could not guess that if the economic status or the racial genius of coloured people had permitted them to run modish hotels or vast and popular department stores her mother would have been there. She drew for herself certain clearly formed conclusions which her subconscious mind thus codified:

First, that the great rewards of life—riches, glamour, pleasure,—are for white-skinned people only. Secondly, that Junius and Virginia were denied these privileges because they were dark; here her reasoning bore at least an element of verisimilitude but she missed the essential fact that her father and sister did not care for this type of pleasure. The effect of her fallaciousness was to cause her to feel a faint pity for her unfortunate relatives and also to feel that coloured people were to be considered fortunate only in the proportion in which they measured up to the physical standards of white people.

One Saturday excursion left a far-reaching impression. Mrs. Murray and Angela had spent a successful and interesting afternoon. They had browsed among the contents of the small exclusive shops in Walnut Street; they had had soda at Adams' on Broad Street and they were standing finally in the portico of the Walton Hotel deciding with fashionable and idle elegance what they should do next. A thin stream of people constantly passing threw an occasional glance at the quietly modish pair, the well-dressed, assured woman and the refined and no less assured daughter. The door-man knew them; it was one of Mrs. Murray's pleasures to proffer him a small tip, much appreciated since it was uncalled for. This was the atmosphere which she loved. Angela had put on her gloves and was waiting for her mother, who was drawing on her own with great care, when she glimpsed in the laughing, hurrying Saturday throng the figures of her father and of Virginia. They were close enough for her mother, who saw them too, to touch them by merely descending a few steps and stretching out her arm. In a second the pair had vanished. Angela saw her mother's face change—with trepidation she thought. She remarked: " It's a good thing Papa didn't see us, you'd have had to speak to him, wouldn't you? " But her mother, giving her a distracted glance, made no reply.

That night, after the girls were in bed, Mattie, perched on the arm of her husband's chair, told him about it. "I was 'at my old game of play-acting again to-day, June, passing you know, and darling, you and Virginia went by within arm's reach and we never spoke to you. I'm so ashamed."

But Junius consoled her. Long before their marriage he had known of his Mattie's weakness and its essential harmlessness. "My dear girl, I told you long ago that where no principle was involved, your passing means nothing to me. It's just a little joke; I don't think you'd be ashamed to acknowledge your old husband anywhere if it were necessary."

"I'd do that if people were mistaking me for a queen," she assured him fondly. But she was silent, not quite satisfied. "After all," she said with her charming frankness, "it isn't you, dear, who make me feel guilty. I really am ashamed to think that I let Virginia pass by without a word. I think I should feel very badly if she were to know it. I don't believe I'll ever let myself be quite as silly as that again."

But of this determination Angela, dreaming excitedly of Saturdays spent in turning her small olive face firmly away from peering black countenances was, unhappily, unaware.

` CHAPTER II

SATURDAY came to be the day of the week for Angela, but her sister Virginia preferred Sundays. She loved the atmosphere of golden sanctity which seemed to hover with a sweet glory about the stodgy, shabby little dwelling. Usually she came downstairs first so as to enjoy by herself the blessed "Sunday feeling" which, she used to declare, would have made it possible for her to recognize the day if she had awakened to it even in China. She was only twelve at this time, yet she had already developed a singular aptitude and liking for the care of the home, and this her mother gratefully fostered. Gradually the custom was formed of turning over to her small hands all the duties of Sunday morning; they were to her a ritual. First the kettle must be started boiling, then the pavement swept. Her father's paper must be carried up and left outside his door. Virginia found a nameless and sweet satisfaction in performing these services.

She prepared the Sunday breakfast which was always the same,—bacon and eggs, strong coffee with good cream for Junius, chocolate for the other three and muffins. After the kettle had boiled and the muffins were mixed it took exactly half an hour to complete preparations. Virginia always went about these matters in the same way. She set the muffins in the oven, pursing her lips and frowning a little just as she had seen her mother do; then she went to the foot of the narrow, enclosed staircase and called " hoo-hoo " with a soft rising inflection, —" last call to dinner," her father termed it. And finally, just for those last few minutes before the family descended she went into the box of a parlour and played hymns, old-fashioned and stately tunes, —" How firm a foundation ", " The spacious firmament on high ", " Am I a soldier of the Cross ". . Her father's inflexible bass, booming down the stairs, her mother's faint alto in thirds mingled with her own sweet treble; a shaft of sunlight, faint and watery in winter, strong and golden in summer, shimmering through the room in the morning dusk completed for the little girl a sensation of happiness which lay perilously near tears.

.   .   .   .   .

After breakfast came the bustle of preparing for church. Junius of course had come down in complete readiness; but the others must change their dresses; Virginia had mislaid her Sunday hair-ribbon again; Angela had discovered a rip in her best gloves and could not be induced to go down until it had been mended. " Wait for me just a minute, Jinny dear, I can't go out looking like this, can I? " She did not like going to church, at least not to their church, but she did care about her appearance and she liked the luxuriousness of being " dressed up " on two successive days. At last the little procession filed out, Mattie hoping that they would not be late, she did hate it so; Angela thinking that this was a stupid way to spend

Sunday and wondering at just what period of
one's life existence began to shape itself as *you*
wanted it. Her father's thoughts were inchoate;
expressed they would have revealed a patriarchal
aspect almost biblical. He had been a poor boy,
homeless, a nobody, yet somehow he had contrived
in his mid-forties to attain to the status of a respectable citizen, house-owner, a good provider. He
possessed a charming wife and two fine daughters,
and as was befitting he was accompanying them to
the house of the Lord. As for Virginia, no one
to see her in her little red hat and her mother's
cut-over blue coat could have divined how near
she was to bursting with happiness. Father,
mother and children, well-dressed, well-fed, united,
going to church on a beautiful Sunday morning;
there was an immense cosmic rightness about all
this which she sensed rather than realized. She
envied no one the incident of finer clothes or a
larger home; this unity was the core of happiness,
all other satisfactions must radiate from this one;
greater happiness could be only a·matter of degree
but never of essence. When she grew up she
meant to live the same kind of life; she would
marry a man exactly like her father and she would
conduct her home exactly as did her mother.
Only she would pray very hard every day for five
children, two boys and two girls and then a last
little one,—it was hard for her to decide whether
this should be a boy or a girl,—which should stay
small for a long, long time. And on Sundays they
would all go to church.

Intent on her dreaming she rarely heard the
sermon. It was different with the hymns, for they
constituted the main part of the service for her

father, and she meant to play them again for him later in the happy, golden afternoon or the grey dusk of early evening. But first there were acquaintances to greet, friends of her parents who called them by their first names and who, in speaking of Virginia and Angela still said: " And these are the babies; my, how they grow! It doesn't seem as though it could be you, Mattie Ford, grown up and with children! "

On Communion Sundays the service was very late, and Angela would grow restless and twist about in her seat, but the younger girl loved the sudden, mystic hush which seemed to descend on the congregation. Her mother's sweetly merry face took on a certain childish solemnity, her father's stern profile softened into beatific expectancy. In the exquisite diction of the sacramental service there were certain words, certain phrases that almost made the child faint; the minister had a faint burr in his voice and somehow this lent a peculiar underlying resonance. to his intonation; he half spoke, half chanted and when, picking up the wafer he began " For in the night " and then broke it, Virginia could have cried out with the ecstasy which filled her. She felt that those who partook of the bread and wine were somehow transfigured; her mother and father wore an expression of ineffable content as they returned to their seats and there was one woman, a middle-aged, mischief-making person, who returned from taking the sacrament, walking down the aisle, her hands clasped loosely in front of her and her face so absolutely uplifted that Virginia used to hasten to get within earshot of her after the church was dismissed, sure that her first words must savour of something mystic

and holy. But her assumption proved always to
be ill-founded.

.   .   .   .   .

The afternoon and the evening repeated the
morning's charm but in a different key.   Usually
a few acquaintances dropped in; the parlour and
dining-room were full for an hour or more of
pleasant, harmless chatter. Mr. Henson, the
policeman, a tall, yellow man with freckles on his
nose and red " bad hair " would clap Mr. Murray
on the back and exclaim " I tell you what, June,"
—which always seemed to Virginia a remarkably
daring way in which to address her tall, dignified
father.   Matthew Henson, a boy of sixteen, would
inevitably be hovering about Angela who found
him insufferably boresome and made no effort
to hide her ennui.   Mrs. Murray passed around
rather hard cookies and delicious currant wine,
talking stitches and patterns meanwhile with two
or three friends of her youth with a frequent injec-
tion of " Mame, do you remember! "
Presently the house, emptied of all but the
family, grew still again, dusk and the lamp light
across the street alternately panelling the walls.
Mrs. Murray murmured something about fixing
a bite to eat, " I'll leave it in the kitchen if anybody wants it ".   Angela reflected aloud that she
had still to get her Algebra or History or French
as the case might be, but nobody moved.   What
they were really waiting for was for Virginia to
start to play and finally she would cross the narrow
absurdity of a room and stretching out her slim,
brown hands would begin her version, a glorified
one, of the hymns which they had sung in church

that morning, and then the old favourites which she had played before breakfast. Even Angela, somewhat remote and difficult at first, fell into this evening mood and asked for a special tune or a repetition: " I like the way you play that, Jinny ". For an hour or more they were as close and united as it is possible for a family to be.

At eight o'clock or thereabouts Junius said exactly as though it had not been in his thoughts all evening: " Play the ' Dying Christian ', daughter ". And Virginia, her treble sounding very childish and shrill against her father's deep, unyielding bass, began Pope's masterpiece on the death of a true believer. The magnificently solemn words: " Vital spark of heavenly flame ", the strangely appropriate minor music filled the little house with an awesome beauty which was almost palpable. It affected Angela so that in sheer self-defence she would go out in the kitchen and eat her share of the cold supper set by her mother. But Mattie, although she never sang this piece, remained while her husband and daughter sang on. Death triumphant and mighty had no fears for her. It was inevitable, she knew, but she would never have to face it alone. When her husband died, she would die too, she was sure of it; and if death came to her first it would be only a little while before Junius would be there stretching out his hand and guiding her through all the rough, strange places just as years ago, when he had been a coachman to the actress for whom she worked, he had stretched out his good, honest hand and had saved her from a dangerous and equivocal position. She wiped away happy and grateful tears.

"The world recedes, it disappears," sang Virginia. But it made no difference how far it drifted away as long as the four of them were together; and they would always be together, her father and mother and she and Angela. With her visual mind she saw them proceeding endlessly through space; there were her parents, arm in arm, and she and—but to-night and other nights she could not see Angela; it grieved her to lose sight thus of her sister, she knew she must be there, but grope as she might she could not find her. And then quite suddenly Angela was there again, but a different Angela, not quite the same as in the beginning of the picture.

And suddenly she realized that she was doing four things at once and each of them with all the intentness which she could muster; she was singing, she was playing, she was searching for Angela and she was grieving because Angela as she knew her was lost forever.

"Oh Death, oh Death, where is thy sting!" the hymn ended triumphantly,—she and the piano as usual came out a little ahead of Junius which was always funny. She said, "Where's Angela?" and knew what the answer would be. "I'm tired, mummy! I guess I'll go to bed."

"You ought to, you got up so early and you've been going all day."

Kissing her parents good-night she mounted the stairs languidly, her whole being pervaded with the fervid yet delicate rapture of the day.

CHAPTER III

MONDAY morning brought the return of the busy, happy week.' It meant wash-day for Mattie, for she and Junius had never been able to raise their ménage to the status either of a maid or of putting out the wash. But this lack meant nothing to her,—she had been married fifteen years and still had the ability to enjoy the satisfaction of having a home in which she had full sway instead of being at the beck and call of others. She was old enough to remember a day when poverty for a coloured girl connoted one of three things: going out to service, working as ladies' maid, or taking a genteel but poorly paid position as seamstress with one of the families of the rich and great on Rittenhouse Square, out West Walnut Street or in one of the numerous impeccable, aristocratic suburbs of Philadelphia.

She had tried her hand at all three of these possibilities, had known what it meant to rise at five o'clock, start the laundry work for a patronizing indifferent family of people who spoke of her in her hearing as " the girl " or remarked of her in a slightly lower but still audible tone as being rather better than the usual run of niggers,—" She never steals, I'd trust her with anything and she isn't what you'd call lazy either." For this family she had prepared breakfast, gone back to her washing, served lunch, had taken down the clothes, sprinkled and folded them, had gone upstairs and made three beds, not including her own and then had returned to the kitchen to prepare dinner. At night she nodded over the dishes and finally stumbling up to the third floor fell into her unmade bed, sometimes not even fully, undressed. And Tuesday morning she would begin on the long and tedious strain of ironing. For this she received four dollars a week with the privilege of every other Sunday and every Thursday off. But she could have no callers.

As a seamstress, life had been a little more endurable but more precarious. The wages were better while they lasted, she had a small but comfortable room; her meals were brought up to her on a tray and the young girls of the households in which she was employed treated her with a careless kindness which while it still had its element of patronage was not offensive. But such families had a disconcerting habit of closing their households and departing for months at a time, and there was Mattie stranded and perilously trying to make ends meet by taking in sewing. But her clientèle was composed of girls as poor as she, who either did their own dressmaking or could afford to pay only the merest trifle for her really exquisite and meticulous work.

.   .   .   .   .

The situation with the actress had really been the best in many, in almost all, respects. But it presented its pitfalls. Mattie was young, pretty and innocent; the actress was young, beautiful and sophisticated. She had been married twice and had been the heroine of many affairs; maidenly modesty, virtue for its own sake, were qualities long since forgotten; high ideals and personal self-respect were too abstract for her slightly coarsened mind to visualize, and at any rate they were incomprehensible and even absurd in a servant, and in a coloured servant to boot. She knew that in spite of Mattie's white skin there was black blood in her veins; in fact she would not have taken the girl on had she not been coloured; all her servants must be coloured, for hers was a carelessly conducted household, and she felt dimly that all coloured people are thickly streaked with immorality. They were naturally loose, she reasoned, when she thought about it at all. " Look at the number of mixed bloods among them; look at Mattie herself for that matter, a perfectly white nigger if ever there was one. I'll bet her mother wasn't any better than she should be."

When the girl had come to her with tears in her eyes and begged her not to send her as messenger to the house of a certain Haynes Brokinaw, politician and well-known man about town, Madame had laughed out loud. " How ridiculous! He'll treat you all right. I should like to know what a girl like you expects. And anyway, if I don't care, why should you? Now run along with the note and don't bother me about this again. I hire you to do what I want, not to do as you want." She was not even jealous,— of a coloured working girl! And anyway, constancy was no virtue in her eyes; she did not possess it herself and she valued it little in others.

Mattie was in despair. She was receiving twenty-five dollars a month, her board, and a comfortable, pleasant room. She was seeing something of the world and learning of its amenities. It was during this period that she learned how very pleasant indeed life could be for a person possessing only a very little extra money and a white skin. But the special attraction which her present position held for her was that every day she had a certain amount of time to call her own, for she was Madame's personal servant; in no wise was she connected with the routine of keeping the house. If Madame elected to spend the whole day away from home, Mattie, once she had arranged for the evening toilette, was free to act and to go where she pleased.

And now here was this impasse looming up with Brokinaw. More than once Mattie had felt his covetous eyes on her; she had dreaded going to his rooms from the very beginning. She had even told his butler, " I'll be back in half an hour for the answer "; and she would not wait in the great square hall as he had indicated for there she was sure that danger lurked. But the third time Brokinaw was standing in the hall. " Just come into my study," he told her, " while I read this and write the answer." And he had looked at her with his cold, green eyes and had asked her why she was so out of breath. " There's no need to rush so, child; stay here and rest. I'm in no hurry, I assure you. Are you really coloured? You know, I've seen lots of white girls not as pretty as you. Sit here and tell me all about your mother,—and your father. Do—do you

30

remember him? " His whole bearing reeked with intention.

Within a week Madame was sending her again and she had suggested fearfully the new coach-man. " No," said Madame. " It's Wednesday, his night off, and I wouldn't send him anyway; coachmen are too hard to keep nowadays ; you're all getting so independent." Mattie had come down from her room and walked slowly, slowly to the corner where the new coachman, tall and black and grave, was just hailing a car. She ran to him and jerked down the arm which he had just lifted to seize the railing. " Oh, Mr. Murray," she stammered. He had been so astonished and so kind. Her halting explanation done, he took the note in silence and delivered it, and the next night and for many nights thereafter they walked through the silent, beautiful square, and Junius had told her haltingly and with fear that he loved her. She threw her arms about his neck: " And I love you too."

" You don't mind my being so dark then? Lots of coloured girls I know wouldn't look at a black man."

But it was partly on account of his colour that she loved him; in her eyes his colour meant safety. " Why should I mind? " she asked with one of her rare outbursts of bitterness, " my own colour has never brought me anything but insult and trouble."

The other servants, it appeared, had told him that sometimes she—he hesitated—" passed ".

" Yes, yes, of course I do," she explained it eagerly, " but never to them. And anyway when I am alone what can I do? I can't label myself.

(

And if I'm hungry or tired and I'm near a place where they don't want coloured people, why should I observe their silly old rules, rules that are unnatural and unjust,—because the world was made for everybody, wasn't it, Junius? "

She had told him then how hard and joyless her girlhood life had been,—she had known such dreadful poverty and she had been hard put to it to keep herself together. But since she had come to live with Madame Sylvio she had glimpsed, thanks to her mistress's careless kindness, something of the life of comparative ease and beauty and refinement which one could easily taste if he possessed just a modicum of extra money and the prerequisite of a white skin.

" I've only done it for fun but I won't do it any more if it displeases you. I'd much rather live in the smallest house in the world with you, Junius, than be wandering around as I have so often, lonely and unknown in hotels and restaurants." Her sweetness disarmed him. There was no reason in the world why she should give up her harmless pleasure unless, he added rather sternly, some genuine principle were involved.

It was the happiest moment of her life when Junius had gone to Madame and told her that both he and Mattie were leaving. " We are going to be married," he announced proudly. The actress had been sorry to lose her, and wanted to give her a hundred dollars, but the tall, black coachman would not let his wife accept it. " She is to have only what she earned," he said in stern refusal. He hated Madame Sylvio for having thrown the girl in the way of Haynes Brokinaw.

They had married and gone straight into the little house on Opal Street which later was to become their own. Mattie her husband considered a perfect woman, sweet, industrious, affectionate and illogical. But to her he was God.

When Angela and Virginia were little children and their mother used to read them fairy tales she would add to the ending, " And so they lived happily ever after, just like your father and me."

All this was passing happily through her mind on this Monday morning. Junius was working somewhere in the neighbourhood; his shop was down on Bainbridge Street, but he tried to devote Mondays and Tuesdays to work up town so that he could run in and help Mattie on these trying days. Before the advent of the washing machine he used to dart in and out two or three times in the course of a morning to lend a hand to the heavy sheets and the bed-spreads. Now those articles were taken care of in the laundry, but Junius still kept up the pleasant fiction.

Virginia attended school just around the corner, and presently she would come in too, not so much to get her own lunch as to prepare it for her mother. She possessed her father's attitude toward Mattie as someone who must be helped, indulged and protected. Moreover she had an unusually keen sense of gratitude toward her father and mother for their kindness and their unselfish ambitions for their children. Jinny never tired of hearing of the difficult childhood of her parents. She knew of no story quite so thrilling as the account of their early trials and difficulties. She thought it wonderfully sweet of them to plan, as they constantly did, better things for their daughters.

"My girls shall never come through my experiences," Mattie would say firmly. They were both to be school-teachers and independent.

It is true that neither of them felt any special leaning toward this calling. Angela frankly despised it, but she supposed she must make her living some way. The salary was fairly good— in fact, very good for a poor girl—and there would be the long summer vacation. At fourteen she knew already how much money she would save during those first two or three years and how she would spend those summer vacations. But although she proffered this much information to her family she kept her plans to herself. Mattie often pondered on this lack of openness in her older daughter. Virginia was absolutely transparent. She did not think she would care for teaching either, that is, not for teaching in the ordinary sense. But she realized that for the present that was the best profession which her parents could have chosen for them. She would spend her summers learning all she could about methods of teaching music.

"And a lot of good it will do you," Angela scoffed. "You know perfectly well that there are no coloured teachers of music in the public schools here in Philadelphia." But Jinny thought it possible that there might be. "When Mamma was coming along there were very few coloured teachers at all, and now it looks as though there'd be plenty of chance for us. And anyway you never know your luck."

By four o'clock the day's work was over and Mattie free to do as she pleased. This was her idle hour. The girls would get dinner, a Monday version of whatever the main course had been the day before. Their mother was on no account to be disturbed or importuned. To-day as usual she sat in the Morris chair in the dining-room, dividing her time between the Sunday paper and the girls' chatter. It was one of her most cherished experiences,—this sense of a day's hard labour far behind her, the happy voices of her girls, her joyous expectation of her husband's home-coming. Usually the children made a game of their preparations, recalling some nonsénse of their early childhood days when it had been their delight to dress up as ladies. Virginia would approach Angela: " Pardon me, is this Mrs. Henrietta Jones? " And Angela, drawing herself up haughtily would reply: " Er,—really you have the advantage of me." Then Virginia: " Oh pardon! I thought you were Mrs. Jones and I had heard my friend Mrs. Smith speak of you so often and since you were in the neighbourhood and passing, I was going to ask you in to have some ice-cream ". The game of course being that Angela should immediately drop her haughtiness and proceed for the sake of the goodies to ingratiate herself into her neighbour's esteem. It was a poor joke, long since worn thin, but the two girls still used the greeting and for some reason it had become part of the Monday ritual of preparing the supper.

But to-night Angela's response lacked spontaneity. She was absorbed and reserved, even a little sulky. Deftly and swiftly she moved about her work, however, and no one who had not attended regularly on those Monday evening preparations could have guessed that there was anything on her mind other than complete absorption in the problem of cutting the bread or garnishing the warmed over roast beef. But Mattie was aware of the quality of brooding in her intense concentration. She had seen it before in her daughter but to-night, though to her practised eye it was more apparent than ever, she could not put her hand on it. Angela's response, if asked what was the matter, would be " Oh, nothing ". It came to her suddenly that her older daughter was growing up; in a couple of months she would be fifteen. Children were often absorbed and moody when they were in their teens, too engaged in finding themselves to care about their effect on others. She must see to it that the girl had plenty of rest; perhaps school had been too strenuous for her to-day; she thought the high school programme very badly arranged, five hours one right after the other were much too long. " Angela, child, I think you'd better not be long out of bed to-night; you look very tired to me."

Angela nodded. But her father came in then and in the little hubbub that arose about his home-coming and the final preparations for supper her listlessness went without further remark.

CHAPTER IV

THE third storey front was Angela's bed-room. She was glad of its loneliness and security to-night, —even if her mother had not suggested her going to bed early she would have sought its shelter immediately after supper. Study for its own sake held no attractions for her; she did not care for any of her subjects really except Drawing and French. And when she was drawing she did not consider that she was studying, it was too naturally a means of self-expression. As for French, she did have to study that with great care, for languages did not come to her with any great readiness, but there was an element of fine lady-ism about the beautiful, logical tongue that made her in accordance with some secret subconscious ambition resolve to make it her own.

The other subjects, History, English, and Physical Geography, were not drudgery, for she had a fair enough mind; but then they were not attractive either, and she was lacking in Virginia's dogged resignation to unwelcome duties. Even when Jinny was a little girl she had been known to say manfully in the face of an uncongenial task: " Well I dotta det it done ". Angela was not like that. But to-night she was concentrating with all her power on her work. During the day she had been badly hurt; she had received a wound whose depth and violence she would not reveal even to her parents,—because, and this only increased the pain, young as she was she knew that there was nothing they could do about it. There was nothing to be done but to get over it. Only she was not developed enough to state this stoicism to herself. She was like a little pet cat that had once formed part of their household; its leg had been badly torn by a passing dog and the poor thing had dragged itself into the house and lain on its cushion patiently, waiting stolidly for this unfamiliar agony to subside. So Angela waited for the hurt in her mind to cease.

But across the history dates on the printed page and through the stately lines of Lycidas she kept seeing Mary Hastings' accusing face, hearing Mary Hastings' accusing voice:

" Coloured! Angela, you never told me that you were coloured ! "

And then her own voice in tragic but proud bewilderment. " Tell you that I was coloured ! Why of course I never told you that I was coloured. Why should I ? "

.   .   .   .   .

She had been so proud of Mary Hastings' friendship. In the dark and tortured spaces of her difficult life it had been a lovely, hidden refuge. It had been an experience so rarely sweet that she had hardly spoken of it even to Virginia. The other girls in her classes had meant nothing to her. At least she had schooled herself to have them mean nothing. Some of them she had known since early childhood; they had lived in her neigh-

bourhood and had gone to the graded schools with
her. They had known that she was coloured, for
they had seen her with Virginia, and sometimes
her tall, black father had come to fetch her home
on a rainy day. There had been pleasant enough
contacts and intimacies; in the quiet of Jefferson
Street they had played " The Farmer in the Dell ",
and " Here come three jolly, jolly sailor-boys ";
dark retreats of the old market had afforded endless
satisfaction for " Hide and Go Seek ". She and
those other children had gone shopping arm in
arm for school supplies, threading their way in and
out of the bustle and confusion that were Columbia
Avenue.

As she grew older many of these intimacies
lessened, in some cases ceased altogether. But
she was never conscious of being left completely
alone; there was always some one with whom to
eat lunch or who was going her way after school.
It was not until she reached the high school that
she began to realize how solitary her life was
becoming. There were no other coloured girls
in her class but there had been only two or three
during her school-life, and if there had been any
she would not necessarily have confined herself
to them; that this might be a good thing to do in
sheer self-defence would hardly have occurred to
her. But this problem did not confront her;
what did confront her was that the very girls
with whom she had grown up were evading
her; when she went to the Assembly none of
them sat next to her unless no other seat were
vacant; little groups toward which she drifted
during lunch, inexplicably dissolved to re-form
in another portion of the room. Sometimes a

girl in this new group threw her a backward glance charged either with a mean amusement or with annoyance.

Angela was proud; she did not need such a hint more than once, but she was bewildered and hurt. She took stories to school to read at recess, or wandered into the drawing laboratory and touched up her designs. Miss Barrington thought her an unusually industrious student.

And then in the middle of the term Mary Hastings had come, a slender, well-bred girl of fifteen. She was rather stupid in her work, in fact she shone in nothing but French and good manners. Undeniably she had an air, and her accent was remarkable. The other pupils, giggling, produced certain uncouth and unheard of sounds, but Mary said in French: " No, I have lent my knife to the brother-in-law of the gardener but here is my cane," quite as though the idiotic phrase were part of an imaginary conversation which she was conducting and appreciating. " She really knows what she's talking about," little Esther Bayliss commented, and added that Mary's family had lost some money and they had had to send her to public school. But it was some time before this knowledge, dispensed by Esther with mysterious yet absolute authenticity, became generally known. Meanwhile Mary was left to her own devices while the class with complete but tacit unanimity " tried her out ". Mary, unaware of this, looked with her near-sighted, slightly supercilious gaze about the room at recess and seeing only one girl, and that girl Angela, who approached in dress, manner and deportment her own rather set ideas, had taken her lunch over to the other pupil's desk and said :

" Come on, let's eat together while you tell me who everybody is."

Angela took the invitation as simply as the other had offered. " That little girl in the purplish dress is Esther Bayliss and the tall one in the thick glasses——"

Mary, sitting with her back to the feeding groups, never troubled to look around. " I don't mean the girls. I expect I'll know them soon enough when I get around to it. I mean the teachers. Do you have to dig for them? " She liked Angela and she showed it plainly and directly. Her home was in some remote fastness of West Philadelphia which she could reach with comparative swiftness by taking the car at Spring Garden Street. Instead she walked half way home with her new friend, up Seventeenth Street as far as Girard Avenue where, after a final exchange of school matters and fare-wells, she took the car, leaving Angela to her happy, satisfied thoughts. And presently she began to know more than happiness and satisfaction, she was knowing the extreme gratification of being the chosen companion of a popular and important girl, for Mary, although not quick at her studies, was a power in everything else. She dressed well, she had plenty of pocket money, she could play the latest marches in the gymnasium, she received a certain indefinable but flattering attention from the teachers, and she could make things " go ". The school paper was moribund and Mary knew how to resuscitate it; she brought in advertisements from her father's business friends; she made her married sisters obtain subscriptions. Without being obtrusive or over-bearing, without conde-scension and without toadying she was the leader of her class. And with it all she stuck to Angela. She accepted popularity because it was thrust upon her, but she was friendly with Angela because the latter suited her.

Angela was happy. She had a friend and the friendship brought her unexpected advantages. She was no longer left out of groups because there could be no class plans without Mary and Mary would remain nowhere for any length of time without Angela. So to save time and argument, and also to avoid offending the regent, Angela was always included. Not that she cared much about this, but she did like Mary; as is the way of a " fidus Achates ", she gave her friendship whole-heartedly. And it was gratifying to be in the midst of things.

.   .   .   .   .

In April the school magazine announced a new departure. Henceforth the editorial staff was to be composed of two representatives from each class ; of these one was to be the chief representative chosen by vote of the class, the other was to be assistant, selected by the chief. The chief representative, said the announcement pompously, would sit in at executive meetings and have a voice in the policy of the paper. The assistant would solicit and collect subscriptions, collect fees, receive and report complaints and in brief, said Esther Bayliss, " do all the dirty work ". But she coveted the position and title for all that.

Angela's class held a brief meeting after school and elected Mary Hastings as representative without a dissenting vote. " No," said Angela holding up a last rather grimy bit of paper. " Here is one for Esther Bayliss." Two or three of the girls giggled; everyone knew that she must have voted for herself; indeed it had been she who had insisted on taking a ballot rather than a vote by acclaim. Mary was already on her feet. She had been sure of the result of the election, would have been astonished indeed had it turned out any other way. " Well, girls," she began in her rather high, refined voice, " I wish to thank you for the—er—confidence you have bestowed, that is, placed in me and I'm sure you all know I'll do my best to keep the old paper going. And while I'm about it I might just as well announce that I'm choosing Angela Murray for my assistant."

There was a moment's silence. The girls who had thought about it at all had known that if Mary were elected, as assuredly she would be, this meant also the election of Angela. And those who had taken no thought saw no reason to object to her appointment. And anyway there was nothing to be done. But Esther Bayliss pushed forward: " I don't know how it is with the rest of you, but I should have to think twice before I'd trust my subscription money to a coloured girl."

Mary said in utter astonishment: " Coloured, why what are you talking about? Who's coloured? "

" Angela, Angela Murray, that's who's coloured. At least she used to be when we all went to school at Eighteenth and Oxford."

Mary said again: " Coloured! " And then, " Angela, you never told me you were coloured! "

Angela's voice was as amazed as her own: " Tell you that I was coloured! Why of course I never told you that I was coloured! Why should I? "

" There," said Esther, " see she never told Mary
that she was coloured. What wouldn't she have
done with our money! "

  .   .   .   .   .

Angela had picked up her books and strolled
out the door. But she flew down the north staircase and out the Brandywine Street entrance and
so to Sixteenth Street where she would meet no
one she knew, especially at this belated hour. At
home there would be work to do, her lessons to
get and the long, long hours of the night must
pass before she would have to face again the hurt
and humiliation of the classroom; before she
would have to steel her heart and her nerves to
drop Mary Hastings before Mary Hastings could
drop her. No one, no one, Mary least of all,
should guess how completely she had been
wounded. Mary and her shrinking bewilderment! Mary and her exclamation: " Coloured! "
This was a curious business, this colour. It was
the one god apparently to whom you could sacrifice everything. On account of it her mother had
neglected to greet her own husband on the street.
Mary Hastings could let it come between her and
her friend.

In the morning she was at school early; the
girls should all see her there and their individual
attitude should be her attitude. She would remember each one's greetings, would store it away for
future guidance. Some of the girls were especially
careful to speak to her, one or two gave her a
meaning smile, or so she took it, and turned away.
Some did not speak at all. When Mary Hastings

came in Angela rose and sauntered unseeing and unheeding deliberately past her through the doorway, across the hall to Miss Barrington's laboratory. As she returned she passed Mary's desk, and the girl lifted troubled but not un-friendly eyes to meet her own; Angela met the glance fully but without recognition. She thought to herself: " Coloured! If they had said to me Mary Hastings is a voodoo, I'd have answered, ' What of it? She's my friend.' "

.   .   .   .   .

Before June Mary Hastings came up to her and asked her to wait after school. Angela who had been neither avoiding nor seeking her gave a cool nod. They walked out of the French class-room together. When they reached the corner Mary spoke:

" Oh, Angela, let's be friends again. It doesn't really make any difference. See, I don't care any more."

" But that's what I don't understand. Why should it have made any difference in the first place? I'm just the same as I was before you knew I was coloured and just the same afterwards. Why should it ever have made any difference at all? "

" I don't know, I'm sure. I was just surprised. It was all so unexpected."

" What was unexpected? "

" Oh, I don't know. I can't explain it. But let's be friends."

" Well," said Angela slowly, " I'm willing, but I don't think it will ever be the same again."

It wasn't. Some element, spontaneity, trustful-
ness was lacking. Mary, who had never thought
of speaking of colour, was suddenly conscious
that here was a subject which she must not discuss. She was less frank, at times even restrained.
Angela, too young to define her thoughts, yet felt
vaguely: " She failed me once,—I was her friend,
—yet she failed me for something with which I
had nothing to do. She's just as likely to do it
again. It's in her."

Definitely she said to herself, " Mary withdrew herself not because I was coloured but
because she didn't know I was coloured. Therefore if she had never known I was coloured she
would always have been my friend. We would
have kept on having our good times together."
And she began to wonder which was the more
important, a patent insistence on the fact of colour
or an acceptance of the good things of life which
could come to you in America if either you were
not coloured or the fact of your racial connections
was not made known.

During the summer Mary Hastings' family,
it appeared, recovered their fallen fortunes. At
any rate she did not return to school in the fall
and Angela never saw her again.

CHAPTER V

Virginia came rushing in. " Angela, where's Mummy? "

" Out. What's all the excitement? "

" I've been appointed. Isn't it great? Won't Mother and Dad be delighted! Right at the beginning of the year too, so I won't have to wait. The official notice isn't out yet but I know it's all right. Miss Herren wants me to report to-morrow. Isn't it perfectly marvellous! Here I graduate from the Normal in June and in the second week of school in September I've got my perfectly good job. Darling child, it's very much better, as you may have heard me observe before, to be born lucky than rich. But I am lucky and I'll be rich too. Think of that salary for my very own! With both of us working, Mummy won't have to want for a thing, nor Father either. Mummy won't have to do a lick of work if she doesn't want to. Well, what have you got to say about it, old Rain-in-the-Face? Or perhaps this isn't Mrs. Henrietta Jones whom I'm addressing of? "

Angela giggled, then raised an imaginary lorgnette.. " Er,—really I think you have the advantage of me. Well, I was thinking how fortunate you were to get your appointment right off the bat and how you'll hate it now that you have got it."

47

She herself, appointed two years previously, had had no such luck. Strictly speaking there are no coloured schools as such in Philadelphia. Yet, by an unwritten law, although coloured children may be taught by white teachers, white children must never receive knowledge at the hands of coloured instructors. As the number of coloured Normal School graduates is steadily increasing, the city gets around this difficulty by manning a school in a district thickly populated by Negroes, with a coloured principal and a coloured teaching force. Coloured children living in that district must thereupon attend that school. But no attention is paid to the white children who leave this same district for the next nearest white or " mixed " school.

Angela had been sixth on the list of coloured graduates. 'Five had been appointed, but there was no vacancy for her, and for several months she was idle with here and there a day, perhaps a week of substituting. She could not be appointed in any but a coloured school, and she was not supposed to substitute in any but this kind of classroom. Then her father discovered that a young white woman was teaching in a coloured school. He made some searching inquiries and was met with the complacent rejoinder that as soon as a vacancy occurred in a white school, Miss Mc-Sweeney would be transferred there and his daughter could have her place.

Just as she had anticipated, Angela did not want the job after she received it. She had expected to loathe teaching little children and her expectation, it turned out, was perfectly well grounded. Perhaps she might like to teach drawing to grown-ups; she would certainly like to have a try at it. Meanwhile it was nice to be independent, to be holding a lady-like, respectable position so different from her mother's early days, to be able to have pretty clothes and to help with the house, in brief to be drawing an appreciably adequate and steady salary. For one thing it made it possible for her to take up work at the Philadelphia Academy of Fine Arts at Broad and Cherry.

.   .   :   .   ..

Jinny was in excellent spirits at dinner. " Now, Mummy darling, you really shall walk in silk attire and siller hae to spare." Angela's appointment had done away with the drudgery of washday. " We'll get Hettie Daniels to come in Saturdays and clean up. I won't have to scrub the front steps any more and everything will be feasting and fun." Pushing aside her plate she rushed over to her father, climbed on his knee and flung her lovely bronze arms around his neck. She still adored him, still thought him the finest man in the world; she still wanted her husband to be just exactly like him; he would not be so tall nor would he be quite as dark. Matthew Henson was of only medium height and was a sort of reddish yellow and he distinctly was not as handsome as her father. Indeed Virginia thought, with a pang of shame at her disloyalty, that it would have been a fine thing if he could exchange his lighter skin for her father's colour if in so doing it he might have gained her father's thick, coarsely grained but beautifully curling, open black hair. Matthew had inherited his father's thick, tight, " bad " hair. Only, thank heaven, it was darker.

Junius tucked his slender daughter back in the hollow of his arm.

" Well, baby, you want something off my plate? " As a child Virginia had been a notorious beggar.

" Darling! I was thinking that now you could buy Mr. Hallowell's car. He's got his eye on a Cadillac, Kate says, and he'd be willing to let Henry Ford go for a song."

Junius was pleased, but he thought he ought to protest. " Do I look as old as all that? I might be able to buy the actual car, now that my girls are getting so monied, but the upkeep, I understand, is pretty steep."

" Oh, nonsense," said Mattie. " Go on and get it, June. Think how nice it will be riding out North Broad Street in the evenings."

And Angela added kindly: " I think you owe it to yourself to get it, Dad. Jinny and I'll carry the house till you get it paid for."

" Well, there's no reason of course why I——" he corrected himself, " why we shouldn't have a car if we want it." He saw himself spending happy moments digging in the little car's inmost mysteries. He would buy new parts, change the engine perhaps, paint it and overhaul her generally. And he might just as well indulge himself. The little house was long since paid for; he was well insured, and his two daughters were grown up and taking care of themselves. He slid Jinny off his knee.

" I believe I'll run over to the Hallowells now and see what Tom'll take for that car. Catch him before he goes down town in it."

Virginia called after him. "Just think! Maybe this time next week you'll be going down town in it."

.   :   .   :   .

She was very happy. Life was turning out just right. She was young, she was twenty, she was about to earn her own living,—" to be about to live "—she said, happily quoting a Latin construction which had always intrigued her. Her mother would never have to work again; her father would have a Henry Ford; she herself would get a new, good music teacher and would also take up the study of methods at the University of Pennsylvania.

Angela could hear her downstairs talking to Matthew Henson whose ring she had just answered. " Only think, Matt, I've been appointed."

" Great! " said Matthew. " Is Angela in? Do you think she'd like to go to the movies with me to-night? She was too tired last time. Run up and ask her, there's a good girl."

Angela sighed. She didn't want to go out with Matthew; he wearied her so. And besides people always looked at her so strangely. She wished he would take it into his head to come and see Jinny.

.   .   .   .   .

Sunday was still a happy day. Already an air of prosperity, of having arrived beyond the striving point, had settled over the family. Mr. Murray's negotiations with Tom Hallowell had been most successful. The Ford, a little four-seater coupé, compact and sturdy, had changed

hands.   Its former owner came around on Sunday
to give Junius a lesson.   The entire household piled
in, for both girls were possessed of the modern
slenderness.   They rode out Jefferson Street and
far, far out Ridge Avenue to the Wissahickon and
on to Chestnut Hill.   From time to time, when the
traffic was thin, Junius took the wheel, anticipating
Tom's instructions with the readiness of the born
mechanic.   They came back laughing and happy
and pardonably proud. ＼ The dense, tender glow of
the late afternoon September sun flooded the little
parlour, the dining-room was dusky and the kitchen
was redolent of scents of ginger bread and spiced
preserves.   After supper there were no lessons
to get.   "It'll be years before I forget all that
stuff I learned in practice school," said Jinny
gaily.

Later on some boys came in; Matthew Henson
inevitably, peering dissatisfied through the autumn
gloom for Angela and immediately content when
he saw her; Arthur Sawyer, who had just entered
the School of Pedagogy and was a little ashamed
of it, for he considered teaching work fit only for
women.   "But I've got to make a living somehow,
ain't I?   And I won't go into that post-office!"

"What's the matter with the post-office?"
Henson asked indignantly.   He had just been
appointed.   In reality he did not fancy the work
himself, but he did not want it decried before
Angela.

"Tell me what better or surer job is there for
a coloured man in Philadelphia?"

"Nothing," said Sawyer promptly, "not a thing
in the world except school teaching.   But that's
just what I object to.   I'm sick of planning my

life with regard to being coloured. I'm not a
bit ashamed of my race. I don't mind in the least
that once we were slaves. Every race in the world
has at some time occupied a servile position. But
I do mind having to take it into consideration
every time I want to eat outside of my home,
every time I enter a theatre, every time I think of
a profession.

"But you do have to take it into consideration,"
said Jinny softly. "At present it's one of the facts
of our living, just as lameness or near-sightedness
might be for a white man."

The inevitable race discussion was on.

"Ah, but there you're all off, Miss Virginia."
A tall, lanky, rather supercilious youth spoke up
from the corner. He had been known to them all
their lives as Franky Porter, but he had taken
lately to publishing poems in the Philadelphia
Tribunal which he signed F. Seymour Porter.
"Really you're all off, for you speak as though
colour itself were a deformity. Whereas, as Miss
Angela being an artist knows, colour may really
be a very beautiful thing, mayn't it?"

"Oh don't drag me into your old discussion,"
Angela answered crossly. "I'm sick of this whole
race business if you ask me. And don't call me
Miss Angela. Call me Angela as you've all done
all our lives or else call me Miss Murray. No, I
don't think being coloured in America is a beautiful
thing. I think it's nothing short of a curse."

"Well," said Porter slowly, "I think its being
or not being a curse rests with you. You've got
to decide whether or not you're going to let it
interfere with personal development and to that
extent it may be harmful or it may be an incentive.

I take it that Sawyer here, who even when we were all kids always wanted to be an engineer, will transmute his colour either into a bane or a blessing according to whether he lets it make him hide his natural tendencies under the bushel of school-teaching or become an inspiration toward making him the very best kind of engineer that there ever was so that people will just have to take him for what he is and overlook the fact of colour."

"That's it," said Jinny. "You know, being coloured often does spur you on."

"And that's what I object to," Angela answered perversely. "I'm sick of this business of always being below or above a certain norm. Doesn't anyone think that we have a right to be happy simply, naturally?"

.   .   .   .   .

Gradually they drifted into music. Virginia played a few popular songs and presently the old beautiful airs of all time, " Drink to me only with thine eyes " and " Sweet and Low ". Arthur Sawyer had a soft, melting tenor and Angela a rather good alto; Virginia and the other boys carried the air while Junius boomed his deep, unyielding bass. The lovely melodies and the peace of the happy, tranquil household crept over them, and presently they exchanged farewells and the young men passed wearied and contented out into the dark confines of Opal Street. Angela and Mattie went upstairs, but Viginia and her father stayed below and sang very softly so as not to disturb the sleeping street; a few hymns and finally the majestic strains of " The Dying Christian " floated up. Mrs. Murray had complained of feeling tired. " I think I'll just lie a moment on your bed, Angela, until your father comes up." But her daughter noticed that she had not relaxed, instead she was straining forward a little and Angela realized that she was trying to catch every note of her husband's virile, hearty voice.

She said, " You heard what we were all talking about before the boys left. You and father don't ever bother to discuss such matters, do you? "

Her mother seemed to strain past the sound of her voice. " Not any more; oh, of course we used to talk about such things, but you get so taken up with the problem of living, just life itself you know, that by and by being coloured or not is just one thing more or less that you have to contend with. But of course there have been times when colour was the starting point of our discussions. I remember how when you and Jinny were little things and she was always running to the piano and you were scribbling all over the walls,—many's the time I've slapped your little fingers for that, Angela,— we used to spend half the night talking about you, your father and I. I wanted you to be great artists but Junius said: ' No, we'll give them a good, plain education and set them in the way of earning a sure and honest living; then if they've got it in them to travel over all the rocks that'll be in their way as coloured girls, they'll manage, never you fear.' And he was right." The music downstairs ceased and she lay back, relaxed and drowsy. " Your father's always right."

Much of this was news to Angela, and she would have liked to learn more about those early nocturnal discussions. But she only said, smiling, " You're still crazy about father, aren't you, darling? "

Her mother was wide awake in an instant. " Crazy! I'd give my life for him ! "

.   .   .   .   .

The Saturday excursions were long since a thing of the past; Henry Ford had changed that. Also the extra work which the girls had taken upon themselves in addition to their teaching,—Angela at the Academy, Virginia at the University,—made Saturday afternoon a too sorely needed period of relaxation to be spent in the old familiar fashion. Still there were times when Angela in search of a new frock or intent on the exploration of a picture gallery asked her mother to accompany her. And at such times the two indulged in their former custom of having tea and a comfortable hour's chat in the luxurious comfort of some exclusive tea-room or hotel. Mattie, older and not quite so lightly stepping in these days of comparative ease as in those other times when a week's ·arduous duties lay behind her, still responded joyously to the call of fashion and grooming, the air of " good living " which pervaded these places. Moreover she herself was able to contribute to this atmos-phere. Her daughters insisted on presenting her with the graceful and dainty clothes which she loved, and they were equally insistent on her wearing them. " No use hanging them in a closet," said Jinny blithely. All her prophecies had come true—her mother had the services of a maid whenever she needed them, she went clad for the most part "in silk attire", and she had "siller to spare" and to spend.

She was down town spending it now. The Ladies' Auxiliary of her church was to give a reception after Lent, and Mattie meant to hold her own with the best of them. "We're getting to be old ladies," she said a bit wistfully, "but we'll make you young ones look at us once or twice just the same." Angela replied that she was sure of that. "And I know one or two little secrets for the complexion that will make it impossible for you to call yourself old."

But those her mother knew already. However she expressed a willingness to accept Angela's offer. She loved to be fussed over, and of late Angela had shown a tendency to rival even Jinny in this particular. The older girl was beginning to lose some of her restlessness. Life was pretty hum-drum, but it was comfortable and pleasant; her family life was ideal and her time at the art school delightful. The instructor was interested in her progress, and one or two of the girls had shown a desire for real intimacy. These intimations she had not followed up very closely, but she was seeing enough of a larger, freer world to make her chafe less at the restrictions which somehow seemed to bind in her own group. As a result of even this slight satisfaction of her cravings, she was indulging less and less in brooding and introspection, although at no time was she able to adapt herself to living with the complete spontaneity so characteristic of Jinny.

But she was young, and life would somehow twist and shape itself to her subsconscious yearnings, just as it had done for her mother, she thought, following Mattie in and out of shops, delivering opinions and lending herself to all the exigencies which shopping imposed. It was not an occupation which she particularly enjoyed, but, like her mother, she adored the atmosphere and its accompaniment of well-dressed and luxuriously stationed women. No one could tell, no one would have thought for a moment that she and her mother had come from tiny Opal Street; no one could have dreamed of their racial connections. "And if Jinny were here," she thought, slowly selecting another cake, "she really would be just as capable of fitting into all this as mother and I; but they wouldn't let her light." And again she let herself dwell on the fallaciousness of a social system which stretched appearance so far beyond being.

From the tea-room they emerged into the damp greyness of the March afternoon. The streets were slushy and slimy; the sky above sodden and dull. Mattie shivered and thought of the Morris chair in the minute but cosy dining-room of her home. She wanted to go to the " Y " on Catherine Street and there were two calls to make far down Fifteenth. But at last all this was accomplished. "Now we'll get the next car and before you know it you'll be home."

"You look tired, Mother," said Angela.

" I am tired," she acknowledged, and, suddenly sagging against her daughter, lost consciousness. About them a small crowd formed, and a man passing in an automobile kindly drove the two women to a hospital in Broad Street two blocks away. It was a hospital to which no coloured woman would ever have been admitted except to char, but there was no such question to be raised in the case of this patient. "She'll be all right presently," the interne announced, "just a little fainting spell brought on by over-exertion. Was that your car you came in? It would be nice if you could have one to get her home in."

"Oh, but I can," and in a moment Angela had rushed to the telephone forgetting everything except that her father was in his shop to-day and therefore almost within reach and so was the car.

Not long after he came striding into the hospital, tall and black and rather shabby in his working clothes. He was greeted by the clerk with a rather hostile, "Yes, and what do you want?"

Angela, hastening across the lobby to him, halted at the intonation.

Junius was equal to the moment's demands. "I'm Mrs. Murray's chauffeur," he announced, hating the deception, but he would not have his wife bundled out too soon. "Is she very badly off, Miss Angela?"

His daughter hastened to reassure him. "No, she'll be down in a few minutes now."

"And meanwhile you can wait outside," said the attendant icily. She did not believe that black people were exactly human; there was no place for them in the scheme of life so far as she could see.

Junius withdrew, and in a half hour's time the young interne and the nurse came out supporting his wan wife. He sprang to the pavement: "Lean on me, Mrs. Murray."

But sobbing, she threw her arms about his neck. "Oh Junius, Junius!"

He lifted her then, drew back for Angela and mounting himself, drove away. The interne

stepped back into the hospital raging about these damn white women and their nigger servants. Such women ought to be placed in a psycho-pathic ward and the niggers burned.

．　　　．　　　．　　　．　　　．

The girls got Mrs. Murray into the Morris chair and ran upstairs for pillows and wraps. When they returned Junius was in the chair and Mrs. Murray in his arms. " Oh, June, dear June, such a service of love."

" Do you suppose she's going to die? " whispered Jinny, stricken. What, she wondered, would become of her father.

But in a few days Mattie was fully recovered and more happy than ever in the reflorescence of love and tenderness which had sprung up between herself and Junius. Only Junius was not so well. He had had a slight touch of grippe during the winter and the half hour's loitering in the treacherous March weather, before the hospital, had not served to improve it. He was hoarse and feverish, though this he did not immediately admit. But a tearing pain in his chest compelled him one morning to suggest the doctor. In a panic Mattie sent for him. Junius really ill! She had never seen him in anything but the pink of condition. The doctor reluctantly admitted pneumonia—" a severe case but I think we can pull him through."

He suffered terribly—Mattie suffered with him, never leaving his bedside. On the fifth day he was delirious. His wife thought, " Surely God isn't going to let him die without speaking to me again."

Toward evening he opened his eyes and saw her tender, stricken face. He smiled. " Dear Mattie," and then, " Jinny, I'd like to hear some music, ' Vital spark '——"

So his daughter went down to the little parlour and played and sang " The Dying Christian ".

Angela thought, " Oh, isn't this terrible! Oh how can she? " Presently she called softly, " Jinny, Jinny come up."

Junius' hand was groping for Mattie's. She placed it in his. " Dear Mattie," he said, " Heaven opens on my eyes,——"

.　　　.　　　.　　　.　　　.

The house was still with the awful stillness that follows a funeral. All the bustle and hurry were over; the end, the fulfilment toward which the family had been striving for the last three days was accomplished. The baked funeral meats had been removed; Virginia had seen to that. Angela was up in her room, staring dry-eyed before her; she loved her father, but not even for him could she endure this aching, formless pain of bereavement. She kept saying to herself fiercely: " I must get over this, I can't stand this. I'll go away."

Mrs. Murray sat in the old Morris chair in the dining-room. She stroked its arms with her plump, worn fingers; she laid her face again and again on its shabby back. One knew that she was remembering a dark, loved cheek. Jinny said, " Come upstairs and let me put you to bed, darling. You're going to sleep with me, you know. You're going to comfort your little girl, aren't you,

Mummy? " Then as there was no response, " Darling, you'll make yourself ill."

Her mother sat up suddenly. " Yes, that's what I want to do. Oh, Jinny, do you think I can make myself ill enough to follow him soon? My daughter, try to forgive me, but I must go to him. I can't live without him. I don't deserve a daughter like you, but,—don't let them hold me back. I want to die, I must die. Say you forgive me,——"

" Darling," and it was as though her husband rather than her daughter spoke, " whatever you want is what I want." By a supreme effort she held back her · tears, but it was years before she forgot the picture of her mother sitting back in the old Morris chair, composing herself for death.

CHAPTER VI

AT the Academy matters progressed smoothly without the flawing of a ripple. Angela looked forward to the hours which she spent there and honestly regretted their passage. Her fellow students and the instructors were more than cordial, there was an actual sense of camaraderie among them. She had not mentioned the fact of her Negro strain, indeed she had no occasion to, but she did not believe that this fact if known would cause any change in attitude. Artists were noted for their broad-mindedness. They were the first persons in the world to judge a person for his worth rather than by any hall-mark. It is true that Miss Henderson, a young lady of undeniable colour, was not received with the same cordiality and attention which Angela was receiving, and this, too, despite the fact that the former's work showed undeniable talent, even originality. Angela thought that something in the young lady's personality precluded an approach to friendship; she seemed to be wary, almost offensively stand-offish. Certainly she never spoke unless spoken to; she had been known to spend a whole session without even glancing at a fellow student.

Angela herself had not arrived at any genuine intimacies. Two of the girls had asked her to their homes but she had always refused; such invitations would have to be returned with similar ones and the presence of Jinny would entail explanations. The invitation of Mr. Shields, the instructor, to have tea at his wife's at home was another matter and of this she gladly availed herself. She could not tell to just what end she was striving. She did not like teaching and longed to give it up. On the other hand she must make her living. Mr. Shields had suggested that she might be able to increase both her earning capacity and her enjoyments through a more practical application of her art. There were directorships of drawing in the public schools, positions in art schools and colleges, or, since Angela frankly acknowledged her unwillingness to instruct, there was such a thing as being buyer for the art section of a department store.

"And anyway," said Mrs. Shields, "you never know what may be in store for you if you just have preparation." She and her husband were both attracted to the pleasant-spoken, talented girl. Angela possessed an undeniable air, and she dressed well, even superlatively. Her parents' death had meant the possession of half the house and half of three thousand dollars' worth of insurance. Her salary was adequate, her expenses light. Indeed even her present mode of living gave her little cause for complaint except that her racial affiliations narrowed her confines. But she was restlessly conscious of a desire for broader horizons. She confided something like this to her new friends.

"Perfectly natural," they agreed. "There's no telling where your tastes and talents will lead you,

—to Europe perhaps and surely to the formation of new and interesting friendships. You'll find artistic folk the broadest, most liberal people in the world."

" There are possibilities of scholarships, too," Mr. Shields concluded more practically. The Academy offered a few in competition. But there were others more liberally endowed and practically without restriction.

Sundays on Opal Street bore still their aspect of something different and special. Jinny sometimes went to church, sometimes packed the car with a group of laughing girls of her age and played at her father's old game of exploring. Angela preferred to stay in the house. She liked to sleep late, get up for a leisurely bath and a meticulous toilet. Afterwards she would turn over her wardrobe, sorting and discarding; read the week's forecast of theatres, concerts and exhibits. And finally she would begin sketching, usually ending up with a new view of Hetty Daniels' head.

Hetty, who lived with them now in the triple capacity, as she saw it, of housekeeper, companion, and chaperone, loved to pose. It satisfied some unquenchable vanity in her unloved, empty existence. She could not conceive of being sketched because she was, in the artist's jargon, " interesting ", " paintable ", or " difficult ". Models, as she understood it, were chosen for their beauty. Square and upright she sat, regaling Angela with tales of the romantic adventures of some remote period which was her youth. She could not be very old, the young girl thought; indeed, from some of her dates she must have been at least twelve years younger than her mother. Yet Mrs. Murray had carried with her to the end some irrefragable quality of girlishness which would keep her memory forever young.

Miss Daniels' great fetish was sex morality. "Them young fellers was always 'round me thick ez bees; wasn't any night they wasn't more fellows in my kitchen then you an' Jinny ever has in yore parlour. But I never listened to none of the' talk, jist held out agin 'em and kept my pearl of great price untarnished. I aimed then and I'm continual to aim to be a verjous woman."

Her unslaked yearnings gleamed suddenly out of her eyes, transforming her usually rather expressionless face into something wild and avid. The dark brown immobile mask of her skin made an excellent foil for the vividness of an emotion which was so apparent, so palpable that it seemed like something superimposed upon the background of her countenance.

"If I could just get that look for Mr. Shields," Angela said half aloud to herself, "I bet I could get any of their old scholarships. . . . So you had lots more beaux than we have, Hetty? Well you wouldn't have to go far to outdo us there."

The same half dozen young men still visited the Murray household on Sundays. None of them except Matthew Henson came as a suitor; the others looked in partly from habit, partly, Jinny used to say, for the sake of Hetty Daniels' good

ginger bread, but more than for any other reason
for the sake of having a comfortable place in which
to argue and someone with whom to conduct the
argument.

"They certainly do argue;" Angela grumbled a
little, but she didn't care. Matthew was usually
the leader in their illimitable discussions, but she
much preferred him at this than at his clumsy
and distasteful love-making. Of course she could
go out, but there was no place for her to visit and
no companions for her to visit with. If she made
calls there would be merely a replica of what she
was finding in her own household. It was true
that in the ultra-modern set Sunday dancing was
being taken up. But she and Virginia did not
fit in here any too well. Her fancy envisaged a
comfortable drawing-room (there *were* folks who
used that term), peopled with distinguished men
and women who did things, wrote and painted and
acted,—people with a broad, cultural background
behind them, or, lacking that, with the originality
of thought and speech which comes from failing,
deliberately failing, to conform to the pattern.
Somewhere, she supposed, there must be coloured
people like that. But she didn't know any of them.
She knew there were people right in Philadelphia
who had left far, far behind them the economic
class to which her father and mother had belonged.
But their thoughts, their actions were still cramped
and confined; they were sitting in their new, even
luxurious quarters, still mental parvenus, still dis-
cussing the eternal race question even as these
boys here.

To-night they were hard at it again with a new
phase which Angela, who usually sat only half

attentive in their midst, did not remember ever having heard touched before. Seymour Porter had started the ball by forcing their attention to one of his poems. It was not a bad poem; as modern verse goes it possessed a touch distinctly above the mediocre.

"Why don't you stop that stuff and get down to brass tacks, Porter?" Matthew snarled. "You'll be of much more service to your race as a good dentist than as a half-baked poet." Henson happened to know that the amount of study which the young poet did at the University kept him just barely registered in the dental college.

Porter ran his hand over his beautifully groomed hair. He had worn a stocking cap in his room all the early part of the day to enable him to perform this gesture without disaster. "There you go, Henson,—service to the race and all the rest of it. Doesn't it ever occur to you that the race is made up of individuals and you can't conserve the good of the whole unless you establish that of each part? Is it better for me to be a first rate dentist and be a cabined and confined personality or a half-baked poet, as you'd call it, and be myself?"

Henson reasoned that a coloured American must take into account that he is usually living in a hostile community. "If you're only a half-baked poet they'll think that you're a representative of your race and that we're all equally no account. But if you're a fine dentist, they won't think, it's true, that we're all as skilled as you, but they will respect you and concede that probably there're a few more like you. Inconsistent, but that's the way they argue."

Arthur Sawyer objected to this constant yielding to an invisible censorship. " If you're coloured you've just got to straddle a bit; you've got to consider both racial and individual integrity. I've got to be sure of a living right now. So in order not to bring the charge of vagrancy against my family I'm going to teach until I've saved enough money to study engineering in comfort."

" And when you get through? " Matthew asked politely.

" When I get through, if this city has come to its senses, I'll get a big job with Baldwin. If not I'll go to South America and take out naturalization papers."

" But you can't do that," cried Jinny, " we'd need you more than ever if you had all that training. You' know what I think? We've all of us got to make up our minds to the sacrifice of something. I mean something more than just the ordinary sacrifices in life, not so much for the sake of the next generation as for the sake of some principle, for the sake of some immaterial quality like pride or intense self-respect or even a saving complacency; a spiritual tonic which the race needs perhaps just as much as the body might need iron or whatever it does need to give the proper kind of resistance. There are some things which an individual might want, but which he'd just have to give up forever for the sake of the more important whole."

" It beats me," said Sawyer indulgently, " how a little thing like you can catch hold of such a big thought. I don't know about a man's giving up his heart's desire forever, though, just because he's coloured. That seems to me a pretty large order."

"Large order or not," Henson caught him up, "she comes mighty near being right. What do you think, Angela?"

"Just the same as I've always thought. I don't see any sense in living unless you're going to be happy."

Angela took the sketch of Hetty Daniels to school. "What an interesting type!" said Gertrude Quale, the girl next to her. "Such cosmic and tragic unhappiness in that face. What is she, not an American?"

"Oh yes she is. She's an old coloured woman who's worked in our family for years and she was born right here in Philadelphia."

"Oh coloured! Well, of course I suppose you would call her an American though I never think of darkies as Americans. Coloured, —yes that would account for that unhappiness in her face. I suppose they all mind it awfully."

It was the afternoon for the life class. The model came in, a short, rather slender young woman with a faintly pretty, shrewish face full of a certain dark, mean character. Angela glanced at her thoughtfully, full of pleasant anticipation. She liked to work for character, preferred it even to beauty. The model caught her eye, looked away and again turned her full gaze upon her with

an insistent, slightly incredulous stare. It was
Esther Bayliss who had once been in the High
School with Angela. She had left not long
after Mary Hastings' return to her boarding
school.

Angela saw no reason why she should speak
to her and presently, engrossed in the portrayal
of the round, yet pointed little face, forgot the
girl's identity. But Esther kept her eyes fixed
on her former school-mate with a sort of intense,
angry brooding so absorbing that she forgot her
pose and Mr. Shield spoke to her two or three
times. On the third occasion he said not unkindly, " You'll have to hold your pose better
than this, Miss Bayliss, or we won't be able to
keep you on."

" I don't want you to keep me on." She spoke
with an amazing vindictiveness. " I haven't got
to the point yet where I'm going to lower myself
to pose for a coloured girl."

He looked around the room in amazement;
no, Miss Henderson wasn't there, she never came
to this class he remembered. " Well after that
we couldn't keep you anyway. We're not taking
orders from our models. But there's no coloured
girl here."

" Oh yes there is, unless she's changed her
name." She laughed spitefully. " Isn't that Angela Murray over there next to that Jew girl? "
In spite of himself, Shields nodded. " Well, she's
coloured though she wouldn't let you know. But
I know. I went to school with her in North
Philadelphia. And I tell you I wouldn't stay
to pose for her not if you were to pay me ten
times what I'm getting. Sitting there drawing

from me just as though she were as good as a
white girl!"

Astonished and disconcerted, he told his wife
about it. "But I can't think she's really coloured,
Mabel. Why she looks and acts just like a white
girl. She dresses in better taste than anybody in
the room. But that little wretch of a model
insisted that she was coloured."

"Well she just can't be. Do you suppose I
don't know a coloured woman when I see one?
I can tell 'em a mile off."

It seemed to him a vital and yet such a dis-
graceful matter. "If she is coloured she should
have told me. I'd certainly like to know, but
hang it all, I can't ask her, for suppose she should
be white in spite of what that little beast of a model
said?" He found her address in the registry and
overcome one afternoon with shamed curiosity
drove up to Opal Street and slowly past her house.
Jinny was coming in from school and Hetty
Daniels on her way to market greeted her on the
lower step. Then Virginia put the key in the lock
and passed inside. "She is coloured," he told his
wife, "for no white girl in her senses would be
rooming with coloured people."

"I should say not! Coloured, is she? Well, she
shan't come here again, Henry."

Angela approached him after class on Saturday. "How is Mrs. Shields? I can't get out
to see her this week but I'll be sure to run in
next."

He blurted out miserably, "But, Miss Murray,
you never told me that you were coloured."

She felt as though she were rehearsing a
well-known part in a play. "Coloured! Of

72

course I never told you that I was coloured.
Why should I? "

.   .   .   .   .

But apparently there was some reason why she
should tell it; she sat in her room in utter dejection
trying to reason it out. Just as in the old days
she had not discussed the matter with Jinny, for
what could the latter do? She wondered if
her mother had ever met with any such experiences. Was there something inherently wrong in
" passing "?

Her mother had never seemed to consider it as
anything but a lark. And on the one occasion,
that terrible day in the hospital when passing or
not passing might have meant the difference
between good will and unpleasantness, her mother
had deliberately given the whole show away. But
her mother, she had long since begun to realize,
had not considered this business of colour or
the lack of it as pertaining intimately to her
personal happiness. She was perfectly satisfied,
absolutely content whether she was part of that
white world with Angela or up on little Opal
Street with her dark family and friends. Whereas it seemed to Angela that all the things which
she most wanted were wrapped up with white
people. All the good things were theirs. Not,
some coldly reasoning instinct within was saying, because they were white. But because for
the present they had power and the badge of
that power was whiteness, very like the colours
on the escutcheon of a powerful house. She
possessed the badge, and unless there was

someone to tell she could possess the power for which it stood.

Hetty Daniels shrilled up: " Mr. Henson's down here to see you."

Tiresome though his presence was, she almost welcomed him to-night, and even accepted his eager invitation to go to see a picture. " It's in a little gem of a theatre, Angela. You'll like the surroundings almost as much as the picture, and that's very good. Sawyer and I saw it about two weeks ago. I thought then that I'd like to take you."

She knew that this was his indirect method of telling her that they would meet with no difficulty in the matter of admission; a comforting assurance, for Philadelphia theatres, as Angela knew, could be very unpleasant to would-be coloured patrons. Henson offered to telephone for a taxi while she was getting on her street clothes, and she permitted the unnecessary extravagance, for she hated the conjectures on the faces of passengers in the street cars; conjectures, she felt in her sensitiveness, which she could only set right by being unusually kind and friendly in her manner to Henson. And this produced undesirable effects on him. She had gone out with him more often in the Ford, which permitted a modicum of privacy. But Jinny was off in the little car to-night.

At Broad and Ridge Avenue the taxi was held up; it was twenty-five minutes after eight when they reached the theatre. Matthew gave Angela a bill. " Do you mind getting the tickets while I settle for the cab? " he asked nervously. He did not want her to miss even the advertisements. This, he almost prayed, would be a perfect night.

74

Cramming the change into his pocket, he rushed into the lobby and joined Angela who, almost as excited as he, for she liked a good picture, handed the tickets to the attendant. He returned the stubs. "All right, good seats there to your left." The theatre was only one storey. He glanced at Matthew.

"Here, here, where do you think you're going?"

Matthew answered unsuspecting: "It's all right. The young lady gave you the tickets."

"Yes, but not for you; she can go in, but you can't." He handed him the torn ticket, turned and took one of the stubs from Angela, and thrust that in the young man's unwilling hand. "Go over there and get your refund."

"But," said Matthew and Angela could feel his very manhood sickening under the silly humiliation of the moment, "there must be some mistake; I sat in this same theatre less than three weeks ago."

"Well, you won't sit in there to-night; the management's ‾ changed hands since then, and we're not selling tickets to coloured people." He glanced at Angela a little uncertainly. "The young lady can come in——"

Angela threw her ticket on the floor. "Oh, come Matthew, come."

Outside he said stiffly, "I'll get a taxi, we'll go somewhere else."

"No, no! We wouldn't enjoy it. Let's go home and we don't need a taxi. We can get the Sixteenth Street car right at the corner."

She was very kind to him in the car; she was so sorry for him, suddenly conscious of the pain which must be his at being stripped before the girl he loved of his masculine right to protect, to appear the hero.

She let him open the two doors for her but stopped him in the box of a hall. " I think I'll say good-night now, Matthew; I'm more tired than I realized. But,—but it was an adventure, wasn't it? "

His eyes adored her, his hand caught hers: " Angela, I'd have given all I hope to possess to have been able to prevent it; you know I never dreamed of letting you in for such humiliation. Oh how are we ever going to get this thing straight? "

" Well, it wasn't your fault." Unexpectedly she lifted her delicate face to his, so stricken and freckled and woebegone, and kissed him; lifted her hand and actually stroked his reddish, stiff, " bad " hair.

Like a man in a dream he walked down the street wondering how long it would be before they married.

.   .   .   .   .

Angela, waking in the middle of the night and reviewing to herself the events of the day, said aloud: " This is the end," and fell asleep again.

The little back room was still Jinny's, but Angela, in order to give the third storey front to Hetty Daniels, had moved into the room which had once been her mother's. She and Virginia had placed the respective head-boards of their narrow, virginal beds against the dividing wall so that they could lie in bed and talk to each other through the communicating door-way, their voices making a circuit from speaker to listener in what Jinny called a hair-pin curve.

Angela called in as soon as she heard her sister moving, " Jinny, listen. I'm going away."

Her sister, still half asleep, lay intensely quiet for another second, trying to pick up the continuity of this dream. Then her senses came to her.

" What'd you say, Angela? "

" I said I was going away. I'm going to leave Philadelphia, give up school teaching, break away from our loving friends and acquaintances, and bust up the whole shooting match."

" Haven't gone crazy, have you? "

" No, I think I'm just beginning to come to my senses. I'm sick, sick, sick of seeing what I want dangled right before my eyes and then of having it snatched away from me and all of it through no fault of my own."

" Darling, you know I haven't the faintest idea of what you're driving at."

" Well, I'll tell you." Out came the whole story, an accumulation of the slights, real and fancied, which her colour had engendered throughout her lifetime; though even then she did not tell of that first hurt through Mary Hastings. That would always linger in some remote, impenetrable fastness of her mind, for wounded trust was there as well as wounded pride and love. " And these two last happenings with Matthew and Mr.

Shields are just too much; besides they've shown me the way."

" Shown you what way? "

Virginia had arisen and thrown an old rose kimono around her. She had inherited her father's thick and rather coarsely waving black hair, enhanced by her mother's softness. She was slender, yet rounded; her cheeks were flushed with sleep and excitement. Her eyes shone. As she sat in the brilliant wrap, cross-legged at the foot of her sister's narrow bed, she made the latter think of a strikingly dainty, colourful robin.

" Well you see as long as the Shields thought I was white they were willing to help me to all the glories of the promised land. And the doorman last night,—he couldn't tell what I was, but he could tell about Matthew, so he put him out; just as the Shields are getting ready in another way to put me out. But as long as they didn't know it didn't matter. Which means it isn't being coloured that makes the difference, it's letting it be known. Do you see?

" So I've thought and thought. I guess really I've had it in my mind for a long time, but last night it seemed to stand right out in my consciousness. Why should I shut myself off from all the things I want most,—clever people, people who do things, Art,— " her voice spelt it with a capital,—" travel and a lot of things which are in the world for everybody really but which only white people, as far as I can see, get their hands on. I mean scholarships and special funds, patronage. Oh Jinny, you don't know, I don't think you can understand the things I want to see and know. You're not like me—— ".

"I don't know why I'm not," said Jinny looking more like a robin than ever. Her bright eyes dwelt on her sister. "After all, the same blood flows in my veins and in the same proportion. Sure you're not laying too much stress on something only temporarily inconvenient?"

"But it isn't temporarily inconvenient; it's happening to me every day. And it isn't as though it were something that I could help. Look how Mr. Shields stressed the fact that I hadn't told him I was coloured. And see how it changed his attitude toward me; you can't think how different his manner was. Yet as long as he didn't know, there was nothing he wasn't willing and glad, glad to do for me. Now he might be willing but he'll not be glad though I need his assistance more than some white girl who will find a dozen people to help her just because she is white." Some faint disapproval in her sister's face halted her for a moment. "What's the matter? You certainly don't think I ought to say first thing: 'I'm Angela Murray. I know I look white but I'm coloured and expect to be treated accordingly!' Now do you?"

"No," said Jinny, "of course that's absurd. Only I don't think you ought to mind quite so hard when they do find out the facts. It seems sort of an insult to yourself. And then, too, it makes you lose a good chance to do something for—for all of us who can't look like you but who really have the same combination of blood that you have."

"Oh that's some more of your and Matthew Henson's philosophy. Now be practical, Jinny;

after all I am both white and Negro and look white. Why shouldn't I declare for the one that will bring me the greatest happiness, prosperity and respect? "

" No reason in the world except that since in this country public opinion is against any infusion of black blood it would seem an awfully decent thing to put yourself, even in the face of appearances, on the side of black blood and say: " Look here, this is what a mixture of black and white really means ! ''

Angela was silent and Virginia, feeling suddenly very young, almost childish in the presence of this issue, took a turn about the room. She halted beside her sister.

" Just what is it you want to do, Angela? Evidently you have some plan."

She had. Her idea was to sell the house and to divide the proceeds. With her share of this and her half of the insurance she would go to New York or to Chicago, certainly to some place where she could by no chance be known, and launch out " into a freer, fuller life ".

" And leave me ! " said Jinny astonished. Somehow it had not dawned on her that the two would actually separate. She did not know what she had thought, but certainly not that. The tears ran down her cheeks.

Angela, unable to endure either her own pain or the sight of it in others, had all of a man's dislike for tears.

" Don't be absurd, Jinny ! How could I live the way I want to if you're with me. We'd keep on loving each other and seeing one another from

time to time, but we might just as well face the
facts. Some of those girls in the art school used
to ask me to their homes; it would have meant
opportunity, a broader outlook, but I never dared
accept because I knew I couldn't return the
invitation."

Under that Jinny winced a little, but she spoke
with spirit. "After that, Angela dear, I'm
beginning to think that you *have* more white
blood in your veins than I, and it was that extra
amount which made it possible for you to make
that remark." She trailed back to her room and
when Hetty Daniels announced breakfast she
found that a bad headache required a longer
stay in bed.

For many years the memory of those next few
weeks lingered in Virginia's mind beside that
other tragic memory of her mother's deliberate
submission to death. But Angela was almost
tremulous with happiness and anticipation. Almost as though by magic her affairs were arranging
themselves. She was to have the three thousand
dollars and Jinny was to be the sole possessor of
the house. Junius had paid far less than this
sum for it, but it had undoubtedly increased in
value. "It's a fair enough investment for you,
Miss Virginia," Mr. Hallowell remarked gruffly.
He had disapproved heartily of this summary
division, would have disapproved more thoroughly
and openly if he had had any idea of the reasons
behind it. But the girls had told no one, not
even him, of their plans. "Some sisters' quarrel,

·I' suppose," he commented to his wife. '" I've never seen any coloured people yêt, relatives that is, who could stand the joint possession of a little money."

A late Easter was casting its charm over the city when Angela trim, even elegant, in her conventional tailored suit, stood in the dining-room of the little house waiting for her taxi. She had burned her bridges behind her, had resigned from school, severed her connection with the Academy, and had permitted an impression to spread that she was going West to visit indefinitely a distant cousin of her mother's. In reality she was going to New York. She had covered her tracks very well, she thought; none of her friends was to see her off; indeed, none of them knew the exact hour of her departure. She was even leaving from the North Philadelphia station so that none of the porters of the main depôt, friends perhaps of the boys who came to her house, and, through some far flung communal instinct familiar to coloured people, acquainted with her by sight, would be able to tell of her going. Jinny, until she heard of this, had meant to accompany her to the station, but Angela's precaution palpably scotched this idea; she made no comment when Virginia announced that it would be impossible for her to see her sister off. An indefinable steeliness was creeping upon them.

Yet when the taxi stood rumbling and snorting outside, Angela, her heart suddenly mounting to her throat, her eyes smarting, put her arm tightly about her sister who clung to her frankly crying. But she only said: " Now, Jinny, there's nothing to cry about. You'll be coming to New York soon. First thing I know you'll be walking up to me: 'Pardon me! Isn't this Mrs. Henrietta Jones?'"

Virginia tried to laugh, "And you'll be saying: 'Really you have the advantage of me.' Oh, Angela, don't leave me!"

The cabby was honking impatiently. "I must, darling. Good-bye, Virginia. You'll hear from me right away."

She ran down the steps, glanced happily back. But her sister had already closed the door.

MARKET

CHAPTER I

FIFTH AVENUE is a canyon; its towering buildings dwarf the importance of the people hurrying through its narrow confines. But Fourteenth Street is a river, impersonally flowing, broad-bosomed, with strange and devious craft covering its expanse. To Angela the famous avenue seemed but one manifestation of living, but Fourteenth Street was the rendezvous of life itself. Here for those first few weeks after her arrival in New York she wandered, almost prowled, intent upon the jostling shops, the hurrying, pushing people, above all intent upon the faces of those people with their showings of grief, pride, gaiety, greed, joy, ambition, content. There was little enough of this last. These men and women were living at a sharper pitch of intensity than those she had observed in Philadelphia. The few coloured people whom she saw were different too; they possessed an independence of carriage, a purposefulness, an assurance in their manner that pleased her. But she could not see that any of these people, black or white, were any happier than those whom she had observed all her life.

But *she* was happier; she was living on the crest of a wave of excitement and satisfaction which would never wane, never break, never be spent. She was seeing the world, she was getting acquainted with life in her own way without restrictions or restraint; she was young, she was temporarily independent, she was intelligent, she was white. She remembered an expression " free, white and twenty-one ",—this was what it meant then, this sense of owning the world, this realization that other things being equal, all things were possible. " If I were a man," she said, " I could be president ", and laughed at herself for the " if " itself proclaimed a limitation. But that inconsistency bothered her little;. she did not want to be a man. Power, greatness, authority, these were fitting and proper for men; but there were sweeter, more beautiful gifts for women, and power of a certain kind too. Such a power she would like to exert in this glittering new world, so full of mysteries and promise. If she could afford it she would have a salon, a drawing-room where men and women, not necessarily great, but real, alive, free, and untrammelled in manner and thought, should come and pour themselves out to her sympathy and magnetism. To accomplish this she must have money and influence; indeed since she was so young she would need even protection; perhaps it would be better to marry . . . a white man. The thought came to her suddenly out of the void; she had never thought of this possibility before. If she were to do this, do it suitably, then all that richness, all that fullness of life which she so ardently craved would be doubly hers. She knew that men had a better time of it than women, coloured men than coloured women, white men than white women. Not that she envied them. Only it would be fun, great fun to capture power and protection in addition to the freedom and independence which she had so long coveted and which now lay in her hand.

But, she smiled to herself, she had no way of approaching these ends. She knew no one in New York; she could conceive of no manner in which she was likely to form desirable acquaintances; at present her home consisted of the four walls of the smallest room in Union Square Hotel. She had gone there the second day after her arrival, having spent an expensive twenty-four hours at the Astor. Later she came to realize that there were infinitely cheaper habitations to be had, but she could not tear herself away from Fourteenth Street. It was Spring, and the Square was full of rusty specimens of mankind who sat on the benches, as did Angela herself, for hours at a stretch, as though they thought the invigorating air and the mellow sun would work some magical burgeoning on their garments such as was worked on the trees. But though these latter changed, the garments changed not nor did their owners. They remained the same, drooping, discouraged down and outers. "I am seeing life," thought Angela, "this is the way people live," and never realized that some of these people looking curiously, speculatively at her wondered what had been her portion to bring her thus early to this unsavoury company.

"A great picture!" she thought. "I'll make a great picture of these people some day and call them 'Fourteenth Street types'." And suddenly a vast sadness invaded her; she wondered if there were people more alive, more sentient to the joy, the adventure of living, even than she, to whom she would also be a "type". But she could not believe this. She was at once almost irreconcilably too concentrated and too objective. Her living during these days was so intense, so almost solidified, as though her desire to live as she did and she herself were so one and the same thing that it would have been practically impossible for another onlooker like herself to insert the point of his discrimination into her firm panoply of satisfaction. So she continued to browse along her chosen thoroughfare, stopping most often in the Square or before a piano store on the same street. There was in this shop a player-piano which was usually in action, and as the front glass had been removed the increased clearness of the strains brought a steady, patient, apparently insatiable group of listeners to a standstill. They were mostly men, and as they were far less given, Angela observed, to concealing their feelings than women, it was easy to follow their emotional gamut. Jazz made them smile but with a certain wistfulness—if only they had time for dancing now, just now when the mood was on them! The young woman looking at the gathering of shabby pedestrians, worn business men and ruminative errand boys felt for them a pity not untinged with satisfaction. *She* had taken what she wanted while the mood was on her. Love songs, particularly those of the sorrowful ballad variety brought to these unmindful faces a strained regret. But there was one expression which Angela could only half interpret. It drifted on to those listening countenances usually at the playing of old Irish and Scottish tunes. She noticed then an acuter attitude of attention, the eyes took on a look of inwardness of utter remoteness. A passer-by engrossed in thought caught a strain and at once his gait and expression fell under the spell. The listeners might be as varied as fifteen people may be, yet for the moment they would be caught in a common, almost cosmic nostalgia. If the next piece were jazz, that particular crowd would disperse, its members going on their meditative ways, blessed or cursed with heaven knew what memories which must not be disturbed by the strident jangling of the latest popular song.

" Homesick," Angela used to say to herself. And she would feel so, too, though she hardly knew for what,—certainly not for Philadelphia and that other life which now seemed so removed as to have been impossible. And she made notes in her sketch book to enable her some day to make a great picture of these " types " too.

    •   •   •   •   •

Of course she was being unconscionably idle; but as her days were filled to overflowing with the impact of new impressions, this signified nothing. She could not guess what life would bring her. For the moment it seemed to her both wise and amusing to sit with idle hands and see what would happen. By a not inexplicable turn of mind she took to going very frequently to the cinema where most things did happen. She found herself studying the screen with a strained and ardent intensity, losing the slight patronizing scepticism which had once been hers with regard to the adventures of these shadowy heroes and heroines; so utterly unforeseen a turn had her own experiences taken. This time last year she had never dreamed of, had hardly dared to long for a life as free and as full as hers was now and was promising to be. Yet here she was on the thresh-hold of a career totally different from anything that a scenario writer could envisage. Oh yes, she knew that hundreds, indeed thousands of white coloured people "went over to the other side ", but that was just the point, she knew the fact without knowing hitherto any of the possi-bilities of the adventure. Already Philadelphia and her trials were receding into the distance. Would these people, she wondered, glancing about her in the soft gloom of the beautiful theatre, begrudge her, if they knew, her cherished freedom and sense of unrestraint? If she were to say to this next woman for instance, " I'm coloured," would she show the occasional dog-in-the-manger attitude of certain white Americans and refuse to sit by her or make a complaint to the usher? But she had no intention of making such an announce-ment. So she spent many happy, irresponsible, amused hours in the marvellous houses on Broad-way or in the dark commonplaceness of her beloved Fourteenth Street. There was a theatre, too, on Seventh Avenue just at the edge of the Village, which she came to frequent, not so much for the sake of the plays, which were the same as elsewhere, as for the sake of the audience, a curiously intimate sort of audience made of numerous still more intimate groups. Their members seemed both purposeful and leisurely. When she came here her loneliness palled on her, however. All unaware her face took on the wistfulness of the men gazing in the music store. She wished she knew some of these pleasant people.

It came to her that she was neglecting her Art. " And it was for that that I broke away from everything and came to New York. ' I must hunt up some classes." This she felt was not quite true, then the real cause rushed up to the surface of her mind: " And perhaps I'll meet some people."

She enrolled in one of the art classes in Cooper Union. This, after all, she felt would be the real beginning of her adventure. For here she must make acquaintances and one of them, perhaps several, must produce some effect on her life, perhaps alter its whole tenor. And for the first time she would be seen, would be met against her new background or rather, against no background. No boyish stowaway on a ship had a greater exuberance in going forth to meet the unknown than had Angela as she entered her class that first afternoon. In the room were five people, working steadily and chatting in an extremely desultory way. The instructor, one of the five, motioned her to a seat whose position made her one of the group. He set up her easel and as she arranged her material she glanced shyly but keenly about her. For the first time she realized how lonely she had been. She thought with a joy which surprised herself: " Within a week I'll be chatting with them too; perhaps going to lunch or to tea with one of them." She arranged herself for a better view,

The young woman nearest her, the possessor of a great mop of tawny hair and smiling clear, slate-grey eyes glanced up at her and nodded, "Am I in your way?" Except for her hair and eyes she was nondescript. A little beyond sat a coloured girl of medium height and build, very dark, very clean, very reserved. Angela, studying her with inner secret knowledge, could feel her constantly withdrawn from her companions. Her refinement was conspicuous but her reserve more so; when asked she passed and received erasers and other articles but she herself did no borrowing nor did she initiate any conversation. Her squarish head capped with a mass of unnaturally straight and unnaturally burnished hair possessed a kind of ugly beauty. Angela could not tell whether her features were good but blurred and blunted by the soft night of her skin or really ugly with an ugliness lost and plunged in that skin's deep concealment. Two students were still slightly behind her. She wondered how she could best contrive to see them.

Someone said: "Hi, there! Miss New One, have *you* got a decent eraser? all mine are on the blink." Not so sure whether or not the term applied to herself she turned to meet the singularly intent gaze of a slender girl with blue eyes, light chestnut hair and cheeks fairly blazing with some unguessed excitement. Angela smiled and offered her eraser.

"It ought to be decent, it's new."

"Yes, it's a very good one; many thanks. I'll try not to trouble you again. My name's Paulette Lister, what's yours?"

"Angèle Mory." She had changed it thus

'slightly when she came to New York. Some troubling sense of loyalty to her father and mother had made it impossible for her to do away with it altogether.

"Mory," said a young man who had been working just beyond Paulette; "that's Spanish. Are you by any chance?"

"I don't think so."

"He is," said Paulette. "His name is Anthony Cruz—isn't that a lovely name? But he changed it to Cross because no American would ever pronounce the z right, and he didn't want to be taken for a widow's cruse."

"That's a shameful joke," said Cross, "but since I made it up, I think you might give me a chance to spring it, Miss Lister. A poor thing but mine own. You might have a heart."

"Get even with her, why don't you, by introducing her as Miss Blister?" asked Angela, highly diverted by the foolish talk.

Several people came in then, and she discovered that she had been half an hour too early, the class was just beginning. She glanced about at the newcomers, a beautiful Jewess with a pearly skin and a head positively foaming with curls, a tall Scandinavian, an obvious German, several more Americans. Not one of them made the photograph on her mind equal to those made by the coloured girl whose name, she learned, was Rachel Powell, the slate-eyed Martha Burden, Paulette Lister and Anthony Cross. Her prediction came true. With in a week she was on jestingly intimate terms with every one of them except Miss Powell, who lent her belongings, borrowed nothing, and spoke only when she was spoken to. At the end of ten days

Miss Burden asked Angela to come and have lunch "at the same place where I go".

. . . . .

On an exquisite afternoon she went to Harlem. At One Hundred and Thirty-fifth Street she left the 'bus and walked through from Seventh Avenue to Lenox, then up to One Hundred and Forty-seventh Street and back down Seventh Avenue to One Hundred and Thirty-ninth Street, through this to Eighth Avenue and then weaving back and forth between the two Avenues through Thirty-eighth, Thirty-seventh down to One Hundred and Thirty-fifth Street to Eighth Avenue where she took the Elevated and went back to the New York which she knew.

But she was amazed and impressed at this bustling, frolicking, busy, laughing great city within a greater one. She had never seen coloured life so thick, so varied, so complete. Moreover, just as this city reproduced in microcosm all the important features of any metropolis, so undoubtedly life up here was just the same, she thought dimly, as life anywhere else. Not all these people, she realized, glancing keenly at the throngs of black and brown, yellow and white faces about her were servants or underlings or end men. She saw a beautiful woman all brown and red dressed as exquisitely as anyone she had seen on Fifth Avenue. A man's sharp, high-bred face etched itself on her memory, —the face of a professional man perhaps,—it might be an artist. She doubted that; he might of course be a musician, but it was unlikely that he would be her kind of an artist, for how could he exist? Ah, there lay the great difference. In all material, even in all practical things these two worlds were alike, but in the production, the fostering of those ultimate manifestations, this world was lacking, for its people were without the means or the leisure to support them and enjoy. And these were the manifestations which she craved, together with the freedom to enjoy them. No, she was not sorry that she had chosen as she had, even though she could now realize that life viewed from the angle of Opal and Jefferson Streets in Philadelphia and that same life viewed from One Hundred and Thirty-fifth Street and Seventh Avenue in New York might present bewilderingly different facets.

Unquestionably there was something very fascinating, even terrible, about this stream of life,—it seemed to her to run thicker, more turgidly than that safe, sublimated existence in which her new friends had their being. It was deeper, more mightily moving even than the torrent of Fourteenth Street. Undoubtedly just as these people,— for she already saw them objectively, doubly so, once with her natural remoteness and once with the remoteness of her new estate,—just as these people could suffer more than others, just so they could enjoy themselves more. She watched the moiling groups on Lenox Avenue; the amazingly well-dressed and good-looking throngs of young men on Seventh Avenue at One Hundred and Thirty-seventh and Thirty-fifth Streets. They were gossiping, laughing, dickering, chaffing, combining the customs of the small town with the astonishing cosmopolitanism of their clothes and manners. Nowhere down town did she see life like this. Oh, all this was fuller, richer, not finer but richer with the difference in quality that there is between velvet and silk. Harlem was a great city, but after all it was a city within a city, and she was glad, as she strained for last glimpses out of the lurching " L " train, that she had cast in her lot with the dwellers outside its dark and serried tents.

CHAPTER II

"WHERE do you live?" asked Paulette, "when you're not here at school?"

Angela blushed as she told her.

"In a hotel? In Union Square? Child, are you a millionaire? Where did you come from? Don't you care anything about the delights of home? Mr. Cross, come closer. Here is this poor child living benightedly in a hotel when she might have two rooms at least in the Village for almost the same price."

Mr. Cross came closer but without saying anything. He was really, Angela thought, a very serious, almost sad young man. He had never continued long the bantering line with which he had first made her acquaintance.

She explained that she had not known where to go. "Often I've thought of moving, and of course I'm spending too much money for what I get out of it,—I've the littlest room."

Paulette opened her eyes very wide which gave an onlooker the effect of seeing suddenly the blue sky very close at hand. Her cheeks took on a flaming tint. She was really a beautiful, even fascinating girl—or woman,—Angela never learned which, for she never knew her age. But her fascination did not rest on her looks, or at least it did not arise from that source; it was more the result of her manner. She was so alive, so intense, so interested, if she were interested, that all her nerves, her emotions even were enlisted to accomplish the end which she might have in view. And withal she possessed the simplicity of a child. There was an unsuspected strength about her also that was oddly at variance with the rather striking fragility of her appearance, the trustingness of her gaze, the limpid unaffectedness of her manner. Mr. Cross, Angela thought negligently, must be in love with her; he was usually at her side when they sketched. But later she came to see that there was nothing at all between these two except a certain friendly appreciation tempered by a wary kindness on the part of Mr. Cross and a negligent generosity on the part of Paulette.

She displayed no negligence of generosity in her desire and eagerness to find Angela a suitable apartment. She did hold out, however, with amazing frankness for one " not too near me but also not too far away ". But this pleased the girl, for she had been afraid that Paulette would insist on offering to share her own apartment and she would not have known how to refuse. She had the complete egoist's desire for solitude.

Paulette lived on Bank Street; she found for her new friend " a duck,—just a duck,—no other word will describe it,—of an apartment " on Jayne Street, two rooms, bath and kitchenette. There was also a tiny balcony giving on a mews. It was more than Angela should have afforded, but the ease with which her affairs were working out gave her an assurance, almost an arrogance of confidence. Besides she planned to save by getting her own meals. The place was already furnished, its former occupant was preparing to go to London for two or more years.

" Two years," Angela said gaily, " everything in the world can happen to me in that time. Oh I wonder what will have happened; what I will be like ! " And she prepared to move in her slender · store of possessions. Anthony, prompted, she suspected by Paulette, offered rather shyly to help her. It was a rainy day, there were several boxes after all, and taxis were scarce, though finally he captured one for her and came riding back in triumph with the driver. Afterwards a few books had to be arranged, pictures must be hung. She had an inspiration.

" You tend to all this and I'll get you the best dinner you ever tasted in your life." Memories of Monday night dinners on Opal Street flooded her memory. She served homely, filling dishes, " fit for a drayman," she teased him. There were corn-beef hash, roasted sweet potatoes, corn pudding, and, regardless of the hour, muffins. After supper she refused to let him help her with the dishes but had him rest in the big chair in the living-room while she laughed and talked with him from the kitchenette at a distance of two yards. Gradually, as he sat there smoking, the sadness and strain faded out of his thin, dark face, he laughed and jested like any other normal young man. When he bade her good-bye he let his slow dark gaze rest in hers for a long silent moment. She closed the door and stood laughing, arranging her hair before the mirror.

" Of course he's loads better looking, but something about him makes me think of Matthew Henson. But nothing doing, young-fellow-me-lad. Spanish and I suppose terribly proud. I wonder what he'd say if he really knew?"

She was to go to Paulette's to dinner. " Just we two," stipulated Miss Lister. " Of course, I could have a gang of men, but I think it will be fun for us to get acquainted." Angela was pleased; she was very fond of Paulette, she liked her for her generous, capable self. And she was not quite ready for meeting men. She must know something more about these people with whom she was spending her life., Anthony Cross had been affable enough, but she was not sure that he, with his curious sadness, his half-proud, half-sensitive tendency to withdrawal, were a fair enough type. However, in spite of Paulette's protestations, there were three young men standing in her large, dark living-room when Angela arrived.

" But you've got to go at once," said Paulette, laughing but firm; " here is my friend,—isn't she beautiful? We've too many things to discuss without being bothered by you."

" Paulette has these fits of cruelty," said one of the three, a short, stocky fellow with an ugly, sensitive face. " She'd have made a good Nero. But anyway I'm glad I stayed long enough to see you. Don't let her hide you from us altogether." Another man made a civil remark; the third one standing back in the gloomy room said nothing, but the girl caught the impression of tallness and blondness and of a pair of blue eyes which stared at her intently. She felt awkward and showed it.

"See, you've made her shy," said Paulette accusingly. "I won't bother introducing them, Angèle, you'll meet them all too soon." Laughing, protesting, the men filed out, and their unwilling hostess closed the door on them with sincere lack of regret. "Men," she mused candidly. "Of course we can't get along without them any more than they can without us, but I get tired of them,—they're nearly all animals. I'd rather have a good woman friend any day." She sighed with genuine sincerity. "Yet my place is always full of men. Would you rather have your chops rare or well done? I like mine cooked to a cinder." Angela preferred hers well done. "Stay here and look around; see if I have anything to amuse you." Catching up an apron she vanished into some smaller and darker retreat which she called her kitchen.

The apartment consisted of the whole floor of a house on Bank Street, dark and constantly within the sound of the opening front door and the noises of the street. "But you don't have the damned stairs when you come in late at night," Paulette explained. The front room was, Angela supposed, the bedroom, though the only reason for this supposition was the appearance of a dressing-table and a wide, flat divan about one foot and a half from the floor, covered with black or purple velvet. The dressing table was a good piece of mahogany, but the chairs were indifferently of the kitchen variety and of the sort which, magazines affirm, may be made out of

a large packing box. In the living room, where
the little table was set, the same anomaly pre-
vailed; the china was fine, even dainty, but the
glasses were thick and the plating had begun to
wear off the silver/ware. On the other hand the
pictures were unusual, none of the stereotyped
things; instead Angela remarked a good copy
of Breughel's " Peasant Wedding ", the head of
Bernini and two etchings whose authors she did
not know. The bookcase held two paper bound
volumes of the poems of Béranger and Villon and
a little black worn copy of Heine. But the other
books were high-brow to the point of austerity:
Ely, Shaw and Strindberg.

" Perhaps you'd like to wash your hands? "
called Paulette. " There's a bathroom down the
corridor there, you can't miss it. You may have
some of my favourite lotion if you want it—up
there on the shelf." Angela washed her hands
and looked up for the lotion. Her eyes opened
wide in amazement. Beside the bottle stood a
man's shaving mug and brush and a case of razors.

The meal, " for you can't call it a dinner," the
cook remarked candidly, was a success. The
chops were tender though smoky; there were
spinach, potatoes, tomato and lettuce salad, rolls,
coffee and cheese. Its rugged quality surprised
Angela not a little; it was more a meal for a working man than for a woman, above all, a woman
of the faery quality of Paulette. " I get so
tired," she said, lifting a huge mouthful, " if I
don't eat heartily; besides it ruins my temper to go
hungry." Her whole attitude toward the meal
was so masculine and her appearance so daintily,

feminine that Angela burst out laughing, explaining with much amusement the cause of her merriment. "I hope you don't mind," she ended, "for of course you are conspicuously feminine. There's nothing of the man about you."

To her surprise Paulette resented this last statement. "There is a great deal of the man about me. I've learned that a woman is a fool who lets her femininity stand in the way of what she wants. I've made a philosophy of it. I see what I want; I use my wiles as a woman to get it, and I employ the qualities of men, tenacity and ruthlessness, to keep it. And when I'm through with it, I throw it away just as they do. Consequently I have no regrets and no encumbrances."

A packet of cigarettes lay open on the table and she motioned to her friend to have one. Angela refused, and sat watching her inhale in deep respirations; she had never seen a woman more completely at ease, more assuredly mistress of herself and of her fate. When they had begun eating Paulette had poured out two cocktails, tossing hers off immediately and finishing Angela's, too, when the latter, finding it too much like machine oil for her taste, had set it down scarcely diminished. "You'll get used to them if you go about with these men. You'll be drinking along with the rest of us."

She had practically no curiosity and on the other hand no reticences. And she had met with every conceivable experience, had visited France, Germany and Sweden; she was now contemplating a trip to Italy and might go to Russia; she would go now, in fact, if it were not that a friend of hers, Jack Hudson, was about to go, there, too, and as she was on the verge of having an affair with him she thought she'd better wait. She didn't relish the prospect of such an event in a foreign land, it put you too much at the man's mercy. An affair, if you were going to have one, was much better conducted on your own *pied à terre.*

"An affair?" gasped Angela.

"Yes,—why, haven't you ever had a lover?"

"A lover?"

"Goodness me, are you a poll parrot? Why yes, a lover. I've had"—she hesitated before the other's complete amazement,—"I've had more than one, I can tell you."

"And you've no intention of marrying?"

"Oh I don't say that; but what's the use of tying yourself up now while you're young? And then, too, this way you don't always have them around your feet; you can always leave them or they'll leave you. But it's better for you to leave them first. It insures your pride." With her babyish face and her sweet, high voice she was like a child babbling precociously. Yet she seemed bathed in intensity. But later she began to talk of her books and of her pictures, of her work and on all these subjects she spoke with the same subdued excitement; her eyes flashed, her cheeks grew scarlet, all experience meant life to her in various manifestations. She had been on a newspaper, one of the New York dailies; she had done press-agenting. At present she was illustrating for a fashion magazine. There was no end to her versatilities.

Angela said she must go.

"But you'll come again soon, won't you, Angèle?"

A wistfulness crept into her voice. "I do so want a woman friend. When a woman really is your friend she's so dependable and she's not expecting anything in return." She saw her guest to the door. "We could have some wonderful times. Good-night, Angèle." Like a child she lifted her face to be kissed.

Angela's first thought as she walked down the dark street was for the unfamiliar name by which Paulette had called her. For though she had signed herself very often as Angèle, no one as yet used it. Her old familiar formula came to her: "I wonder what she would think if she knew." But of one thing she was sure: if Paulette had been in her place she would have acted in exactly the same way. "She would have seen what she wanted and would have taken it," she murmured and fell to thinking of the various confidences which Paulette had bestowed upon her,—though so frank and unreserved were her remarks that "confidences" was hardly the name to apply to them. Certainly, Angela thought, she was in a new world and with new people. Beyond question some of the coloured people of her acquaintance must have lived in a manner which would not bear inspection, but she could not think of one who would thus have discussed it calmly with either friend or stranger. Wondering what it would be like to conduct oneself absolutely according to one's own laws, she turned into the dark little vestibule on Jayne Street. As usual the Jewish girl who lived above her was standing blurred in the thick blackness of the hall, and as usual Angela did not realize this until, touching the button and turning on the light, she caught sight of Miss Salting straining her face upwards to receive her lover's kiss.

CHAPTER III

FROM the pinnacle of her satisfaction in her studies, in her new friends and in the joke which she was having upon custom and tradition she looked across the class-room at Miss Powell who preserved her attitude of dignified reserve. Angela thought she would try to break it down; on Wednesday she asked the coloured girl to have lunch with her and was pleased to have the invitation accepted. She had no intention of taking the girl up as a matter either of patronage or of loyalty. But she thought it would be nice to offer her the ordinary amenities which their common student life made natural and possible. Miss Powell it appeared ate generally in an Automat or in a cafeteria, but Angela knew of a nice tea-room. " It's rather arty, but they do serve a good meal and it's cheap." Unfortunately on Wednesday she had to leave before noon; she told Miss Powell to meet her at the little restaurant. " Go in and get a table and wait for me, but I'm sure I'll be there as soon as you will." After all she was late, but, what was worse, she found to her dismay that Miss Powell, instead of entering the tea-room, had been awaiting her across the street. There were no tables and the two had to wait almost fifteen minutes before being served,

" Why on earth didn't you go in? " asked Angela a trifle impatiently, " you could have held the table." Miss Powell answered imperturbably: " Because I didn't know how they would receive me if I went in by myself." Angela could not pretend to misunderstand her. " Oh, I think they would have been all right," she murmured, blushing at her stupidity. How quickly she had forgotten those fears and uncertainties. She had never experienced this sort of difficulty herself, but she certainly knew of them from Virginia and others.

The lunch was not a particularly pleasant one. Either Miss Powell was actually dull or she had made a resolve never to let herself go in the presence of white people; perhaps she feared being misunderstood, perhaps she saw in such encounters a lurking attempt at sociological investigations; she would lend herself to no such procedure, that much was plain. Angela could feel her effort to charm, to invite confidence, glance upon and fall back from this impenetrable armour. She had been amazed to find both Paulette and Martha Burden already gaining their living by their sketches. Miss Burden indeed was a caricaturist of no mean local reputation; Anthony Cross was frankly a commercial artist, though he hoped some day to be a recognised painter of portraits. She was curious to learn of Miss Powell's prospects. Inquiry revealed that the young lady had one secret aspiration; to win or earn enough money to go to France and then after that, she said with sudden ardour, " anything could happen ". To this end she had worked, saved, scraped, gone without pleasures and clothes. Her

work was creditable, indeed above the average,
but not sufficiently imbued, Angela thought, with
the divine promise to warrant this sublimation of
normal desires.

Miss Powell seemed to read her thought. "And
then it gives me a chance to show America that
one of us can stick; that we have some idea above
the ordinary humdrum of existence."

She made no attempt to return the luncheon
but she sent Angela one day a bunch of beautiful
jonquils,—and made no further attempt at friendship. To one versed in the psychology of this
proud, sensitive people the reason was perfectly
plain. "You've been awfully nice to me and I
appreciate it but don't think I'm going to thrust
myself upon you. Your ways and mine lie along
different paths."

Such contacts, such interpretations and investigations were making up her life, a life that for
her was interesting and absorbing, but which had
its perils and uncertainties. She had no purpose,
for it was absurd for her, even with her ability, to
consider Art an end. She was using it now deliberately, as she had always used it vaguely, to get in
touch with interesting people and with a more
attractive atmosphere. And she was spending
money too fast; she had been in New York eight
months, and she had already spent a thousand
dollars. At this rate her little fortune which had
seemed at first inexhaustible would last her less
than two years; at best, eighteen months more.
Then she must face,—what? Teaching again?

Never, she'd had enough of that. Perhaps she could earn her living with her brush, doing menu cards, Christmas and birthday greetings, flowers, Pierrots and Pierrettes on satin pillow tops. She did not relish that. True there were the specialities of Paulette and of Martha Burden, but she lacked the deft sureness of the one and the slightly mordant philosophy underlying the work of the other. Her own speciality she felt sure lay along the line of reproducing, of interpreting on a face the emotion which lay back of that expression. She thought of her Fourteenth Street " types ",—that would be the sort of work which she would really enjoy, that and the depicting of the countenance of a purse-proud but lonely man, of the silken inanity of a society girl, of the smiling despair of a harlot. Even in her own mind she hesitated before the use of that terrible word, but association was teaching her to call a spade a spade.

Yes, she might do worse than follow the example of Mr. Cross and become a portrait painter. But somehow she did not want to have to do this; necessity would, she was sure, spoil her touch; besides, she hated the idea of the position in which she would be placed, fearfully placating and flattering possible patrons, hurrying through with an order because she needed the cheque, accepting patronage and condescension. No, she hoped to be sought after, to have the circumstances which would permit her to pick and choose, to refuse if the whim pleased her. It should mean something to be painted by " Mory ". People would say, " I'm going to have my portrait done by ' Mory ' ". But all this would call for position, power, wealth.

And again she said to herself .'. . " I might marry—a white man. Marriage is the easiest way for a woman to get those things, and white men have them." But she knew only one white man, Anthony Cross, and he would never have those qualities, at least not by his deliberate seeking. They might come eventually but only after long years. Long, long years of struggle with realities. There was a simple, genuine stead-fastness in him that made her realize that he would seek for the expression of truth and of himself even at the cost of the trimmings of life. And she was ashamed, for she knew that for the vanities and gewgaws of a leisurely and irresponsible existence she would sacrifice her own talent, the integrity of her ability to interpret life, to write down a history with her brush.

．　　　　．　　　　．　　　　．　　　　．

Martha Burden was as strong and as pronounced a personage as Paulette; even stronger perhaps because she had the great gift of silence. Paulette, as Angela soon realized, lived in a state of con-stant defiance. " I don't care what people think," was her slogan; men and women appealed to her in proportion to the opposition which they, too, proclaimed for the established thing. Angela was surprised that she clung as persistently as she did to a friendship with a person as conventional and reactionary as herself. But Martha Burden was not like that. One could not tell whether or not she was thinking about other people's opinions. It was probable that the other people and their attitude never entered her mind. She was cool and slightly aloof, with the coolness and aloofness of her slaty eyes and her thick, tawny hair. Neither the slatiness nor the tawniness proclaimed warmth —only depth, depth and again depth. It was impossible to realize what she would be like if impassioned or deeply stirred to anger. There would probably be something implacable, god-like about her; she would be capable of a long, slow, steady burning of passion. Few men would love Martha though many might admire her. But a man once enchanted might easily die for her.

Angela liked her house with its simple elegance, its fine, soft curtains and steady, shaded glow of light that stood somehow for home. She liked her husband, Ladislas Starr, whom Martha produced without a shade of consciousness that this was the first intimation she had given of being married. They were strong individualists, molten and blended in a design which failed to obscure their emphatic personalities. Their apartment in the Village was large and neat and sunny; it bore no trace of palpable wealth, yet nothing conducing to comfort was lacking. Book-cases in the dining-room and living-room spilled over; the *Nation*, the *Mercury*, the *Crisis*, *a magazine of the darker races*, left on the broad arm of an easy chair, mutely invited; it was late autumn, almost winter, but there were jars of fresh flowers. The bedroom where Angela went to remove her wrap was dainty and restful.

The little gathering to which Martha had invited her was made up of members as strongly individual as the host and hostess. They were all specialists in their way, and specialists for the most part in some offshoot of a calling or movement which was itself already highly specialized. Martha presented a psychiatrist, a war correspondent,— " I'm that only when there is a war of course," he explained to Angela's openly respectful gaze,— a dramatist, a corporation lawyer, a white-faced, conspicuously beautiful poet with a long evasive Russian name, two press agents, a theatrical manager, an actress who played only Shakespeare rôles, a teacher of defective children and a medical student who had been a conscientious objector and had served a long time at Leavenworth. He lapsed constantly into a rapt self-communing from whch he only roused himself to utter fiery tirades against the evils of society.

In spite of their highly specialised interests they were all possessed of a common ground of knowledge in which such subjects as Russia, Consumers' Leagues, and the coming presidential election figured most largely. There was much laughter and chaffing but no airiness, no per- siflage. One of the press agents, Mrs. Cecil, entered upon a long discussion with the corpora- tion lawyer on a Bill pending before Congress; she knew as much as he about the matter and held her own in a long and almost bitter argu- ment which only the coming of refreshments broke up.

Just before the close of the argument two other young men had come in, but Angela never learned their vocation. Furthermore she was interested in observing the young teacher of defective children. She was coloured; small and well-built, exquisitely dressed, and of a beautiful tint, all bronze and soft red, " like Jinny " thought Angela, a little aston- ished to observe how the warmth of her appearance overshadowed or rather overshone everyone else in the room. The tawniness even of Miss Burden's hair went dead beside her. The only thing to cope with her richness was the classical beauty of the Russian poet's features. He seemed unable to keep his eyes away from her; was punctiliously attentive to her wants and leaned forward several times during the long political discussion to whisper low spoken and apparently amusing comments. The young woman, perfectly at ease in her deep chair, received his attentions with a slightly detached, amused objectivity; an objectivity which she had for everyone in the room including Angela at whom she had glanced once rather sharply. But the detachment of her manner was totally different from Miss Powell's sensitive dignity. Totally without self-consciousness she let her warm dark eyes travel from one face to another. She might have been saying: " How far you are away from the things that really matter, birth and death and hard, hard work! " The Russian poet must have realized this, for once Angela heard him say, leaning forward, " *You* think all this is futile, don't you? "

Martha motioned for her to wait a moment until most of the other guests had gone, then she came forward with one of the two young men who had come in without introduction. " This is Roger Fielding, he'll see you home."

He was tall and blond with deeply blue eyes which smiled on her as he said: " Would you like to walk or ride? It's raining a little."

Angela said she preferred to walk.

116

" All right then.   Here, Starr, come across with that umbrella I lent you."

They went out into the thin, tingling rain of late Autumn.   " I was surprised," said Roger, " to see you there with the high-brows.   I didn't think you looked that way when I met you at Paulette's."

" We've met before?   I'm—I'm sorry, but I don't seem to remember you."

" No I don't suppose you would.   Well, we didn't exactly meet; I saw you one day at Paulette's.   That's why I came this evening, because I heard you'd be here and I'd get a chance to see you again; but I was surprised because you didn't seem like that mouthy bunch.   They make me tired taking life so plaguey seriously. Martha and her old high-brows!" he ended ungratefully.

Angela, a little taken back with the frankness of his desire to meet her, said she hadn't thought they were serious.

" Not think them serious?   Great Scott! what kind of talk are you used to?   You look as though you'd just come out of a Sunday-school!   Do you prefer bible texts? "

But she could not explain to him the picture which she saw in her mind of men and women at her father's home in Opal Street,—the men talking painfully of rents, of lynchings, of building and loan associations; the women of child-bearing and the sacrifices which must be made to put Gertie through school, to educate Howard.   " I don't mean for any of my children to go through what I did."   And in later years in her own first maturity, young Henson and Sawyer and the others in the tiny parlour talking of ideals and inevitable sacrifices for the race; the burnt-offering of individualism for some dimly glimpsed racial whole. This was seriousness, even sombreness, with a great sickening vital upthrust of reality. But these other topics, peaks of civilization superimposed upon peaks, she found, even though interesting, utterly futile.

They had reached the little hall now. "We must talk loud," she whispered.

"Why?" he asked, speaking obediently very loud indeed.

"Wait a minute; no, she's not there. The girl above me meets her young man here at night and just as sure as I forget her and come in quietly there they are in the midst of a kiss. I suspect she hates me."

In his young male sophistication he thought at first that this was a lead, but her air was so gay and so childishly guileless that he changed his opinion. "Though no girl in this day and time could be as simple and innocent as *she* looks."

But aloud he said, "Of course she doesn't hate you, nobody could do that. I assure you I don't."

She thought his gallantries very amusing. "Well, it relieves me to hear you say so; that'll keep me from worrying for one night at least." And withdrawing her hand from his retaining grasp, she ran upstairs.

A letter from Virginia lay inside the door. Getting ready for bed she read it in bits.

" Angela darling, wouldn't it be fun if I were to come to New York too? Of course you'd keep on living in your Village and I'd live in famous Harlem, but we'd both be in the same city, which is where two only sisters ought to be,—dumb I calls it to live apart the way we do. The man out at the U. of P. is crazy to have me take an exam. in music; it would be easy enough and much better pay than I get here. So there are two perfectly good reasons why I should come. He thinks I'll do him credit and I want to get away from this town."

Then between the lines the real reason betrayed itself :

" I do have such awful luck. Edna Brown had a party out in Merion not long ago and Matthew took me. And you know what riding in a train can do for me,—well that night of all nights I had to become car-sick. Matthew had been so nice. He came to see me the next morning, but, child, he's never been near me from that day to this. I suppose a man can't get over a girl's being such a sight as I was that night. Can't things be too hateful ! "

Angela couldn't help murmuring: " Imagine anyone wanting old Matthew so badly that she's willing to break up her home to get over him. Now why couldn't he have liked her instead of me ? "

And pondering on such mysteries she crept into bed. But she fell to thinking again about the evening she had spent with Martha and the people whom she had met. And again it seemed to her that they represented an almost alarmingly un-necessary class. If any great social cataclysm were to happen they would surely be the first to be swept out of the running. Only the real people could survive. Even Paulette's mode of living, it seemed to her, had something more forthright and vital.

CHAPTER IV

In the morning she was awakened by the ringing of the telephone. The instrument was an extravagance, for, save for Anthony's, she received few calls and made practically none. But the woman from whom she had taken the apartment had persuaded her into keeping it. Still, as she had never indicted the change in ownership, its value was small. She lay there for a moment blinking drowsily in the thin but intensely gold sunshine of December thinking that her ears were deceiving her.

Finally she reached out a rosy arm, curled it about the edge of the door jamb and, reaching the little table that stood in the other room just on the other side of the door, set the instrument up in her bed. The apartment was so small that almost everything was within arm's reach.

" Hello," she murmured sleepily.

" Oh, I thought you must be there; I said to myself: ' She couldn't have left home this early '. What time do you go to that famous drawing class of yours anyway? "

" I beg your pardon! Who is this speaking, please? "

" Why, Roger, of course,—Roger Fielding. Don't say you've forgotten me already. This is Angèle, isn't it? "

" Yes this is Angèle Mory speaking, Mr. Field-ing."

" Did I offend your Highness, Miss Mory? Will you have lunch with me to-day and let me tell you how sorry I am? "

But she was lunching with Anthony. " I have an engagement."

" Of course you have. Well, will you have tea, dinner, supper to-day,—breakfast and all the other meals to-morrow and so on for a week? You might just as well say ' yes ' because I'll pester you till you do.".

" I'm engaged for tea, too, but I'm not really as popular as I sound. That's my last engagement for this week; I'll be glad to have dinner with you."

" Right-oh! Now don't go back and finish up that beauty sleep, for if you're any more charm-ing than you were last night I won't answer for myself. I'll be there at eight."

Inexperienced as she was, she was still able to recognize his method as a bit florid; she preferred, on the whole, Anthony's manner at lunch when he leaned forward and touching her hand very lightly said: " Isn't it great for us to be here! I'm so content, Angèle. Promise me you'll have lunch with me every day this week. I've had a streak of luck with my drawings."

She promised him, a little thrilled herself with his evident sincerity and with the niceness of the smile which so transfigured his dark, thin face, robbing it of its tenseness and strain.

Still something, some vanity, some vague pre-monition of adventure, led her to linger over her dressing for the dinner with Roger. There was never very much colour in her cheeks, but her skin was warm and white; there was vitality beneath her pallor; her hair was warm, too, long and thick and yet so fine that it gave her little head the effect of being surrounded by a nimbus of light; rather wayward, glancing, shifting light for there were little tendrils and wisps and curls in front and about the temples which no amount of coaxing could subdue. She touched up her mouth a little, not so much to redden it as to give a hint of the mondaine to her appearance. Her dress was flame-colour—Paulette had induced her to buy it,—of a plain, rather heavy beautiful glowing silk. The neck was high in back and girlishly modest in front. She had a string of good artificial pearls and two heavy silver bracelets. Thus she gave the effect of a flame herself; intense and opaque at the heart where her dress gleamed and shone, transparent and fragile where her white warm neck and face rose into the tenuous shadow of her hair. Her appearance excited herself.

Roger found her delightful. As to women he considered himself a connoisseur. This girl pleased him in many respects. She was young; she was, when lighted from within by some indescribable mechanism, even beautiful; she had charm and, what was for him even more important, she was puzzling. In repose, he noticed, studying her closely, her quiet look took on the resemblance of an arrested movement, a composure on tip-toe so to speak, as though she had been stopped in the swift transition from one mood to another. And back of that momentary cessation of action one could see a mind darting, quick, restless, indefatigable, observing, tabulating perhaps even mocking. She had for him the quality of the foreigner, but she gave this quality an objectivity as though he were the stranger and she the well-known established personage taking note of his peculiarities and apparently boundlessly diverted by them.

But of all this Angela was absolutely unaware. No wonder she was puzzling to Roger, for, in addition to the excitement which she—a young woman in the high tide of her youth, her health, and her beauty—would be feeling at receiving in the proper setting the devotion and attention which all women crave, she was swimming in the flood of excitement created by her unique position. Stolen waters are the sweetest. And Angela never forgot that they were stolen. She thought: "Here I am having everything that a girl ought to have just because I had sense enough to suit my actions to my appearance." The realization, the secret fun bubbling back in some hidden recess of her heart, brought colour to her cheeks, a certain temerity to her manner. Roger pondered on this quality. If she were reckless!

The dinner was perfect; it was served with elegance and beauty. Indeed she was surprised at the surroundings, the grandeur even of the hotel to which he had brought her. She had no idea of his means, but had supposed that his circumstances were about those of her other new friends; probably he was better off than Anthony, whose poverty she instinctively sensed, and she judged that his income, whatever it might be, was not so perilous as Paulette's. But she would have put him on the same footing as' the Starrs. This sort of expenditure, however, meant money, " unless he 'really does like me and is splurging this time just for 'me ". The idea appealed to her vanity and gave her a sense of power; she' looked at Roger with a warm smile. At once his intent, considering gaze filmed; he was already leaning toward her but' he bent even farther across the perfect little table and asked in a' low, eager tone: " Shall we stay here and dance or go to your. house and talk and smoke a bit? "

" Oh we'll stay and dance; it would be so late by the time we get home that we'd only have a few minutes."

Presently the golden evening was over and they were in the vestibule at Jayne Street. Roger said very loudly: " Where's that push button? " Then lower: " Well, your young lovers aren't here to-night either. I'm beginning to' think you made that story up, Angèle."

She assured him, laughing, that she had' told the truth. " You come here some time and you'll see them for yourself." But she wished she could think of something more ordinary to say. His hands held hers very tightly; they were very strong and for the first time she noticed that the veins stood up on them like cords. She tried to pull her own away and he released' them' and, taking her key, turned the lock in the inner' door, then stood looking down at her.

" Well I'm glad they're not here to-night to take their revenge." And as he handed her back the key he kissed her on the lips. His knowledge of women based on many, many such experiences, told him that her swift retreat was absolutely unfeigned.

As on a former occasion she stood, after she had gained her room, considering herself in the glass. She had been kissed only once before, by Matthew Henson, and that kiss had been neither as casual nor as disturbing as this. She was thrilled, excited, and vaguely displeased. "He is fresh, I'll say that for him." And subsiding into the easy chair she thought for a long time of Anthony Cross and his deep respectful ardour.

In the morning there were flowers.

.   .   .   .   "   .

From the class-room she went with Paulette to deliver the latter's sketches. "Have tea to-day with me; we'll blow ourselves at the Ritz. This is the only time in the month that I have any money, so we'll make the best of it."

Angela looked about the warm, luxurious room at the serene, luxurious women, the super-groomed, super-deferential, tremendously confident men. She sighed. "I love all this, love it."

Paulette, busy blowing smoke-rings, nodded. "I blew sixteen that time. Watch me do it again. There's nothing really to this kind of life, you know."

"Oh don't blow smoke-rings! It's the only thing in the world that can spoil your looks. What do you mean there's nothing to it?"

" Well for a day-in-and-day-out existence, it just doesn't do. It's too boring. It's fun for you and me to drift in here 'twice a year when we've just had a nice, fat cheque which we've got to spend. But there's nothing to it for every day; it's too much like reaching the harbour where you would be. The tumult and the shouting are all over. I'd rather live just above the danger line down on little old Bank Street, and think up a way to make five hundred dollars so I could go to the French Riviera second class and bum around those little towns, Villefranche, Beaulieu, Cagnes,—you must see them, Angèle— and have a spanking affair with a real man with honest to God blood in his veins than to sit here and drink tea and listen to the nothings of all these tame tigers, trying you out, seeing how much it will take to buy you."

Angela was bewildered by this outburst. " I thought you said you didn't like affairs unless you could conduct them on your own *pied à terre*."

" Did I? Well that was another time—not to-day. By the way, what would you say if I were to tell you that I'm going to Russia? "

She glanced at her friend with the bright shamelessness of a child, for she knew that Angela had heard of Jack Hudson's acceptance as newspaper correspondent in Moscow.

" I wouldn't say anything except that I'd much rather be here in the warmth and cleanliness of the Ritz than be in Moscow where I'm sure it will be cold and dirty."

" That's because you've never wanted anyone." Her face for a moment was all desire. Beautiful but terrible too. " She actually looks like Hetty Daniels," thought Angela in astonishment. Only, alas, there was no longer any beauty in Hetty's face.

" When you've set your heart on anybody or on anything there'll be no telling what you'll do, Angèle. For all your innocence you're as deep, you'll be as desperate as Martha Burden once you're started. I know your kind. Well, if you must play around in the Ritz, etcet., etcet., I'll tell Roger Fielding. He's a good squire and he can afford it."

" Why? Is he so rich? "

" Rich! If all the wealth that he—no, not he, but his father—if all the wealth that old man Fielding possesses were to be converted into silver dollars there wouldn't be space enough in this room, big as it is, to hold it."

Angela tried to envisage it. " And Roger, what does he do? "

" Spend it. What is there for him to do? Nothing except have a good time and keep in his father's good graces. His father's some kind of a personage and all that, you know, crazy about his name and his posterity. Roger doesn't dare get drunk and lie in the gutter and he mustn't make a misalliance. Outside of that the world's his oyster and he eats it every day. There's a boy who gets everything he wants."

" What do you mean by a misalliance? He's not royalty."

" Spoken like a good American. No, he's not. But he mustn't marry outside certain limits. No chorus girl romances for his father. The old man wouldn't care a rap about money but he would insist on blue blood and the Mayflower. The funny thing is that Roger, for all his appearing so democratic, is that way too. But of course he's been so run after the marvel is that he's as unspoiled as he is. But it's the one thing I can't stick in him. I don't mind a man's not marrying me; but I can't forgive him if he thinks I'm not good enough to marry him. Any woman is better than the best of men." Her face took on its intense, burning expression; one would have said she was consumed with excitement.

Angela nodded, only half-listening. Roger a multi-millionaire! Roger who only two nights ago had kissed and mumbled her fingers, his eyes avid and yet so humble and beseeching!

"One thing, if you do start playing around with Roger be careful. He's a good bit of a rotter, and he doesn't care what he says or spends to gain his ends." She laughed at the inquiry in her friend's eyes. "No, I've never given Roger five minutes' thought. But I know his kind. They're dangerous. It's wrong for men to have both money and power; they're bound to make some woman suffer. Come on up the Avenue with me and I'll buy a hat. I can't wear this whang any longer. It's too small, looks like a peanut on a barrel."

.   .   .   .   .

Angela was visual minded. She saw the days of the week, the months of the year in little narrow divisions of space. She saw the past years of her life falling into separate, uneven compartments whose ensemble made up her existence. Whenever she looked back on this period from Christmas to Easter she saw a bluish haze beginning in a white mist and flaming into something red and terrible; and across the bluish haze stretched the name: Roger.

Roger! She had never seen anyone like him: so gay, so beautiful, like a blond, glorious god, so overwhelming, so persistent. She had not liked him so much at first except as one likes the sun or the sky or a singing bird, anything jolly and free. There had been no touching points for their minds. He knew nothing of life except what was pleasurable; it is true his idea of the pleasurable did not always coincide with hers. He had no fears, no restraints, no worries. Yes, he had one; he did not want to offend his father. He wanted ardently and unswervingly his father's money. he did not begrudge his senior a day, an hour, a moment of life; about this he had a queer, unselfish sincerity. The old financial war horse had made his fortune by hard labour and pitiless fighting. He had given Roger his being, the *entrée* into a wonderful existence. Already he bestowed upon him an annual sum which would have kept several families in comfort. If Roger had cared to save for two years he need never have asked his father for another cent. With any kind of luck he could have built up for himself a second colossal fortune. But he did not care to do this. He did not wish his father one instant's loss of life or of its enjoyment. But he did want final possession of those millions.

Angela liked him best when he talked about

"my dad"; he never mentioned the vastness of his wealth, but by now she could not have helped guessing even without Paulette's aid that he was a wealthy man. She would not take jewellery from him, but there was a steady stream of flowers, fruit, candy, books, fine, copies of the old masters. She was afraid and ashamed to express a longing in his presence. And with all this his steady, constant attendance. And an odd watchfulness which she felt but could not explain.

"He must love me," she said to herself, thinking of his caresses. She had been unable to keep him from kissing her. Her uneasiness had amused and charmed him: he laughed at her Puritanism, succeeded in shaming her out of it. "Child, where have you lived? Why there's nothing in a kiss. If I didn't kiss you I couldn't come to see you. And I have to see you, Angèle!" His voice grew deep; the expression in his eyes made her own falter.

Yet he did not ask her to marry him. "But I suppose it's because he can see I don't love him yet." And she wondered what it would be like to love. Even Jinny knew more about this than she, for she had felt, perhaps still did feel, a strong affection for Matthew Henson. Well, anyway, if they married she would probably come to love him; most women learned to love their husbands. At first after her conversation with Paulette about Roger she had rather expected a diminution at any time of his attentions, for after all she was unknown; from Roger's angle she would be more than outside the pale. But she was sure now that he loved and

would want to marry her, for it never occurred
to her that men bestowed attentions such as these
on a passing fancy. She saw her life rounding
out like a fairy tale. Poor, coloured—coloured in
America; unknown, a nobody! And here at her
hand was the forward thrust shadow of love
and of great wealth. She would do lots of good
among coloured people; she would see that Miss
Powell, for instance, had her scholarship. Oh
she would hunt out girls and men like Seymour
Porter,—she had almost forgotten his name,—
or was it Arthur Sawyer?—and give them a taste of
life in its fullness and beauty such as they had
never dreamed of.

To-night she was to go out with Roger. She
wore her flame-coloured dress again; a pretty green
one was also hanging up in her closet, but she wore
the flame one because it lighted her up from within
—lighted not only her lovely, fine body but her
mind too. Her satisfaction with her appearance
let loose some inexplicable spring of gaiety and
merriment and simplicity so that she seemed
almost daring.

Roger, sitting opposite, tried to probe her mood,
tried to gauge the invitation of her manner and its
possibilities. She touched him once or twice,
familiarly; he thought almost possessively. She
seemed to be within reach now if along with that
accessibility she had recklessness. It was this
attribute which for the first time to-night he
thought to divine within her. If in addition to
her insatiable interest in life—for she was always
asking him about people and places,—she possessed
this recklessness, then indeed he might put to her a
proposal which had been hanging on his lips for

weeks and months. Something innocent, pathetically untouched about her had hitherto kept him
back. But if she had the requisite daring! They
were dining in East Tenth Street in a small *café*
—small contrasted with the Park Avenue Hotel
to which he had first taken her. But about them
stretched the glitter and perfection of crystal and
silver, of marvellous napery and of obsequious
service. Everything, Angela thought, looking
about her, was translated. The slight odour of
food was, she told Fielding, really an aroma:
the mineral water which he was drinking because he could not help it and she because
she could not learn to like wine, was nectar; the
bread, the fish, the, courses were ambrosia.
The food, too, in general was to be spoken of
as viands.

" Vittles, translated," she said laughing.

" And you, you, too, are translated. Angèle,
you are wonderful, you are charming," his lips
answered but his senses beat and hammered.
Intoxicated with the magic of the moment and the
surroundings, she turned her smiling countenance
a little nearer, and saw his face change, darken.
A cloud over the sun.

" Excuse me," he said and walked hastily across
the room back of her. In astonishment she
turned and looked after him. At a table behind
her three coloured people (under the direction of a
puzzled and troubled waiter,) were about to take
a table. Roger went up and spoke to the head-
waiter authoritatively, even angrily. The latter
glanced about the room, nodded obsequiously
and crossing, addressed the little group. There
was a hasty, slightly acrid discussion. Then the

three filled out, past Angela's table this time, their heads high.

She turned back to her plate, her heart sick. For her the evening was ended. Roger came back, his face flushed, triumphant, " Well I put a spoke in the wheel of those ' coons '! They forget themselves so quickly, coming in here spoiling white people's appetites. I told the manager if they brought one of their damned suits I'd be responsible. I wasn't going to have them here with you, Angèle. I could tell that night at Martha Burden's by the way you looked at that girl that you had no time for darkies. I'll bet you'd never been that near to one before in your life, had you? Wonder where Martha picked that one up."

She was silent, lifeless. He went on recounting instances of how effectively he had " spoked the wheel " of various coloured people. He had black-balled Negroes in Harvard, aspirants for small literary or honour societies. " I'd send 'em all back to Africa if I could. There's been a darkey up in Harlem's got the right idea, I understand; though he must be a low brute to cave in on his race that way; of course it's merely a matter of money with him. He'd betray them all for a few thousands. Gosh, if he could really pull it through I don't know but what I'd be willing to finance it."

To this tirade there were economic reasons to oppose, tenets of justice, high ideals of humanity. But she could think of none of them. Speechless, she listened to him, her appetite fled.

" What's the matter, Angèle? Did it make you sick to see them? "

" No, no not that. I—I don't mind them; you're mistaken about me and that girl at Martha Burden's. It's you, you're so 'violent. I didn't know you were that way!"

" And I've made you afraid of me? Oh, I don't want to do that." But he was flattered to think that he had affected her. " See here, let's get some air. I'll take you for a spin around the Park and then run you home."

But she did not want to go to the Park; she wanted to go home immediately. His little blue car was outside; in fifteen minutes they were at Jayne Street. She would not permit him to come inside, not even in the vestibule; she barely gave him her hand.

" But Angèle, you can't leave me like this; why what have I done? Did it frighten you because I swore a little? But I'd never swear at you. Don't go like this."

She was gone, leaving him staring and nonplussed on the sidewalk. Lighting a cigarette, he climbed back in her car. " Now what the devil!" He shifted his gears. " But she likes me. I'd have sworn she liked me to-night. Those damn niggers! I bet she's thinking about me this minute."

.   .   .   .   .

He would have lost his bet. She was thinking about the coloured people.

She could visualize them all so plainly; she could interpret their changing expressions as completely as though those changes lay before her in a book. There were a girl and two men, one

young, the other the father perhaps of either of the
other two. The fatherly-looking person, for so
her mind docketed him, bore an expression of
readiness for any outcome whatever. She knew
and understood the type. His experiences of
surprises engendered by this thing called prejudice
had been too vast for them to appear to him as
surprises. If they were served this was a lucky
day; if not he would refuse to let the incident
shake his stout spirit.

It was to the young man and the girl that her
interest went winging. In the mirror behind
Roger she had seen them entering the room and
she had thought: "Oh, here are some of them
fighting it out again. O God! please let them be
served, please don't let their evening be spoiled."
She was so happy herself and she knew that the
reception of fifty other *maîtres d'hôtel* could not
atone for a rebuff at the beginning of the game.
The young fellow was nervous, his face tense,—
thus might he have looked going to meet the
enemy's charge in the recent Great War; but
there the odds were even; here the cards were
already stacked against him. Presently his expression would change for one of grimness,
determination and despair. Talk of a lawsuit
would follow; apparently did follow; still a lawsuit at best is a poor substitute for an evening's
fun.

But the girl, the girl in whose shoes she herself
might so easily have been! She was so clearly a
nice girl, with all that the phrase implies. To
Angela watching her intently and yet with the indifference of safety she recalled Virginia, so
slender, so appealing she was and so brave. So

very brave! Ah, that courage! It affected at first a gay hardihood: "Oh I know it isn't customary for people like us to come into this café, but everything is going to be all right." It met Angela's gaze with a steadiness before which her own quailed, for she thought: "Oh, poor thing! perhaps she thinks that I don't want her either." And when the blow had fallen the courage had had to be translated anew into a comforting assurance. "Don't worry about me, Jimmy," the watching guest could just hear her. "Indeed, indeed it won't spoil the evening, I should say not; there're plenty of places where they'd be all right. We just happened to pick a lemon."

The three had filed out, their heads high, their gaze poised and level. But the net result of the evening's adventure would be an increased cynicism in the elderly man, a growing bitterness for the young fellow, and a new timidity in the girl, who, even after they had passed into the street, could not relieve her feelings, for she must comfort her baffled and goaded escort.

Angela wondered if she had been half as consoling to Matthew Henson,—was it just a short year ago? And suddenly, sitting immobile in her arm-chair, her evening cloak slipping unnoticed to the floor, triumph began to mount in her. Life could never cheat her as it had cheated that coloured girl this evening, as it had once cheated her in Philadephia with Matthew. She was free, free to taste life in all its fullness and sweetness, in all its minutest details. By exercising sufficient courage to employ the unique weapon which an accident of heredity had placed in her grasp she

was able to master life. How she blessed her
mother for showing her the way! In a country
where colour or the lack of it meant the difference
between freedom and fetters how lucky she was!

But, she told herself, she was through with Roger
Fielding.

CHAPTER V

Now it was Spring, Spring in New York. Washington Square was a riot of greens that showed up bravely against the great red brick houses on its north side. The Arch viewed from Fifth Avenue seemed a gateway to Paradise. The long deep streets running the length of the city invited an exploration to the ends where pots of gold doubtless gleamed. On the short crosswise streets the April sun streamed in splendid banners of deep golden light.

In two weeks Angela had seen Roger only once. He telephoned every day, pleading, beseeching, entreating. On the one occasion when she did permit him to call there were almost tears in his eyes. "But, darling, what did I do? If you'd only tell me that. Perhaps I could explain away whatever it is that's come between us." But there was nothing to explain she told him gravely, it was just that he was harder, more cruel than she had expected; no, it wasn't the coloured people, she lied and felt her soul blushing, it was that now she knew him when he was angry or displeased, and she could see how ruthless, how determined he was to have things his way. His willingness to pay the costs of the possible lawsuit had filled her with a sharp fear. What could one do against a man, against a group of men such as he and his kind represented who would spend time and money to maintain a prejudice based on a silly, time-worn tradition?

Yet she found she did not want to lose sight of him completely. The care, the attention, the flattery with which he had surrounded her were beginning to produce their effect. In the beautiful but slightly wearying balminess of the Spring she missed the blue car which had been constantly at her call; eating a good but homely meal in her little living room with the cooking odours fairly overwhelming her from the kitchenette, she found herself longing unconsciously for the dainty food, the fresh Spring delicacies which she knew he would be only too glad to procure for her. Shamefacedly she had to acknowledge that the separation which she was so rigidly enforcing meant a difference in her tiny exchequer, for it had now been many months since she had regularly taken her main meal by herself and at her own expense.

To-day she was especially conscious of her dependence upon him, for she was to spend the afternoon in Van Cortlandt Park with Anthony. There had been talk of subways and the Elevated. Roger would have had the blue car at the door and she would have driven out of Jayne Street in state. Now it transpired that Anthony was to deliver some drawings to a man, a tricky customer, whom it was best to waylay if possible on Saturday afternoon. Much as he regretted it he would probably be a little late. Angela, therefore, to save time must meet him at Seventy-second Street. Roger would never have made a request like that; he would have brought his lawyer or his business man along in the car with him and, dismissing him with a curt " Well I'll see if I can finish this to-morrow," would have hastened to her with his best Walter Raleigh manner, and would have produced the cloak, too, if she would but say so. Perhaps she'd have to take him back. Doubtless later on she could manage his prejudices if only he would speak. But how was she to accomplish that?

Still it was lovely being here with Anthony in the park, so green and fresh, so new with the recurring newness of Spring. Anthony touched her hand and said as he had once before, " I'm so content to be with you, Angel. I may call you Angel, mayn't I? You are that to me, you know. Oh if you only knew how happy it makes me to be content, to be satisfied like this. I could get down on my knees and thank God for it like a little boy." He looked like a little boy as he said it. " Happiness is a hard thing to find and harder still to keep."

She asked him idly, " Haven't you always been happy? "

His face underwent a startling change. Not only did the old sadness and strain come back on it, but a great bitterness such as she had never before seen.

" No," he said slowly as though thinking through long years of his life. " I haven't been happy for years, not since I was a little boy. Never once have I been happy nor even at ease until I met you."

But she did not want him to find his happiness in her. That way would only lead to greater unhappiness for him. So she said, to change the subject: " Could you tell me about it? "

But there was nothing to tell, he assured her, his face growing darker, grimmer. " Only my father was killed when I was a little boy, killed by his enemies. I've hated them ever since; I never stopped hating them until I met you." But this was just as dangerous a road as the other plus the possibilities of re-opening old wounds. So she only shivered and said vaguely, " Oh, that was terrible! Too terrible to talk about. I'm sorry, Anthony!" And then as a last desperate topic: " Are you ever going back to Brazil?" For she knew that he had come to the United States from Rio de Janeiro. He had spent Christmas at her house, and had shown her pictures of the great, beautiful city and of his mother, a slender, dark-eyed woman with a perpetual sadness in her eyes.

The conversation languished. She thought: " It must be terrible to be a man and to have these secret hates and horrors back of one." Some Spanish feud, a matter of hot blood and ready knives, a sudden stroke, and then this deadly memory for him.

" No," he said after a long pause. " I'm never going back to Brazil. I couldn't." He turned to her suddenly. " Tell me, Angel, what kind of girl are you, what do you think worth while? Could you, for the sake of love, for the sake of being loyal to the purposes and vows of someone you loved, bring yourself to endure privation and hardship and misunderstanding, hardship that would be none the less hard because it really could be avoided?"

She thought of her mother who had loved her father so dearly, and of the wash-days which she

142

had endured for him, the long years of household
routine before she and Jinny had been old enough
to help her first with their hands and then with
their earnings. She thought of the little, dark,
shabby house, of the made-over dresses and turned
coats. And then she saw Roger and his wealth
and his golden recklessness, his golden keys which
could open the doors to beauty and ease and—
decency! Oh, it wasn't decent for women to have
to scrub and work and slave and bear children
and sacrifice their looks and their pretty hands,—
she saw her mother's hands as they had always
looked on wash day, they had a white, boiled
appearance. No, she would not fool herself nor
Anthony. She was no sentimentalist. It was not
likely that she, a girl who had left her little sister
and her home to go out to seek life and happiness
would throw it over for poverty,—hardship. If
a man loved a woman how could he ask her
that?

So she told him gently: "No, Anthony, I
couldn't," and watched the blood drain from his
face and the old look of unhappiness drift into
his eyes.

He answered inadequately. "No, of course you
couldn't." And turning over,—he had been sitting
on the grass at her feet—he lay face downward on
the scented turf. Presently he sat up and giving
her a singularly sweet but wistful smile, said: "I
almost touched happiness, Angèle. Did you by
any chance ever happen to read Browning's 'Two
in the Roman Campagna'?"

But she had read very little poetry except what
had been required in her High School work, and
certainly not Browning.

He began to interpret the fragile, difficult beauty of the poem with its light but sure touch on evanescent, indefinable feeling. He quoted:

> "How is it under our control
> To love or not to love?"

And again:

> "Infinite yearning and the pang
> Of finite hearts that yearn."

They were silent for a long time. And again she wondered how it would feel to love. He watched the sun drop suddenly below some tree tops and rose to his feet shivering a little as though its disappearance had made him immediately cold.

"'So the good moment goes.' Come, Angel, we'll have to hasten. It's getting dark and it's a long walk to the subway."

.   .   .   .   .

The memory of the afternoon stayed by her, shrouding her thoughts, clinging to them like a tenuous, adhering mantle. But she said to herself: "There's no use thinking about that. I'm not going to live that kind of life." And she knew she wanted Roger and what he could give her and the light and gladness which he always radiated. She wanted none of Anthony's poverty and privation and secret vows,—he meant, she supposed, some promise to devote himself to REAL ART,— her visual mind saw it in capitals. Well, she was sick of tragedy, she belonged to a tragic race.

" God knows it's time for one member of it to be having a little fun."

" Yes," she thought all through her class, painting furiously—for she had taken up her work in earnest since Christmas—" yes, I'll just make up my mind to it. I'll take Roger back and get married and settle down to a pleasant, safe, beautiful life." And useful. It should be very useful. Perhaps she'd win Roger around to helping coloured people. She'd look up all sorts of down-and-outers and give them a hand. And she'd help Anthony, at least she'd offer to help him; she didn't believe he would permit her.

Coming out of the building a thought occurred to her: " Take Roger back, but back to what? To his old status of admiring, familiar, generous friend? Just that and no more? " Here was her old problem again. She stopped short to consider it.

Martha Burden overtook her. " Planning the great masterpiece of the ages, Angèle? Better come along and work it out by my fireside. I can give you some tea. Are you coming? "

" Yes," said Angela, still absorbed.

" Well," said Martha after they had reached the house. " I've never seen any study as deep as that. Come out of it Angèle, you'll drown. You're not by any chance in love, are you? "

" No," she replied, " at least I don't know. But tell me, Martha, suppose—suppose I were in love with one of them, what do you do about it, how do you get them to propose? "

Martha lay back and laughed. " Such candour have I not met, no, not in all Flapperdom. Angèle, if I could answer that I'd be turning women away from my door and handing out my knowledge to the ones I did admit at a hundred dollars a throw."

"But there must be some way. Oh, of course, I know lots of them propose, but how do you get a proposal from the ones you want,—the,—the interesting ones?"

"You really want to know? The only answer I can give you is Humpty Dumpty's dictum to Alice about verbs and adjectives: 'It depends on which is the stronger.'" She interpreted for her young guest was clearly mystified. "It depends on (A) whether you are strong enough to make him like you more than you like him; (B) whether if you really do like him more than he does you you can conceal it. In other words, so far as liking is concerned you must always be ahead of the game, you must always like or appear to like him a little less than he does you. And you must make him want you. But you mustn't give. Oh yes, I know that men are always wanting women to give, but they don't want the women to want to give. They want to take,—or at any rate to compel the giving."

"It sounds very complicated, like some subtle game."

A deep febrile light came into Martha's eyes. "It is a game, and the hardest game in the world for a woman, but the most fascinating; the hardest in which to strike a happy medium. You see, you have to be careful not to withhold too much and yet to give very little. If we don't give enough we lose them. If we give too much we lose ourselves. Oh, Angèle, God doesn't like women,"

˒ " But," said Angela thinking of her own mother,
" there are some women who give all and men
like them the better for it."

" Oh, yes, that's true. Those are the blessed
among women. They ought to get down on their
knees every 'day and thank God for permitting
them to be their normal selves and not having
to play a game." For a moment her still, proud
face broke into deeps of pain. " Oh, Angèle,
think of loving and never, never being able to
show it until you're asked for it; think of living
a game every hour of your life!" Her face
quivered back to its normal immobility.

Angela walked home through the purple twilight musing no longer on her own case but on
this unexpected revelation. " Well," she said,
" I certainly shouldn't like to love like that."
She thought of Anthony: " A woman could be her
true self with him." But she had given him up.

.   .   .   .   .

If the thing to do were to play a game she would
play one. Indeed she rather enjoyed the prospect.
She was playing a game now, a game against
public tradition on the one hand and family
instinct on the other; the stakes were happiness
and excitement, and almost anyone looking at
the tricks which she had already taken would
prophesy that she would be the winner. She
decided to follow all the rules as laid down by
Martha Burden and to add any workable ideas
of her own. When Roger called again she was
still unable to see him, but her voice was a shade
less curt over the telephone; she did not cut him

off so abruptly. "I must not withhold too much," she reminded herself. He was quick to note the subtle change in intonation. "But you're going to let me come to see you soon, Angèle," he pleaded. "You wouldn't hold out this way against me forever. Say when I may come."

"Oh, one of these days; I must go now, Roger. Good-bye."

After the third call she let him come to spend Friday evening. She heard the blue car rumbling in the street and a few minutes later he came literally staggering into the living-room so laden was he with packages. Flowers, heaps of spring posies had come earlier in the day, lilacs, jonquils, narcissi. Now this evening there were books and candy, handkerchiefs,—"they were so dainty and they looked just like you," he said fearfully, for she had never taken an article of dress from him, —two pictures, a palette and some fine brushes and last a hamper of all sorts of delicacies. "I thought if you didn't mind we'd have supper here; it would be fun with just us two."

How much he pleased her he could not divine; it was the first time he had ever given a hint of any desire for sheer domesticity. Anthony had sought nothing better than to sit and smoke and watch her flitting about in her absurd red or violet apron. Matthew Henson had been speechless with ecstasy when on a winter night she had allowed him to come into the kitchen while she prepared for him a cup of cocoa. But Roger's palate had been so flattered by the concoctions of chefs famous in London, Paris and New York that he had set no store by her simple cooking.

148

Indeed his inevitable comment had been: "Here, what do you want to get yourself all tired out for? Let's go to a restaurant. It's heaps less bother."

But to-night he, too, watched her with humble, delighted eyes. She realized that he was conscious of her every movement; once he tried to embrace her, but she whirled out of his reach without reproach but with decision. He subsided, too thankful to be once more in her presence to take any risks. And when he left he had kissed her hand.

She began going about with him again, but with condescension, with kindness. And with the new vision gained from her talk with Martha she could see his passion mounting. "Make him want you," —that was the second rule. It was clear that he did, no man could be as persevering as this otherwise. Still he did not speak. They were to meet that afternoon in front of the school to go "anywhere you want, dear, I'm yours to command". It was the first time that he had called for her at the building, and she came out a litttle early, for she did not want any of the three, Martha, Paulette, nor Anthony, to see whom she was meeting. It would be better to walk to the corner, she thought, they'd be just that much less likely to recognize him. She heard footsteps hurrying behind her, heard her name and turned to see Miss Powell, pleased and excited. She laid her hand on Angela's arm but the latter shook her off. Roger must not see her on familiar terms like this with a coloured girl for she felt that the afternoon portended something and she wanted no side issues. The coloured girl gave her a penetrating glance; then her habitual reserve settled down blotting out the eagerness, leaving her face blurred and heavy. "I beg your pardon, Miss Mory, I'm sure," she murmured and stepped out into the tempestuous traffic of Fourth Avenue. Angela was sorry; she would make it up to-morrow, she thought, but she had not dismissed her a moment too soon for Roger came rushing up, his car resplendent and resplendent himself in a grey suit, soft grey hat and blue tie. Angela looked at him approvingly. "You look just like the men in the advertising pages of the Saturday *Evening Post*," she said, and the fact that he did not wince under the compliment proved the depth of his devotion, for every one of his outer garments, hat, shoes, and suit, had been made to measure.

They went to Coney Island. "The ocean will be there, but very few people and only a very few amusements," said Roger. They had a delightful time; they were like school children, easily and frankly amused; they entered all the booths that were open, ate pop-corn and hot dogs and other local dainties. And presently they were flying home under the double line of trees on Ocean Parkway and entering the bosky loveliness of Prospect Park. Roger slowed down a little.

"Oh," said Angela. "I love this car."

He bent toward her instantly. "Does it please you? Did you miss it when you made me stay away from you?"

She was afraid she had made a mistake: "Yes, but that's not why I let you come back."

"I know that. But you do like it, don't you, comfort and beauty and dainty surroundings?"

" Yes," she said solemnly, " I love them all."

He was silent then for a long, long time, his face a little set, a worried line on his forehead.

" Well now what's he thinking about? " she asked herself, watching his hands and their clever manipulation of the steering wheel though his thoughts, she knew, were not on that.

He turned to her with an air of having made up his mind. " Angèle, I want you to promise to spend a day out riding with me pretty soon. I— I have something I want to say to you." He was a worldly young man about town but he was actually mopping his brow. " I've got to go south for a week for my father,—he owns some timber down there with which he used to supply saw-mills but since the damned niggers have started running north it's been something of a weight on his hands. He wants me to go down and see whether it's worth his while to hold on to it any longer. It's so rarely that he asks anything of me along a business line that I'd hate to refuse him. But I'll be back the morning of the twenty-sixth. I'll have to spend the afternoon and evening with him out on Long Island but on the twenty-seventh could you go out with me? "

She said as though all this preamble portended nothing: " I couldn't give you the whole day, but I'd go in the afternoon."

" Oh," his face fell a little. " Well, the after-noon then. Only of course we won't be able to go far out. Perhaps you'd like me to arrange a lunch and we'd go to one of the Parks, Central or the Bronx, or Van Cortlandt,——"

" No, not Van Cortlandt," she told him. That park was sacred to Anthony Cross.

" Well, wherever you say. We can settle it even that day. The main thing is that you'll go."

She said to herself. " Aren't men funny! He could have asked me five times over while he was making all these arrangements." But she was immensely relieved, even happy. She felt very kindly toward him; perhaps she was in love after all, only she was not the demonstrative kind. It was too late for him to come in, but they sat in the car in the dark security of Jayne Street and she let him take her in his arms and kiss her again again. For the first time she returned his kisses.

Weary but triumphant she mounted the stairs almost stumbling. from a sudden, overwhelming fatigue. She had been under a strain! But it was all over now; she had conquered, she had been the stronger. She had secured not only him but an assured future, wealth, protection, influence, even power. She herself was power,—like the women one reads about, like Cleopatra,—Cleopatra's African origin intrigued her, it was a fitting comparison. Smiling, she took the last steep stairs lightly, springily, suddenly reinvigorated.

As she opened the door a little heap of letters struck her foot. Switching on the light she sat in the easy chair and incuriously turned them over. They were bills for the most part, she had had to dress to keep herself dainty and desirable for Roger. At the bottom of the heap was a letter from Virginia. When she became Mrs. Roger Fielding she would never have to worry about a bill again; how she would laugh when she remembered the small amounts for which these called! Never again would she feel the slight quake of dismay which always overtook her when she saw she words: " Miss Angèle Mory in account with,——" Outside of the regular monthly statement for gas she had never seen a bill in her father's house. Well, she'd have no difficulty in getting over her squeamish training.

Finally she opened Jinny's letter. Her sister had written:

" Angela I'm coming up for an exam. on the twenty-eighth. I'll arrive on the twenty-sixth or I could come the day before. You'll meet me, won't you? I know where I'm going to stay,"—she gave an address on 139th Street—" but I don't know how to get there; I don't know your school hours, write and tell me so I can arrive when you're free. There's no reason why I should put you out."

So Virginia was really coming to try her luck in New York. It would be nice to have her so near. " Though I don't suppose we'll be seeing so much of each other," she thought, absently reaching for her schedule. " Less than ever now, for I suppose Roger and I will live in Long Island; yes, that would be much wiser. I'll wear a veil when I go to meet her, for those coloured porters stare at you so and they never forget you."

The twenty-seventh came on Thursday; she had classes in the morning; well, Jinny would be coming in the afternoon anyway, and after twelve she had, —Oh heavens that was *the* day, the day she was to go out with Roger, the day that he would put the great question. And she wrote to Virginia:

"Come the twenty-sixth, Honey, any time after four. I couldn't possibly meet you on the twenty-seventh. But the twenty-sixth is all right. Let me know when your train comes in and I'll be there. And welcome to our city."

CHAPTER VI

THE week was one of tumult, almost of agony.
After all, matters were not completely settled, you
never could tell. She would be glad when the
twenty-seventh had come and gone, for then, then
she would be rooted, fixed. She and Roger would
marry immediately. But now he was so far away,
in Georgia; she missed him and evidently he missed
her for the first two days brought her long tele-
grams almost letters. " I can think of nothing but
next Thursday, are you thinking of it too? " The
third day brought a letter which said practically
the same thing, adding, " Oh, Angèle, I wonder
what you will say ! "

" But he could ask me and find out," she said
to herself and suddenly felt assured and triumphant.
Every day thereafter brought her a letter reiterat-
ing this strain. " And I know how he hates to
write ! "

The letter on Wednesday read, " Darling, when
you get this I'll actually be in New York; if I can
I'll call you up but I'll have to rush like mad so
as to be free for Thursday, so perhaps I can't
manage."

She made up her mind not to answer the telephone even if it did ring, she would strike one last
note of indifference though only she herself would
be aware of it.

It was the day on which Jinny was to arrive.
It would be fun to see her, talk to her, hear all the
news about the queer, staid people whom she had
left so far behind. Farther now than ever.
Matthew Henson was still in the post-office, she
knew. Arthur Sawyer was teaching at Sixteenth
and Fitzwater; she could imagine the sick distaste
that mantled his face every time he looked at
the hideous, discoloured building. Porter had
taken his degree in dentistry but he was not prac-
tising, on the contrary he was editing a small weekly,
getting deeper, more and more hopelessly into
debt she was sure. . . . It would be fun some
day to send him a whopping cheque; after all,
he had taken a chance just as she had; she
recognized his revolt as akin to her own, only he
had not had her luck. She must ask Jinny about
all this.

It was too bad that she had to meet her sister,
—but she must. Just as likely as not she'd be car
sick and then New York was terrifying for the
first time to the stranger,—she had known an
instant's sick dread herself that first day when
she had stood alone and ignorant in the great
rotunda of the station. But she was different
from Jinny; nothing about life ever made her
really afraid; she might hurt herself, suffer, meet
disappointment, but life could not alarm her;
she loved to come to grips with it, to force it to
a standstill, to yield up its treasures. But Jinny
although brave, had secret fears, she was really
only a baby. Her little sister! For the first time
in months she thought of her with a great surge
of sisterly tenderness.

It was time to go. She wore her most un-

156

obtrusive clothes, a dark blue suit, a plain white silk shirt, a dark blue, bell-shaped hat—a *cloche* —small and fitting down close over her eyes. She pulled it down even farther and settled her modish veil well over the tip of her nose. It was one thing to walk about the Village with Miss Powell. There were practically no coloured people there. But this was different. Those curious porters should never be able to recognize her. Seymour Porter had worked among them one summer at Broad Street station in Philadelphia. He used to say: "They aren't really curious, you know, but their job makes them sick; so they're always hunting for the romance, for the adventure which for a day at least will take the curse off the monotonous obsequiousness of their lives."

She was sorry for them, but she could not permit them to remedy their existence at her expense.

· · · · ·

In her last letter she had explained to Jinny about those two troublesome staircases which lead from the train level of the New York Pennsylvania Railroad [station to] the street level. "There's no use my trying to tell you which one to take in order to bring you up to the right hand or to the left hand side of the elevator because I never know myself. So all I can say, dear, is when you do get up to the elevator just stick to it and eventually I'll see you or you'll see me as I revolve around it. Don't you move, for it might turn out that we were both going in the same direction."

True to her own instructions, she was stationed between the two staircases, jerking her neck now toward one staircase, now toward the other, stopping short to look at the elevator itself. She thrust up her veil to see better.

A man sprinted by in desperate haste, brushing so closely by her that the corner of his suit-case struck sharply on the thin inner curve of her knee.

" My goodness ! " she exclaimed involuntarily.

For all his haste he was a gentleman, for he pulled off his hat, threw her a quick backward glance and began : " I beg your—why darling, darling, you don't mean to say you came to meet me ! "

" Meet you ! I thought you came in this morning." It was Roger, Roger and the sight of him made her stupid with fear.

He stooped and kissed her, tenderly, possessively. " I did,—oh Angela you *are* a beauty ! Only a beauty can wear plain things like that. I did come in this morning but I'm trying to catch Kirby, my father's lawyer, he ought to be coming in from Newark just now and I thought I'd take him down to Long Island with me for the night. I've got a lot of documents for him here in this suitcase—that Georgia business was most complicated—that way I won't have to hunt him up in the morning and I'll have more time to—to arrange for our trip in the afternoon. What are you doing here ? "

What was she doing there ? Waiting for her sister Jinny who was coloured and who showed it. And Roger hated Negroes. She was lost, ruined, unless she could get rid of him. She told the first lie that came into her mind,

" I'm waiting for Paulette." All this could be fixed up with Paulette later. Miss Lister would think as little of deceiving a man, any man, as she would of squashing a mosquito. They were fair game and she would ask no questions.

His face clouded. " Can't say I'm so wild about your waiting for Paulette. Well we can wait together—is she coming up from Philadelphia? That train's bringing my man too from Newark." He had the male's terrible clarity of understanding for train connections.

" What time does your train go to Long Island? I thought you wanted to get the next one."

" Well, I'd like to but they're only half an hour apart. I can wait. Better the loss of an hour to-day than all of to-morrow morning. We can wait together; see the people are beginning to come up. I wish I could take you home but the minute he shows up I'll have to sprint with him."

" Now God be on my side," she prayed. Sometimes these trains were very long. If Mr. Kirby were in the first car and Jinny toward the end that would make all of ten minutes' difference. If only she hadn't given those explicit directions!

There was Jinny, her head suddenly emerging into view above the stairs. She saw Angela, waved her hand. In another moment she would be flinging her arms about her sister's neck; she would be kissing her and saying, " Oh, Angela, Angela darling! "

And Roger, who was no fool, would notice the name Angela—Angèle; he would know no coloured girl would make a mistake like this.

She closed her eyes in a momentary faintness, opened them again.

"What's the matter?" said Roger sharply, "are you sick?"

Jinny was beside her. Now, now the bolt would fall. She heard the gay, childish voice saying laughingly, assuredly:

"I beg your pardon, but isn't this Mrs. Henrietta Jones?"

Oh, God was good! Here was one chance if only Jinny would understand! In his astonishment Roger had turned from her to face the speaker. Angela, her eyes beseeching her sister's from under her close hat brim, could only stammer the old formula: "Really you have the advantage of me. No, I'm not Mrs. Jones."

Roger said rudely, "Of course she isn't Mrs. Jones. Come, Angèle." Putting his arm through hers he stooped for the suitcase.

But Jinny, after a second's bewildered but incredulous stare, was quicker even than they. Her slight figure, her head high, preceded them; vanished into a telephone booth.

Roger glared after her. "Well of all the damned cheek!"

.   .   .   .   .

For the first time in the pursuit of her chosen ends she began to waver. Surely no ambition, no pinnacle of safety was supposed to call for the sacrifice of a sister. She might be selfish,—oh, undoubtedly she had been selfish all these months to leave Jinny completely to herself—but she had never meant to be cruel. She tried to picture the tumult of emotions in her sister's mind, there must have been amazement,—oh she had seen it all on her face, the utter bewilderment, the incredulity and then the settling down on that face of a veil of dignity and pride—like a baby trying to harden its mobile features. She was in her apartment again now, pacing the floor, wondering what to do. Already she had called up the house in 139th Street, it had taken her a half-hour to get the number for she did not know the householder's name and "Information" had been coy,—but Miss Murray had not arrived yet. Were they expecting her? Yes, Miss Murray had written to say that she would be there between six and seven; it was seven-thirty now and she had not appeared. Was there any message? "No, no!" Angela explained she would call again.

But where was Jinny? She couldn't be lost, after all she was grown-up and no fool, she could ask directions. Perhaps she had taken a cab and in the evening traffic had been delayed,—or had met with an accident. This thought sent Angela to the telephone again. There was no Miss Murray as yet. In her wanderings back and forth across the room she caught sight of herself in the mirror. Her face was flushed, her eyes shining with remorse and anxiety. Her vanity reminded her: " If Roger could just see me now ". Roger and to-morrow! He would have to speak words of gold to atone for this breach which for his sake she had made in her sister's trust and affecton.

At the end of an hour she called again. Yes, Miss Murray had come in. So great was her relief that her knees sagged under her. Yes of

L 161

course they would ask her to come to the telephone. After a long silence the voice rang again over the wire. "I didn't see her go out but she must have for she's not in her room."

"Oh all right," said Angela, "the main thing was to know that she was there." But she was astonished. Jinny's first night in New York and she was out already! She could not go to see her Thursday because of the engagement with Roger, but she'd make good the next day; she'd be there the first thing, Friday morning. Snatching up a sheet of note-paper she began a long letter full of apologies and excuses. "And I can't come to-morrow, darling, because as I told you I have a very important engagement, an engagement that means very much to me. Oh you'll understand when I tell you about it." She put a special delivery stamp on the letter.

Her relief at learning that Jinny was safe did not ease her guilty conscience. In a calmer mood she tried now to find excuses for herself, extenuating circumstances. As soon as Jinny understood all that was involved she would overlook it. After all, Jinny would want her to be happy. "And anyway," she thought to herself sulkily, "Mamma didn't speak to Papa that day that we were standing on the steps of the Hotel Walton." But she knew that the cases were not analogous; no principle was involved, her mother's silence had not exposed her husband to insult or contumely, whereas Roger's attitude to Virginia had been distinctly offensive. "And moreover," her thoughts continued with merciless clarity, "when a principle *was* at stake your mother never hesitated a moment to let those hospital attendants know of the true status of affairs. In fact she was not aware that she was taking any particular stand. Her husband was her husband and she was glad to acknowledge that relationship."

A sick distaste for her action, for her daily deception, for Roger and his prejudices arose within her. But with it came a dark anger against a country and a society which could create such an issue. And she thought: "If I had spoken to Jinny, had acknowledged her, what good would it have done me or her either? After it was all over she would have been exactly where she was before and I would have lost everything. And I do so want to be happy, to have a good time. At this very hour to-morrow I'll probably be one of the most envied girls in New York. And afterwards I can atone for it all. I'll be good to all sorts of people; I'll really help humanity, lots of coloured folks will be much better off on account of me. And if I had spoken to Jinny I could never have helped them at all." Once she murmured: "I'll help Jinny too, the darling! She shall have everything in the world she wants." But in her heart she knew already that Jinny would want nothing.

CHAPTER VII

THURSDAY came and Thursday sped as Thursdays will. For a long time Angela saw it as a little separate entity of time shut away in some hidden compartment of her mind, a compartment whose door she dreaded to open.

On Friday she called up her sister early in the morning. "Is that you, Jinny? Did you get my letter? Is it all right for me to come up?"

"Yes," said Jinny noncommittally, to all questions, then, laconically: "But you'd better come right away if you want to catch me. I take the examination to-day and haven't much time."

Something in the matter-of-factness of her reply disconcerted Angela. Yet there certainly was no reason why her sister should show any enthusiasm over seeing her. Only she did want to see her, to talk to some one of her very own to-day. She would like to burrow her head in Virginia's shoulder and cry! But a mood such as Jinny's voice indicated did not invite confidences.

A stout brown-skinned bustling woman suggesting immense assurance and ability opened the door. "Miss Murray told me that she was expecting some-one. You're to go right on up. Her's is the room right next to the third storey front."

164

" She was expecting someone." Evidently
Virginia had been discreet. This unexpected,
unsought for carefulness carried a sting with it.
" Hello," said Jinny, casually thrusting a dishevelled but picturesque head out of the door. " Can
you find your way in? This room's larger than
any two we ever had at home, yet already it looks
like a ship at sea." She glanced about the dis-
ordered place. " I wonder if this is what they
mean by ' shipshape '. Here I'll hang up this
suit, then you can sit down. Isn't it a sweetie?
Got it at Snellenburg's."

She had neither kissed nor offered to shake
hands with her sister, yet her manner was friendly
enough, even cordial. " See I've bobbed my
hair," she went on. " Like it? I'm wild about
it even if it does take me forever to fix it." Standing before a mirror she began shaping the ends
under with a curling iron.

Angela thought she had never seen any one so
pretty and so colourful. Jinny had always shown
a preference for high colours; to-day she was
revelling in them; her slippers were high heeled
small red mules; a deep green dressing-gown hung
gracefully from her slim shoulders and from its
open collar flamed the rose and gold of her smooth
skin. Her eyes were bright and dancing. Her
hair, black, alive and curling, ended in a thick
velvety straightness like cut plush.

Angela said stiffly, " I hope I didn't get you up,
telephoning so early."

Virginia smiled, flushing a little more deeply
under the dark gold of her skin. " Oh dear no!
I'd already had an earlier call than that this morning."

"You had!" exclaimed Angela, astonished. "I didn't know you knew anyone in New York." She remembered her sister's mysterious disappearance the first night of her arrival. "And see here, Jinny, I'm awfully sorry about what happened the other night. I wouldn't have had it happen for a great deal. I wish I could explain to you about it." How confidently she had counted on having marvellous news to tell Virginia and now how could she drag to the light yesterday's sorry memory? "But I called you up again and again and you hadn't arrived and then when they finally did tell me that you had come, it appeared that you had gone out. Where on earth did you go?"

Jinny began to laugh, to giggle in fact. For a moment she was the Virginia of her school days, rejoicing in some innocent mischief, full of it. "I wasn't out. There's a wash-room down the hall and I went there to wash my face,——" it clouded a moment. "And when I came back I walked as I thought into my room. Instead of that I had walked into the room of another lodger. And there he sat——"

"Oh," said Angela inattentively. "I'm glad you weren't out. I was quite worried. Listen, Virginia," she began desperately, "I know you think that what I did in the station the other day was unspeakable; it seems almost impossible for me to explain it to you. But that man with me was a very special friend,——"

"He must have been indeed," Jinny interrupted drily, "to make you cut your own sister." She was still apparently fooling with her hair, her head perched on one side, her eyes glued to the mirror. But she was not making much progress and her lips were trembling.

Angela proceeded unheeding, afraid to stop. " A special friend, and we had come to a very crucial point in our relationship. It was with him that I had the engagement yesterday."

" Well, what about it? Were you expecting him to ask you to marry him? Did he? "

" No," said Angela very low, " that's just what he didn't do though he,—he asked everything else."

Virginia, dropping the hair-brush, swung about sharply. " And you let him talk like that? "

" I couldn't help it once he had begun,—I was so taken by surprise, and, besides, I think that his ultimate intentions are all right."

' " His ultimate intentions ! Why, Angela what are you talking about? You know perfectly well what his ultimate intentions are. Isn't he a white man? Well, what kind of intentions would he have toward a coloured woman? "

" Simple ! He doesn't know I'm coloured. And besides some of them are decent. You must remember that I know something about these people and you don't, you couldn't, living that humdrum little life of yours at home."

" I know enough about them and about men in general to recognize an insult when I hear one. Some men bear their character stamped right on their faces. Now this man into whose room I walked last night by mistake,——"

" I don't see how you can do very much talking walking into strange men's rooms at ten o'clock at night."

The triviality of the retort left Jinny dumb.
It was their first quarrel.

.   .

.   .   .   .   .

They sat in silence for a few minutes, for several
minutes. Virginia, apparently completely composed, was letting the tendrils of her mind reach
far, far out to the ultimate possibilities of this
impasse in relationship between herself and her
sister. She thought: " I really have lost her,
she's really gone out of my ken just as I used to
lose her years ago when father and I would be
singing ' The Dying Christian '. I'm twenty-three
years old and I'm really all alone in the world."
Up to this time she had always felt she had Angela's
greater age and supposedly greater wisdom to
fall back on, but she banished this conjecture
forever. " Because if she could cut me when she
hadn't seen me for a year for the sake of a man
who she must have known meant to insult her, she
certainly has no intention of openly acknowledging
me again. And I don't believe I want to be a
sister in secret. I hate this hole and corner business."
She saw again the scene in the station, herself
at first so serene, so self-assured, Angela's confused
coldness, Roger's insolence. Something hardened,
grew cold within her. Even his arrogance had
failed to bring Angela to her senses, and suddenly
she remembered that it had been possible in slavery
times for white men and women to mistreat their
mulatto relations, their own flesh and blood, selling
them into deeper slavery in the far South or standing by watching them beaten, almost, if not com-

pletely, to death. Perhaps there was something fundamentally different between white and coloured blood after all. Aloud she said: " You know before you went away that Sunday morning you said that you and I were different. Perhaps you're right, Angela; perhaps there is an extra infusion of white blood in your veins which lets you see life at another angle. If that's the case I have no right to judge you. You must forgive my ignorant comments."

She began slipping into a ratine dress of old blue trimmed with narrow collars and cuffs and a tiny belt of old rose. Above the soft shades the bronze and black of her head etched themselves sharply; she might have been a dainty bird of Paradise cast in a new arrangement of colours but her tender face was set in strange and implacable lines.

Angela looked at her miserably. She had not known just what, in her wounded pride and humiliation, she had expected to gain from her sister, but certainly she had hoped for some balm. And in any event not this cool aloofness. She had forgotten that her sister might be suffering from a wound as poignant as her own. The year had made a greater breach than she had anticipated; she had never been as outspoken, as frank with Virginia as the latter had been with her, but there had always been a common ground between them, a meeting place. In the household Jinny had had something of a reputation for her willingness to hear all sides of a story, to find an excuse or make one.

An old aphorism of Hetty Daniels returned to her. " He who would have friends must show himself friendly." And she had done anything but that; she had neglected Jinny, had failed to answer her letters, had even planned,—was it only day before yesterday!—to see very little of her in what she had dreamed would be her new surroundings. Oh she had been shameful! But she would make it up to Jinny now—and then she could come to her at this, this crisis in her life which so frightened and attracted her. She was the more frightened because she felt that attraction. She would make her sister understand the desires and longings which had come to her in this strange, dear, free world, and then together they would map out a plan of action. Jinny might be a baby but she had strength. So much strength, said something within her, that just as likely as not she would say: "Let the whole thing go, Angela, Angela! You don't want to be even on the outskirts of a thing like this."

Before she could begin her overtures Jinny was speaking. "Listen, Angela, I've got to be going. I don't know when we'll be seeing each other again, and after what happened Wednesday you can hardly expect me to be looking you up, and as you doubtless are very busy you'd hardly be coming 'way up here. But there are one or two things I want to talk to you about. First about the house."

"About the house? Why it's yours. I've nothing more to do with it."

"I know, but I'm thinking of selling it. There is such a shortage of houses in Philadelphia just now; Mr. Hallowell says I can get at least twice as much as father paid for it. And in that case you've some more money coming to you."

If only she had known of this,—when?—twenty-four hours earlier, how differently she might have received Roger's proposition. If she had met Virginia Wednesday and had had the talk for which she had planned!

" Well of course it would be awfully nice to have some more money. But what I don't understand is how are you going to live? What are you going to do? "

" If I pass this examination I'm coming over here, my appointment would be only a matter of a few months. I'm sure of that. This is May and I'd only have to wait until September. Well, I wouldn't be working this summer anyway. And there's no way in the world which I could fail to pass. In fact I'm really thinking of taking a chance and coming over here to substitute. Mr. Holloster, the University of Pennsylvania man, has been investigating and he says there's plenty of work. And I guess I'm due to have a change; New York rather appeals to me. And there certainly is something about Harlem! " In spite of her careless manner Angela knew she was thinking about Matthew Henson. She stretched out her hand, pulled Jinny's head down on her shoulder. " Oh darling, don't worry about him. Matthew really wasn't the man for you."

" Well," said Virginia, " as long as I think he was, the fact that he wasn't doesn't make any real difference, does it? At least not at first. But I certainly shan't worry about it."

" No don't,—I,——" It was on the tip of her tongue to say " I know two or three nice young men whom you can play around with. I'll introduce you to them." But could she? Jinny understood her silence; smiled and nodded. "It's all right, honey, you can't do anything; you would if you could. We've just got to face the fact that you and I are two separate people and we've got to live our lives apart, not like the Siamese twins. And each of us will have to go her chosen way. After all each of us is seeking to get all she can out of life! and if you can get more out of it by being white, as you undoubtedly can, why, why shouldn't you? Only it seems to me that there are certain things in living that are more fundamental even than colour,—but I don't know. I'm all mixed up. But evidently you don't feel that way, and you're just as likely to be right as me."

"Jinny!"

"My dear, I'm not trying to reproach you. I'm trying to look at things without sentiment. After all, in a negative way, merely by saying nothing, you're disclaiming your black blood in a country where it is an inconvenience,—oh! there's not a doubt about that. You may be proud of it, you may be perfectly satisfied with it—I am—but it certainly can shut you out of things. So why shouldn't you disclaim a living manifestation of that blood?"

Before this cool logic Angela was silent. Virginia looked at her sister, a maternal look oddly apparent on her young face. When she was middle-aged she would be the embodiment of motherhood. How her children would love her!

"Angela, you'll be careful!"

"Yes, darling. Oh if only I could make you understand what it's all about."

"Yes, well, perhaps another time. I've got to

172

fly now." She hesitated, took Angela by the arms and gazed into her eyes. " About this grand white party that you were in the station with. Are you awfully in love with him? "

" I'm not in love with him at all."

" Oh, pshaw! " said innocent Virginia, " you've got nothing to worry about! Why, what's all the shooting for? "

PLUM BUN

CHAPTER I

ANGELA wanted to ride downtown with her sister. ",Perhaps I might bring you luck." But on this theme Jinny was adamant. " You'd be much more" likely to bring yourself bad luck. No, there's no sense in taking a chance. I'll take the elevated; I my landlady said it would drop me very near the school where I'm taking the examination. You go some other way." Down in the hall Mrs. Gloucester was busy dusting, her short bustling figure alive with housewifely ardour. Virginia' paused near her and held out her hand to Angela: " Good-bye, Miss Mory," she said wickedly, " it was very kind of you to give me so much 'time. If you can ever tear yourself away from your beloved Village, come up and I'll try to show you Harlem. I don't think it's going to take me long to learn it."

Obediently Angela let her go her way and walking over to Seventh Avenue mounted the 'bus, smarting a little under Jinny's generous precautions. But presently she began to realize their value, for at One Hundred and Fourteenth Street Anthony Cross entered. He sat down beside her. " I never expected to see you in my neighbourhood."

" Oh is this where you live? I've often wondered."

"As it happens I've just come here, but I've lived practically all over New York." He was thin, restless, unhappy. His eyes dwelt ceaselessly on her face. She said a little nervously:

"It seems to me I hardly ever see you any more. What do you do with yourself?"

"Nothing that you would be interested in."

She did not dare make the obvious reply and after all, though she did like him very much, she was not interested in his actions. For a long moment she sought for some phrase which would express just the right combination of friendliness and indifference.

"It's been a long time since we've had lunch together; come and have it to-day with me. You be my guest." She thought of Jinny and the possible sale of the house. "I've just found out that I'm going to get a rather decent amount of money, certainly enough to stand us for lunch."

"Thank you, I have an engagement; besides I don't want to lunch with you in public."

This was dangerous ground. Flurried, she replied unwisely: "All right, come in some time for tea; every once in a while I make a batch of cookies; I made some a week ago. Next time I feel the mood coming on me I'll send you a card and you can come and eat them, hot and hot."

"You know you've no intention of doing any such thing. Besides you don't know my address."

"An inconvenience which can certainly be rectified," she laughed at him.

But he was in no laughing mood. "I've no cards with me, but they wouldn't have the address anyway." He tore a piece of paper out of his notebook, scribbled on it. "Here it is. I have to get off now." He gave her a last despairing look. "Oh, Angel, you know you're never going to send for me!"

The bit of paper clutched firmly in one hand, she arrived finally at her little apartment. Naturally of an orderly turn of mind she looked about for her address book in which to write the street and number. But some unexplained impulse led her to smooth the paper out and place it in a corner of her desk. That done she took off her hat and gloves, sat down in the comfortable chair and prepared to face her thoughts.

·　　·　　·　　·　　·

Yesterday! Even now at a distance of twenty-four hours she had not recovered her equilibrium. She was still stunned, still unable to realize the happening of the day. Only she knew that she had reached a milestone in her life; a possible turning point. If she did not withdraw from her acquaintanceship with Roger now, even though she committed no overt act she would never be the same; she could never again face herself with the old, unshaken pride and self-confidence. She would never be the same to herself. If she withdrew, then indeed, indeed she would be the same old Angela Murray, the same girl save for a little sophistication that she had been before she left Philadelphia, only she would have started on an adventure and would not have seen it to its finish, she would have come to grips with life and would have laid down her arms at the first onslaught. Would she be a coward or a wise, wise woman?

She thought of two poems that she had read in
" Hart's Class-Book ", an old, old book of her
father's,—one of them ran:

> 'He either fears his fate too much
>   Or his deserts are small,
> Who dares not put it to the touch
>   For fear of losing all.'

The other was an odd mixture of shrewdness
and cowardice:

> 'He who fights and runs away
>   Shall live to fight another day
> But he who is in battle slain
>   Has fallen ne'er to rise again.'

Were her deserts small or should she run away
and come back to fight another day when she was
older, more experienced? More experienced!
How was she to get that experience? Already she
was infinitely wiser, she would, if occasion required
it, exercise infinitely more wariness than she had
yesterday with Roger. Yet it was precisely because of that experience that she would know how
to meet, would even know when to expect similar
conditions.

She thought that she knew which verse she
would follow if she were Jinny, but, back once
more in the assurance of her own rooms, she knew
that she did not want to be Jinny, that she and
Jinny were two vastly different persons. "But,"
she said to herself, " if Jinny were as fair as I and
yet herself and placed in the same conditions as
those in which I am placed her colour would save

her. It's a safeguard for Jinny; it's always been a curse for me."

Roger had come for her in the blue car. There were a hamper and two folding chairs and a rug stored away in it. It was a gorgeous day. "If we can," he said, "we'll picnic." He was extremely handsome and extremely nervous. Angela was nervous too, though she did not show it except in the loss of her colour. She was rather plain to-day; to be so near the completion of her goal and yet to have to wait these last few agonizing moments, perhaps hours, was deadly. They were rather silent for a while, Roger intent on his driving. Traffic in New York is a desperate strain at all hours, at eleven in the morning it is deadly; the huge leviathan of a city is breaking into the last of its stride. For a few hours it will proceed at a measured though never leisurely pace and then burst again into the mad rush of the homeward bound.

But at last they were out of the city limits and could talk. For the first time since she had known him he began to speak of his possessions. "Anything, anything that money can buy, Angèle, I can get and I can give." His voice was charged with intention. They were going in the direction of Forest Hills; he had a cottage out there, perhaps she would like to see it. And there was a grove not far away. "We'll picnic there," he said, "and—and talk." He certainly was nervous, Angela thought, and liked him the better for it.

The cottage or rather the house in Forest Hills was beautiful, absolutely a gem.   And it was completely furnished with taste and marked daintiness.   " What do you keep it furnished for? " asked Angela wondering.   Roger murmured that it had been empty for a long time but he had seen this equipment and it had struck him that it was just the thing for this house so he had bought it; thereby insensibly reminding his companion again that he could afford to gratify any whim.   They drove away from the exquisite little place in silence.   Angela was inclined to be amused; surely no one could have asked for a better opening than that afforded by the house. What would make him talk, she wondered, and what, oh what would he say?   Something far, far more romantic than poor Matthew Henson could ever have dreamed of,—yes and far, far less romantic, something subconscious prompted her, than Anthony Cross had said.   Anthony with his poverty and honour and desperate vows!

They had reached the grove, they had spread the rug and a tablecloth; Roger had covered it with dainties.   He would not let her lift a finger, she was the guest and he her humble servant.   She looked at him smiling, still forming vague contrasts with him and Matthew and Anthony.

Roger dropped his sandwich, came and sat behind her.   He put his arm around her and shifted his shoulder so that her head lay against it.

" Don't look at me that way Angèle, Angèle! I can't stand it."

So it was actually coming.   " How do you want me to look at you? "

He bent his head down to hers and kissed her.
" Like this, like this! Oh Angèle, did you like
the house? "

" Like it? I loved it."

" Darling, I had it done for you, you know. I
thought you'd like it."

It seemed a strange thing to have done without
consulting her, and anyway she did not want to
live in a suburb. Opal Street had been suburb
enough for her. She wanted, required, the noise
and tumult of cities.

" I don't care for suburbs, Roger." How
strange for him to talk about a place to live in
and never a word of love!

" My dear girl, you don't have to live in a
suburb if you don't want to. I've got a place, an
apartment in Seventy-second Street, seven rooms;
that would ·be enough for you and your maid,
wouldn't it? I could have this furniture moved
over there, or if you think it too cottagey, you could
have new stuff altogether."

Seven rooms for three people! Why she'wanted
a drawing-room and a studio and where would he
put his things? This sudden stinginess was quite
inexplicable.

" But Roger, seven rooms wouldn't be big
enough."

He laughed indulgently, his face radiant with
relief and triumph. " So she wants a palace,
does she? Well, she shall have it. A whole
ménage if you want it, a place on Riverside Drive,
servants and a car. Only somehow I hadn't
thought of you as caring about that kind of thing.
After that little hole in the wall you've been living
in on Jayne Street I'd have expected you to find

the place in Seventy-second Street as large as you'd care for."

A little hurt, she replied: "But I was thinking of you too. There wouldn't be room for your things. And I thought you'd want to go on living in the style you'd been used to." A sudden welcome explanation dawned on her rising fear. "Are you keeping this a secret from your father? Is that what's the trouble?"

Under his thin, bright skin he flushed. "Keeping what a secret from my father? What are you talking about, Angèle?"

She countered with his own question. "What are *you* talking about, Roger?"

He tightened his arms about her, his voice stammered, his eyes were bright and watchful. "I'm asking you to live in my house, to live for me; to be my girl; to keep a love-nest where I and only I may come." He smiled shamefacedly over the cheap current phrase.

She pushed him away from her; her jaw fallen and slack but her figure taut. Yet under her stunned bewilderment her mind was racing. So this was her castle, her fortress of protection, her refuge. And what answer should she make? Should she strike him across his eager, half-shamed face, should she get up and walk away, forbidding him to follow? Or should she stay and hear it out? Stay and find out what this man was really like; what depths were in him and, she supposed, in other men. But especially in this man with his boyish, gallant air and his face as guileless and as innocent apparently as her own.

ˌThat was what she hated in herself, she told that self fiercely, shut up with her own thoughts the next afternoon in her room. She hated herself for staying and listening. It had given him courage to talk and talk. But what she most hated had been the shrewdness, the practicality which lay beneath that resolve ˌto hear it out. She had thought of those bills; she had thought of her poverty, of her helplessness, and she had thought too of Martha Burden's dictum: "You must make him want you." Well here was a way to make him want her and to turn that wanting to account. "Don't," Martha said, "withhold too much. Give a little." Suppose she gave him just the encouragement of listening to him, of showing him that she did like him a little; while he meanwhile went on wanting, wanting—men paid a big price for their desires. Her price would be marriage. It was a game, she knew, which women played all over the world although it had never occurred to her to play it; a dangerous game at which some women burned their fingers. "Don't give too much," said Martha, ˌ"for then you lose yourself." Well, she would give nothing and she would not burn her fingers. Oh, it would beˌa great game.

Another element entered too. He had wounded her pride and he should salve it. And the only unguent possible would be a proposal of marriage. Oh if only she could be a girl in a book and when he finally did ask her for her hand, she would be able to tell him that she was going to marry someone else, someone twice as eligible, twice as handsome, twice as wealthy.

·　　·　　·　　·　　·

Through all these racing thoughts penetrated the sound of Roger's voice, pleading, persuasive, seductive. She was amazed to find a certain shamefaced timidity creeping over her; yet it was he who should have shown the shame. And she could not understand either why she was unable to say plainly: "You say you care for me, long for me so much, why don't you ask me to come to you in the ordinary way?" But some pride either unusually false or unusually fierce prevented her from doing this. Undoubtedly Roger with his wealth, his looks and his family connections had already been much sought after. He knew he was an "eligible". Poor, unknown, stigmatized, if he but knew it, as a member of the country's least recognized group she could not bring herself to belong even in appearance to that band of young women who so obviously seek a "good match".

When he had paused a moment for breath she told him sadly: "But, Roger, people don't do that kind of thing, not decent people."

"Angèle, you are such a child! This is exactly the kind of thing people do do. And why not? Why must the world be let in on the relationships of men and women? Some of the sweetest unions in history have been of this kind."

"For others perhaps, but not for me. Relationships of the kind you describe don't exist among the people I know." She was thinking of her parents, of the Hallowells, of the Hensons whose lives were indeed like open books.

He looked at her curiously, "The people you know! Don't tell me you' haven't guessed about Paulette!"

She had forgotten about Paulette! "Yes I know about her. She told me herself. I like her, she's been a mighty fine friend, but, Roger, you surely don't want me to be like her."

"Of course I don't. It was precisely because you weren't like her that I became interested. You were such a babe in the woods. Anyone could see you'd had no experience with men."

This obvious lack of logic was too bewildering. She looked at him like the child which, in these matters, she really was. "But,—but Roger, mightn't that be a beginning of a life like Paulette's? What would become of me after we, you and I, had separated? Very often these things last only for a short time, don't they?"

"Not necessarily; certainly not between you and me. And I'd always take care of you, you'd be provided for." He could feel her gathering resentment. In desperation he played a cunning last card: "And besides who knows, something permanent may grow out of this. I'm not entirely my own master, Angèle."

Undoubtedly he was referring to his father whom he could not afford to offend. It never occurred to her that he might be lying, for why should he?

.   .   .   .   .

To all his arguments, all his half-promises and implications she returned a steady negative. As twilight came on she expressed a desire to go home; with the sunset her strength failed her; she felt beaten and weary. Her unsettled future, her hurt pride, her sudden set-to with the realities of the society in which she had been moving, bewildered

and frightened her. Resentful, puzzled, intro-
spective, she had no further words for Roger;
it was impossible for him to persuade her to agree
or to disagree with his arguments. During the long
ride home she was resolutely mute.

Yet on the instant of entering Jayne Street she
felt she could not endure spending the long evening hours by herself and she did not want to be
alone with Roger. She communicated this distaste
to him. While not dishevelled they were not
presentable enough to invade the hotels farther
uptown. But, anxious to please her, he told her
they could go easily enough to one of the small
cabarets in the Village. A few turns and windings
and they were before a house in a dark side street
knocking on its absurdly barred door, entering its
black, myterious portals. In a room with a highly
polished floor, a few tables and chairs, some rather
bizarre curtains, five or six couples were sitting,
among them Paulette, Jack Hudson, a tall, rather
big, extremely blonde girl whose name Angela
learned was Carlotta Parks, and a slender, black-
avised man whose name she failed to catch. Paulette hailed him uproariously; the blonde girl rose
and precipitately threw her arms about Fielding's
neck.

" Roger ! "

" Don't," he said rather crossly. " Hello, Jack."
He nodded to the dark man whom he seemed to
know indifferently well. " What have they got to
eat here, you fellows? Miss Mory and I are tired
and hungry. We've been following the pike all
day." Miss Parks turned and gave Angela a long,
considering look.

" Sit here," said Paulette, " there's plenty of

room. Jack, you order for them, the same things we've been having. You get good cooking here." She was radiant - with happiness and content. Under the influence of the good, stimulating food Angela began to recover, to look around her.

Jack Hudson, a powerfully built bronze figure of a man, beamed on Paulette, saying nothing and in his silence saying everything. The dark man kept his eyes' on Carlotta, who was oblivious to everyone but Roger, clearly her friend of long standing. She sat clasping one of his hands, her head almost upon his shoulder. " Roger it's so good to see you again! I've thought of you so often! I've been meaning to write to you; we're having a big house party this summer. You must come! Dad's asking up half of Washington; attachés, 'Prinzessen, Countessen and serene English Altessen'; he'll come up for week-ends."

A member of the *haut monde*, evidently she was well-connected, powerful, even rich. A girl of Roger's own set amusing herself in this curious company. Angela felt her heart contract with a sort of helpless jealousy.

The dark man, despairing of recapturing Carlotta's attention, suddenly asked Angèle if she would care to dance. He was a superb partner and for a moment or two, reinvigorated by the food and the snappy music, she became absorbed in the smooth, gliding motion and in her partner's pleasant conversation. Glancing over her shoulder she noted Carlotta still talking to Roger. The latter, however, was plainly paying the girl no attention. His eyes fixed on Angela, he was moodily following her every motion, almost straining, she thought, to catch her words. His eyes met hers and a long,

long look passed between them so fraught, it seemed to her, with a secret understanding and sympathy, that her heart shook with a moment's secret wavering.

Her partner escorted her back to the table. Paulette, flushed and radiant, with the mien of a dishevelled baby, was holding forth while Hudson listened delightedly. As a *raconteuse* she had a faint, delicious malice which usually made any recital of her adventures absolutely irresistible. "Her name," she was saying loudly, regardless of possible listeners, "was Antoinette Spewer, and it seems she had it in for me from the very first. She told Sloane Corby she wanted to meet me and he invited both of us to lunch. When we got to the restaurant she was waiting for me in the lobby; Sloane introduced us and—she pulled a lorgnette on me,—a lorgnette on *me*!" She said it very much as a Westerner might speak of someone "pulling" a revolver. "But I fixed that. There were three or four people passing near us. I drew back until they were well within hearing range, and then I said to her: 'I beg pardon but what did you say your last name was?' Well, when a person's named Spewer she can't shout it across a hotel lobby! Oh, she came climbing down off her high horse; she respects me to this day, I tell you."

Roger rose. "We must be going; I can't let Miss Mory get too tired." He was all attention and courtesy. Miss Parks looked at her again, narrowing her eyes.

In the car Roger put his arm about her. "Angèle, when you were dancing with that fellow I couldn't stand it! And then you looked at me,—

oh such a look! You were thinking about me, I felt it, I knew it."

Some treacherous barrier gave way within her. "Yes, and I could tell you were thinking about me."

"Of course you could! And without a word! Oh, darling, darling, can't you see that's the way it would be? If you'd only take happiness with me there we would be with a secret bond, an invisible bond, existing for us alone and no one else in the world the wiser. But we should know and it would be all the sweeter for that secrecy."

Unwittingly he struck a responsive chord within her,—stolen waters were the sweetest, she of all people knew that.

Aloud she said: "Here we are, Roger. Some of the day has been wonderful; thank you for that."

"You can't go like this! You're going to let me see you again?"

She knew she should have refused him, but again some treacherous impulse made her assent. He drove away, and, turning, she climbed the long, steep flights of stairs, bemused, thrilled, frightened, curious, the sense of adventure strong upon her. To-morrow she would see Jinny, her own sister, her own flesh and blood, one of her own people. To-gether they would thresh this thing out.

CHAPTER II

A CURIOUS period of duelling ensued. Roger was young, rich and idle. Nearly every wish he had ever known had been born within him only to be satisfied. He could not believe that he would fail in the pursuit of this baffling creature who had awakened within him an ardour and sincerity of feeling which surprised himself. The thought occurred to him more than once that it would have been a fine thing if this girl had been endowed with the name and standing and comparative wealth of—say Carlotta Parks,—but it never occurred to him to thwart in this matter the wishes of his father who would, he knew, insist immediately on a certified account of the pedigree, training and general fitness of any strange aspirant for his son's hand. Angela had had the good sense to be frank; she did not want to become immeshed in a tissue of lies whose relationship, whose sequence and inter-dependence she would be likely to forget. To Roger's few questions she had said quite truly that she was the daughter of " poor but proud parents "; —they had laughed at the hackneyed phrase,—that her father had been a boss carpenter and that she had been educated in the ordinary public schools and for a time had been a school teacher. No one would ever try to substantiate these statements, for clearly the person to whom they applied would not be falsifying such a simple account. There would be no point in so doing. Her little deceits had all been negative, she had merely neglected to say that she had a brown sister and that her father had been black.

Roger found her unfathomable. His was the careless, unreasoned cynicism of the modern, worldly young man. He had truly, as he acknowledged, been attracted to Angela because of a certain incurious innocence of hers apparent in her observations and in her manner. He saw no reason why he should cherish that innocence. If questioned he would have answered: " She's got to learn about the world in which she lives sometime; she might just as well learn of it through me. And I'd always look out for her." In the back of his mind, for all his unassuming even simple attitude toward his wealth and power, lurked the conviction that that same wealth and power could heal any wound, atone for any loss. Still there were times when even he experienced a faint, inner qualm, when Angela would ask him: " But afterwards, what would become of me, Roger? " It was the only question he could not meet. Out of all his hosts of precedents from historical Antony and Cleopatra down to notorious affinities discovered through blatant newspaper " stories " he could find for this only a stammered " There's no need to worry about an afterwards, Angèle, for you and I would always be friends."

Their frequent meetings now were little more than a trial of strength. Young will and determination were pitted against young will and determination. On both the excitement of the chase was strong, but each was pursuing a different quarry. To all his protestations, arguments and demands, Angela returned an insistent: " What you are asking is impossible." Yet she either could not or would not drive him away, and gradually, though she had no intention of yielding to his wishes, her first attitude of shocked horror began to change.

For three months the conflict persisted. Roger interposed the discussion into every talk, on every occasion. Gradually it came to be the *raison d'être* of their constant comradeship. His arguments were varied and specious. " My dearest girl, think of a friendship in which two people would have every claim in the world upon each other and yet no claim. Think of giving all, not because you say to a minister ' I will ', but from the generosity of a powerful affection. That is the very essence of free love. I give you my word that the happiest couples in the world are those who love without visible bonds. Such people are bound by the most durable ties. Theirs is a state of the closest because the freest, most elastic union in the world."

A singularly sweet and curious intimacy was growing up between them. Roger told Angela many anecdotes about his father and about his dead mother, whom he still loved, and for whom he even grieved in a pathetically boyish way. " She was so sweet to me, she loved me so. I'll never forget her. It's for her sake that I try to please my father, though Dad's some pumpkins on his own account." In turn she was falling into the habit of relating to him the little happenings of her every-day life, a life which she was beginning to realize must, in his eyes, mean the last word in the humdrum and the monotonous. And yet how full of adventure, of promise, even of mystery did it seem compared with Jinny's!

Roger had much intimate knowledge of people and told her many and dangerous secrets. "See how I trust you, Angèle; you might trust me a little!"

If his stories were true, certainly she might just as well trust him a great deal, for all her little world, judging it by the standards by which she was used to measuring people, was tumbling in ruins at her feet. If this were the way people lived then what availed any ideals? The world was made to take pleasure in; one gained nothing by exercising simple virtue, it was after all an extension of the old formula which she had thought out for herself many years ago. Roger spent most of his time with her, it seemed. Anything which she undertook to do delighted him. She would accept no money, no valuable presents. "And I can't keep going out with you to dinners and luncheons forever, Roger. It would be different if,—if we really meant anything to each other." He deliberately misunderstood her. "But nothing would give me more pleasure than for us to mean the world to one another." He sent her large hampers of fruit and even the more ordinary edibles; then he would tease her about being selfish. In order to get rid of the food she had asked him to lunch, to dinner, since nothing that she could say would make him desist from sending it.

Nothing gave her greater joy really than this playful housekeeping. She was very lonely; Jinny had her own happy interests; Anthony never came near her nor did she invite him to come; Martha Burden seemed engrossed in her own affairs, she was undergoing some secret strain that made her appear more remote, more strongly self-sufficient, more mysterious than ever. Paulette, making overt preparations to go to Russia with Hudson, was impossibly, hurtingly happy. Miss Powell,—but she could not get near her; the young coloured girl showed her the finest kind of courtesy, but it had about it a remote and frozen quality, unbreakable. However, Angela for the moment did not desire to break it; she must run no more risks with Roger, still she put Miss Powell on the list of those people whom she would some day aid,—when everything had turned out all right.

The result of this feeling of loneliness was, of course, to turn her more closely to Roger. He paid her the subtle compliment of appearing absolutely at home in her little apartment; he grew to like her plain, good cooking and the experiments which sometimes she made frankly for him. And afterwards as the fall closed in there were long, pleasant evenings before an open fire, or two or three last hours after a brisk spin in the park in the blue car. And gradually she had grown to accept and even inwardly to welcome his caresses. She perched with an air of great unconsciousness on the arm of the big chair in which he was sitting but the transition became constantly easier from the arm of the chair to his knee, to the steely embrace of his arm, to the sound of the hard beating of his heart, to his murmured: " This is where you belong, Angèle, Angèle." He seemed an anchor for her frail, insecure bark of life.

It was at moments like these that he told her amazing things about their few common acquaintances. There was not much to say about Paulette. "I think," said Roger judicially, "that temperamentally she is a romantic adventurer. Something in her is constantly seeking a change but she will never be satisfied. She's a good sport, she takes as she gives, asking nothing permanent and promising nothing permanent." Angela thought it rather sad. But Roger dismissed the theme with the rather airy comment that there were women as there were men " like that ". She wondered if he might not be a trifle callous.

More than once they had spoken of Martha Burden; Angela confessed herself tremendously intrigued by the latter, by that tense, brooding personality. She learned that Martha, made of the stuff which dies for causes, was constantly being torn between theory and practice.

" She's full," said Roger, " of the most highfalutin, advanced ideas. Oh I've known old Martha all my life, we were brought up together, it's through her really that I began to know the people in this part of town. She's always been a sort of sister. More than once I've had to yank her by the shoulders out of difficulties which she herself created. I made her marry Starr."

" Made her marry him,—didn't she want him? "

" Yes, she wanted him all right, but she doesn't believe in marriage. She's got the courage of her convictions, that girl. Why actually she lived with Starr two years while I was away doing Europe. When I came back and found out what had happened I told Starr I'd beat him into pulp if he didn't turn around and make good."

" But why the violence? Didn't he want to? "

" Yes, only," he remembered suddenly his own hopes, " not every man is capable of appreciating a woman who breaks through the conventions for him. Some men mistake it for cheapness but others see it for what it is and love more deeply and gratefully." Softly, lingeringly he touched the soft hair shadowing her averted cheek. " I'm one of those others, Angèle."

She wanted to say: " But why shouldn't we marry? Why not make me safe as well as Martha? " But again her pride intervened. Instead she remarked that Martha did not seem always happy.

" No, well that's because she's got this fool idea of hers that now that they are bound the spontaneity is lacking. She wants to give without being obliged to give; to take because she chooses and not because she's supposed to. Oh she's as true as steel and the best fighter in a cause, but I've no doubt but that she leads old Starr a life with her temperament."

Angela thought that there were probably two sides to this possibility. A little breathlessly she asked Roger if he knew Anthony Cross.

" Cross, Cross! A sallow, rather thin fellow? I think I saw him once or twice at Paulette's. No, I don't really know him. A sullen, brooding sort of chap I should say. Frightfully self-absorbed and all that."

For some reason a little resentment sprang up in her. Anthony might brood, but his life had been lived on dark, troublesome lines that invited brooding; he had never known the broad, golden highway of Roger's existence. And anyway she did not believe, if Martha Burden had been Anthony's lifelong friend, almost his sister, that he would have told his sweetheart or his wife either of those difficult passages in her life. Well, she would have to teach Roger many things. Aloud she spoke of Carlotta Parks.

"She's an interesting type. Tell me about her."

But Roger said rather shortly that there was nothing to tell. "Just a good-hearted, high-spirited kid, that's all, who lets the whole world know her feelings."

.   .   .   .   .

According to Paulette there was more than this to be told about Miss Parks. "I don't know her myself, not being a member of that crowd. But I've always heard that she and Roger were childhood sweethearts, only they've just not pulled it off. Carlotta's family is as old as his. Her people have always been statesmen, her father's in the Senate. I don't think they have much money now. But the main thing is she pleases old man Fielding. Nothing would give him more pleasure than to see Carlotta Roger's wife. I may be mistaken, but I think nothing would give Carlotta more pleasure either."

"Doesn't he care for her?" Queer how her heart tightened, listening for the answer.

"Yes, but she likes him too much and shows it. So he thinks he doesn't want her. Roger will never want any woman who comes at his first

call. Don't you hate that sort of man? They are
really the easiest to catch; all you've got to do
provided they're attracted at all, is to give one
inviting glance and then keep steadily retreating.
And they'll come—like Bo Peep's sheep. But I
don't want a man like that; he'd cramp my
style. His impudence, expecting a woman to re-
press or evoke her emotions just as he wants them!
Hasn't a woman as much right to feel as a man
and to feel first? Never mind, some woman is
going to 'get' Roger yet. He doesn't think it
possible because he has wealth and position. He'll
be glad to come running to Carlotta then. I
don't care very much for her,—she's a little too
loud for me," objected the demure and conservative Miss Lister, " but I do think she likes Roger
for himself and not for what he can give her! "

    •   •   •   •   •

Undoubtedly this bit of knowledge lent a new
aspect; the adventure began to take on fresh
interest. Everything seemed to be playing into
her hands. Roger's interest and longing were
certainly undiminished. Martha Burden's advice,
confirmed by Paulette's disclosure, was bound to
bring results. She had only to " keep retreating ".
But there was one enemy with whom she had
never thought to reckon, she had never counted
on the treachery of the forces of nature; she had
never dreamed of the unaccountable weakening of
those forces within. Her weapons were those furnished by the conventions but her fight was against
conditions; impulses, yearnings which antedated
both those weapons and the conventions, which

furnished them. Insensibly she began to see in
Roger something more than a golden way out of
her material difficulties; he was becoming more
than a means through which she should be admitted to the elect of the world for whom all
things are made. Before her eyes he was changing to the one individual who was kindest,
most thoughtful of her, the one whose presence
brought warmth and assurance. Furthermore, his
constant attention, flatteries and caresses were pro-
ducing their inevitable effect. She was naturally
cold; unlike Paulette, she was a woman who
would experience the grand passion only once,
perhaps twice, in her life and she would always
have to be kindled from without; in the last
analysis her purity was a matter not of morals,
nor of religion, nor of racial pride; it was a matter
of fastidiousness. Bit by bit Roger had forced
his way closer and closer into the affairs of her
life, and his proximity had not offended that
fastidiousness. Gradually his demands seemed to
her to represent a very natural and beautiful impulse; his arguments and illustrations began to
bear fruit; the conventions instead of showing in
her eyes as the codified wisdom based on the
experiences of countless generations of men and
women, seemed to her prudish and unnecessary.
Finally her attitude reduced itself to this: she
would have none of the relationship which
Roger urged so insistently, not because according
to all the training which she had ever received,
it was unlawful, but because viewed in the
light of the great battle which she was wag-
ing for pleasure, protection and power, it was
inexpedient.

The summer and the early fall had passed. A cold, rainy autumn was closing in; the disagreeable weather made motoring almost impossible. There were always the theatres and the cabarets, but Roger professed himself as happy nowhere else but at her fireside. And she loved to have him there, tall and strong and beautiful, sometimes radiant with hope, at others sulking with the assurance of defeat. He came in one day ostensibly to have tea with her; he had an important engagement for the evening but he could not let the day pass without seeing her. Angela was tired and a little dispirited. Jinny had sold the house and had sent her twelve hundred dollars as her share, but the original three thousand was almost dissipated. She must not touch this new gift from heaven; her goal was no nearer; the unwelcome possibility of teaching, on the contrary, was constantly before her. Moreover, she was at last realising the danger of this constant proximity, she was appalled by her thoughts and longings. Upon her a great fear was creeping not only of Roger but of herself.

Always watchful, he quickly divined her distrait mood, resolved to try its possibilities for himself. In a tense silence they drank their tea and sat gazing at the leaping, golden flames. The sullen night closed in. Angela reminded him presently that he must go but on he sat and on. At eight o'clock she reminded him again; he took out his watch and looked at it indifferently. " It's too late for me to keep it now, besides I don't want to go. Angèle be kind, don't send me away."

" But you've had no dinner."

"Nor you either. I'm like the beasts of the field keeping you like this. Shall we go out somewhere?" But she was languid; she did not want to stir from the warm hearth out into the chilly night.

"No, I don't want to go. But you go, Roger. I can find something here in the house for myself, but there's not a thing for you. I hate to be so inhospitable."

"Tell you what, suppose I go around to one of these *delicatessens* and get something. Too tired to fix up a picnic lunch?"

In half an hour he returned, soaked. "It's raining in torrents! Why I never saw such a night!" He shook himself, spattering rain-drops all over the tiny apartment.

"Roger! You'll have to take off your coat!"

He sat in his shirt-sleeves before the fire, his hair curling and damp, his head on his hand. He looked so like a little boy that her heart shook within her. Turning he caught the expression in her eyes, sprang towards her. "Angèle you know, you *know* you like me a little!"

"I like you a very great deal." He put his arm about her, kissed her; her very bones turned to water. She freed herself, finding an excuse to go into the kitchenette. But he came and stood towering over her in the doorway, his eyes on her every motion. They ate the meal, a good one, almost as silently as they had drunk the tea; a terrible awareness of each other's presence was upon them, the air was charged with passion. Outside the rain and wind beat and screamed.

"It's a terrible night," she said, but he made no reply. She said again, "Roger, it's getting late,

you must go home." Very reluctantly then, his
eyes still on hers, he rose to his feet, got into his
overcoat and, hat in hand, stooped to kiss her
good-night. His arm stole about her, holding her
close against him. She could feel him trembling,
she was trembling herself. Another second and the
door had closed behind him.

Alone, she sat looking at the fire and thinking:
" This is awful. I don't believe anything is going
to come of this. I believe I'll send him a note
to-morrow and tell him not to come any more."

Someone tapped on the door; astonished that
a caller should appear at such an hour, but not
afraid, she opened it. It was Roger. He came
striding into the room, flinging off his wet coat,
and yet almost simultaneously catching her up in
his arms. " It's such a terrible night, Angèle; you
can't send me out in it. Why should I go when the
fire is here and you, so warm and soft and
sweet ! "

All her strength left her; she could not even
struggle, could not speak. He swept her up in his
arms, cradling her in them like a baby with her
face beneath his own. " You know that we were
meant for each other, that we belong to each
other ! "

A terrible lassitude enveloped her out of which
she heard herself panting: " Roger, Roger let me
go ! Oh, Roger, must it be like this? Can't it be
any other way? "

And from a great distance she heard his voice
breaking, pleading, promising: " Everything will
be all right, darling, darling. I swear it. Only
trust me, trust me ! "

Life rushed by on a great, surging tide. She could not tell whether she was utterly happy or utterly miserable.   All that she could do was to feel; feel that she was Roger's totally. Her whole being turned toward him as a flower to the sun. Without him life meant nothing; with him it was everything. For the time being she was nothing but emotion; he was amazed himself at the depth of feeling which he had aroused in her.

Now for the first time she felt possessive; she found herself deeply interested in Roger's welfare because, she thought, he was hers and she could not endure having a possession whose qualities were unknown. She was not curious about his money nor his business affairs but she thirsted to know how his time away from her was spent, whom he saw, what other places he frequented. Not that she begrudged him a moment away from her side, but she must be able to account for that moment.

Yet if she felt possessive of him her feeling also recognized his complete absorption of her, so completely, so exhaustively did his life seem to envelop hers. For a while his wishes, his pleasure were the end and aim of her existence; she told herself with a slight tendency toward self-mockery that this was the explanation of being, of her being; that men had other aims, other uses but that the sole excuse for being a woman was to be just that,—a woman. Forgotten were her ideals about her Art; her ambition to hold a salon; her desire to help other people; even her intention of marrying in order to secure her future. Only something quite outside herself, something watchful, proud, remote from the passion and rapture which flamed within her, kept her free and independent. She would not accept money, she would not move to the apartment on Seventy-second Street; she still refused gifts so ornate that they were practically bribes. She made no explanations to Roger, but he knew and she knew too that her surrender was made out of the lavish fullness and generosity of her heart; there was no calculation back of it; if this were free love the freedom was the quality to be stressed rather than the emotion.

Sometimes, in her inchoate, wordless intensity of feeling which she took for happiness, she paused to take stock of that other life, those other lives which once she had known; that life which had been hers when she had first come to New York before she had gone to Cooper Union, in those days when she had patrolled Fourteenth Street and had sauntered through Union Square. And that other life which she knew in Opal Street,—æons ago, almost in another existence. She passed easily over those first few months in New York because even then she had been approaching a threshold, getting ready to enter on a new, undreamed of phase of being. But sometimes at night she lay for hours thinking over her restless, yearning childhood, her fruitless days at the Academy, the abortive wooing of Matthew Henson. The Hensons, the Hallowells, Hetty Daniels,—Jinny! How far now she was beyond their pale! Before her rose the eager, starved face of Hetty Daniels; now she herself was cognizant of phases of life for which Hetty longed but so contemned. Angela could imagine the envy back of the tone in which Hetty, had she but known it, would have expressed her disapproval of her former charge's manner of living. " Mattie Murray's girl, Angela, has gone straight to the bad; she's living a life of sin with some man in New York." And then the final, blasting indictment. " He's a white man, too. Can you beat that? "

CHAPTER III

ROGER's father, it appeared, had been greatly pleased with his son's management of the saw-mills in Georgia; as a result he was making more and more demands on his time. And the younger man half through pride, half through that steady determination never to offend his father, was always ready to do his bidding. Angela liked and appreciated her lover's filial attitude, but even in the period of her warmest interest she resented, secretly despised, this tendency to dependence. He was young, superbly trained; he had the gift of forming friendships whose strength rested on his own personality, yet he distrusted too much his own powers or else he was lazy—Angela could never determine which. During this phase of their acquaintanceship she was never sure that she loved him, but she was positive that if at this time he had been willing to fling aside his obsequious deference to his father's money and had said to her: " Angèle, if you'll help me, we'll build up a life, a fortune of our own," she would have adored him.

Her strong, independent nature, buffeted and sickened and strengthened by the constant attrition of colour prejudice, was unable to visualise or to pardon the frame of mind which kept Roger from joining battle with life when the odds were already so overwhelmingly in his favour. Alone, possessed of a handicap which if guessed at would have been as disabling as a game leg or an atrophied body, she had dared enter the lists. And she was well on the way to winning a victory. It was to cost her, she was beginning to realize, more than she had anticipated. But having entered she was not one to draw back,—unless indeed she changed her goal. Hers was a curious mixture of materialism and hedonism, and at this moment the latter quality was uppermost in her life. But she supposed that in some vague future she and Roger would marry. His ardour rendered her complacent.

But she was not conscious of any of these inner conflicts and criticisms; she was too happy. Now she was adopting a curious detachment toward life tempered by a faint cynicism,—a detachment which enabled her to say to herself: " Rules are for ordinary people but not for me." She remembered a verse from a poet, a coloured woman about whom she had often wondered. The lines ran:

> "The strong demand, contend, prevail.
> The beggar is a fool!"

She would never be a beggar. She would ask no further counsel nor advice of anyone. She had been lucky thus far in seeking advice only from Paulette and Martha Burden, two people of markedly independent methods of thought and action. They had never held her back. Now she would no longer consult even them. She would live her life as an individualist, to suit herself without regard for the conventions and established ways of life. Her native fastidiousness, she was sure, would keep her from becoming an offence in her own eyes.

In spite of her increasing self-confidence and self-sufficiency Roger's frequent absences left her lonely. Almost then, without any conscious planning on her part, she began to work at her art with growing vigour and interest. She was gaining in assurance; her technique showed an increased mastery; above all she had gained in the power to compose, a certain sympathy, a breadth of comprehension, the manifestation of that ability to interpret which she had long suspected lay within her, lent themselves to her hand. Mr. Paget, the instructor, spoke of her paintings with increased respect; the attention of visitors was directed thereto. Martha Burden and even Paulette, in the intervals of her ecstatic preparations, admitted her to the freemasonry of their own assured standing. Anthony Cross reminded her of the possibilities for American students at Fontainebleau. But she only smiled wisely; she would have no need of such study, but she hoped with all her heart that Miss Powell would be the recipient of a prize which would enable her to attend there.

"If she isn't," she promised herself, "I'll make Roger give her her expenses. I'd be willing to take the money from him for that."

To her great surprise her other interest besides her painting lay in visiting Jinny. If anyone had asked her if she were satisfied with her own life, her reply would have been an instant affirmative. But she did not want such a life for her sister. For Virginia there must be no risks, no secrets, no irregularities. Her efforts to find out how her sister spent her free hours amazed herself; their fruitlessness filled her with a constant irritation which Virginia showed no inclination to allay. The younger girl had passed her examination and had been appointed; she was a successful and enthusiastic teacher; this much Angela knew, but beyond this nothing. She gathered that Virginia spent a good deal of time with a happy, intelligent, rather independent group of young coloured men and women; there was talk occasionally of the theatre, of a dance, of small clubs, of hikes, of classes at Columbia or at New York City College. Angela even met a gay, laughing party, consisting of Virginia and her friends *en route* to Brooklyn, she had been later informed briefly. The girls were bright birds of paradise, the men, her artist's eye noted, were gay, vital fauns. In the subway beside the laughing, happy groups, white faces showed pale and bloodless, other coloured faces loomed dull and hopeless. Angela began tardily to recognize that her sister had made her way into that curious, limited, yet shifting class of the " best " coloured people; the old Philadelphia phrase came drifting back to her, " people that you know." She was amazed at some of the names which Virginia let drop from her lips in her infrequent and laconic descriptions of certain evenings which she had spent in the home of Van Meier, a great coloured American, a littérateur, a fearless and dauntless apostle of the rights of man; his name was known, Martha Burden had assured her, on both sides of the water.

Such information she picked up as best she might for Virginia vouchsafed nothing; nor did she, on the infrequent occasions on which she ran across her sister, even appear to know her. This, Angela pointed out, was silly. "You might just as well speak," she told Jinny petulantly, remembering uncomfortably the occasion when she herself had cut her sister, an absolute stranger in New York. "Plenty of white and coloured people are getting to know each other and they always acknowledge the acquaintanceship. Why shouldn't we? No harm could come of it." But in Virginia's cool opinion no good could come of it either. Usually the younger girl preserved a discreet silence; whatever resolves she might have made with regard to the rupture between herself and her sister, she was certainly able to keep her own counsel. It was impossible to glean from her perfect, slightly distrait manner any glimpse of her inner life and her intentions. Frequently she showed an intense preoccupation from which she awakened to let fall a remark which revealed to Angela a young girl's normal reactions to the life about her, pleasant, uneventful and tinged with a cool, serene happiness totally different from the hot, heady, turgid rapture which at present was Angela's life.

· · · · ·

The Jewish girl, Rachel Salting, who lived on the floor above, took to calling on Angela. "We're young and here by ourselves," she said smiling, "it's stupid for us not to get acquainted, don't you think so?" Hers was a charming smile and a charming manner. Indeed she was a very pretty girl, Angela thought critically. Her skin

was very, very pale, almost pearly, her hair jet
black and curling, her eyes large and almond-
shaped. Her figure was straight and slender but
bore none the less some faint hint of an exotic
voluptuousness. Her interests, she informed her
new friend, were all with the stage, her ideal being
Raquel Meller.

Angela welcomed her friendliness. A strange
apathy, an unusual experience for her, had invaded her being; her painting claimed, it is true,
a great deal of time and concentration; her hours
with Virginia, while not always satisfactory, were
at least absorbing; but for the first time in her
knowledge, her whole life was hanging on the
words, the moods, the actions of some one else—
Roger. Without him she was quite lost; not only
was she unable to order her days without him in
mind, she was even unable to go in quest of new
adventures in living as was once her wont. Consequently she received with outstretched arms
anything beyond the ordinary which might break
the threatening monotony of her life.

Rachel Salting was like a fresh breeze, a curious
mixture of Jewish conservatism and modernity.
Hers was a keen, clear mind, well trained in the
New York schools and colleges with many branch-
ing interests. She spoke of psychiatry, housing
problems, Zionism, child welfare, with a knowledge and zest which astounded Angela, whose
training had been rather superficial and who had
begun to adopt Paulette's cleverness and Martha
Burden's slightly professional, didactic attitude
toward things in general as norms for herself.
Rachel, except when dwelling on the Jewish
problem, seemed to have no particular views to

set forth. Her discussions, based on her wide reading, were purely academic, she had no desire to proselyte, she was no reformer. She was merely a "nice", rather jolly, healthy young woman, an onlooker at life which she had to get through with and which she was finding for the moment at any rate, extremely pleasant.

She was very happy; happy like Virginia with a happiness vastly different from what Angela was calling by that name; a breathless, constant, smiling happiness, palpable, transparent, for all the world to see. Within a few weeks after their acquaintanceship had started, Rachel with smiles and blushes revealed her great secret. She was going to be married.

"To the very best man in the world, Angèle."

"Yes, I'm sure of it."

"He's very good-looking, tall,———"

"As though I didn't know that."

"How could you know?"

"Darling child, haven't I seen him, at least the outline of him, often enough in the hall when I'd come in and turn on that wretched light? I didn't think you'd ever forgive me for it. It did seem as though I were doing it on purpose."

"Oh, I knew you weren't. Then you have seen him?"

"Yes, he's tall and blond. Quite a nice foil for your darkness. See, I'm always the artist."

"Yes," Rachel said slowly, "he is blond."

Angela thought she detected a faint undertone of worry in her hitherto triumphant voice but decided that that was unlikely.

But Rachel confirmed this impression by her next words: "If only everything will turn out all right."

Angel's rather material mind prompted her to ask: "What's the matter, is he very poor?"

Rachel stared. "Poor? As though that mattered. Yes, he's poor, but I don't care about that."

"Well, if you don't care about that, what's the trouble then? He's free, white and twenty-one, isn't he?"

"Yes, yes, it's only—oh you wouldn't understand, you lucky girl! It's nothing you'd ever have to bother about. You see we've got to get our parents' consent first. We haven't spoken of it yet. When we do, I'm afraid there'll be a row."

Some ritual inherent in her racial connections, Angela decided, and asked no further questions. Indeed, she had small chance, for Rachel, once launched, had begun to expound her gospel of marriage. It was an old, old story. Angela could have closed her eyes and imagined her own mother rhapsodizing over her future with Junius. They would be poor, very poor at first but only at first, and they would not mind poverty a bit. It would be fun together. There were little frame houses in the Bronx that rented comparatively cheap. Perhaps Angela knew of them.

Angela shuddering inwardly, acknowledged that she had seen them, dull brown, high-shouldered affairs, perched perilously on stoops. The rooms would be small, square, ugly,——

Rachel would help her John in every way. They would economize. "I won't wash and iron, for that is heart-breaking work, and I want to keep myself dainty and pretty for him, so that when we do become better off he won't have to be ashamed of me. And all the time even in our hardest days

I'll be trying my luck at play-writing." She spoke
with the unquenchable ambition which was her
racial dowry. "I'll be attending lectures and
sitting up in the galleries of theatres where they
have the most successful plays. And some day
I'll land." Her fanciful imagination carried her
years ahead. "On our First Night, Angela, you
must be in our box and I'll have an ermine coat.
Won't it be wonderful? But nothing will be more
wonderful than those first few years when we'll
be absolutely dependent on each other; I on what
he makes, he on the way I run the home. That
will be heaven."

Confidences such as these left Angela unmoved
but considerably shaken. There must be something in the life of sacrifice, even drudgery which
Rachel had depicted. Else why should so many
otherwise sensible girls take the risk? But there,
it was silly for her to dwell on such pictures and
scenes. Such a life would never come to her. It
was impossible to conceive of such a life with
Roger. Yet there were times in her lonely room
when she pondered long and deeply, drawing
pictures. The time would be summer; she would
be wearing a white dress, would be standing in
the doorway of a house in the suburbs very, very
near New York. There'd be the best possible
dinner on the table. She did love to cook. And a
tall, strong figure would be hurrying up the walk:
" I had the best luck to-day, Angèle, and I brought
you a present." And presently after dinner she
would take him upstairs to her little work-room
and she'd draw aside the curtain and show him a
portrait of a well-known society woman. " She's
so pleased with it; and she's going to get me lots

of orders,——" Somehow she was absolutely sure
that the fanciful figure was not Roger.

.   .   .   .   .

Her lover, back from a three weeks' trip to
Chicago, dissipated that sureness. He was glad,
overwhelmingly glad to be back and to see Angèle.
He came to her apartment directly from the train,
not stopping even to report to his father. " I
can see him to-morrow. To-night is absolutely
yours. What shall we do, Angèle? We can
go out to dinner and the theatre or run out to
the Country Club or stay here. What do you
say? "

" We'll have to stay here, Roger; I'll fix up a
gorgeous dinner, better than anything you've had
to eat in any of your old hotels. But directly after,
I'll have to cut and run because I promised Martha
Burden faithfully to go to a lecture with her to-
night."

" I never knew you to be interested in a lecture
before."

She was worried and showed it. " But this is a
different sort of lecture. You know how crazy
Martha is about race and social movements. Well,
Van Meier is to speak to-night and Martha is
determined that a lot of her friends shall hear him.
I'm to go with her and Ladislas."

" What's to keep me from going? "

" Nothing, only he's coloured, you know."

" Well, I suppose it won't rub off. I've heard
of him. They say he really has brains. I've
never seen a nigger with any yet; so this bids fair
to be interesting. And, anyway, you don't think
I'm going to let my girl run off from me the

very moment I come home, do you? Suppose
I have Reynolds bring the big car here and we'll
take Martha and Ladislas along and anyone else
she chooses to bring."

The lecture was held in Harlem in East One
Hundred and Thirty-fifth Street. The hall was
packed, teeming with suppressed excitement and
a certain surcharged atmosphere. Angela radiant,
calmed with the nearness and devotion of Roger,
looked about her with keen, observing eyes. And
again she sensed that fullness, richness, even thick-
ness of life which she had felt on her first visit to
Harlem. The stream of living ran almost molten;
little waves of feeling played out from groups within
the audience and beat against her consciousness
and against that of her friends, only the latter were
without her secret powers of interpretation. The
occasion was clearly one of moment. " I'd come
any distance to hear Van Meier speak," said a
thin-faced dark young man behind them. " He
always has something to say and he doesn't talk
down to you. To hear him is like reading a classic,
clear and beautiful and true."

Angela, revelling in types and marshalling bits
of information which she had got from Virginia,
was able to divide the groups. There sat the most
advanced coloured Americans, beautifully dressed,
beautifully trained, whimsical, humorous, bitter,
impatiently responsible, yet still responsible. In
one section loomed the dark, eager faces of West
Indians, the formation of their features so markedly
different from that of the ordinary American as
to give them a wild, slightly feral aspect. These
had come not because they were disciples of Van
Meier but because they were earnest seekers after

truth. But unfortunately their earnestness was slightly married by a stubbornness and an unwillingness to admit conviction. Three or four coloured Americans, tall, dark, sleek young men sat within earshot, speaking with a curious didactic precision. " They're quoting all the sociologists in the world," Ladislas Starr told his little group in astonishment.

Martha, with her usual thoroughness, knew all about them. They were the editors of a small magazine whose chief bid to fame lay in the articles which they directed monthly against Van Meier; articles written occasionally in a spirit of mean jealousy but usually in an effort to gain a sort of inverted glory by carrying that great name on its pages.

Here and there a sprinkling of white faces showed up plainly, startlingly distinct patterns against a back-ground of patient, softly stolid black faces; faces beaten and fashioned by life into a mold of steady, rock-like endurance, of unshakable, unconquered faith. Angela had seen such faces before in the churches in Philadelphia; they brought back old pictures to her mind.

" There he is ! " exclaimed Martha triumphantly. " That's Van Meier ! Isn't he wonderful? " Angela saw a man, bronze, not very tall but built with a beautiful symmetrical completeness, cross the platform and sit in the tall, deep chair next to the table of the presiding officer. He sat with a curious immobility, gazing straight before him like a statue of an East Indian idol. And indeed there was about him some strange quality which made one think of the East; a completeness, a superb lack of self-consciousness, an odd, arresting beauty wrought by the perfection of his fine, straight nose and his broad, scholarly forehead. One look, however casual, gave the beholder the assurance that here indeed was a man, fearless, dauntless, the captain of his fate.

He began to speak on a clear, deep, bell-like note. Angela thought she had never heard its equal for beauty, for resonance, for culture. And as the young man had said, he did not talk down. His English was the carefully sifted language of the savant, his periods polished, almost poetical. He was noted on two continents for his sociological and economic contributions, but his subject was racial sacrifice. He urged the deliberate introduction of beauty and pleasure into the difficult life of the American Negro. These objects should be theirs both as racial heritage and as compensation. Yet for a time, for a long time, there would have to be sacrifices, many sacrifices made for the good of the whole. "Our case is unique," the beautiful, cultured voice intoned; "those of us who have forged forward, who have gained the front ranks in money and training, will not, are not able as yet to go our separate ways apart from the unwashed, untutored herd. We must still look back and render service to our less fortunate, weaker brethren. And the first step toward making this a workable attitude is the acquisition not so much of a racial love as a racial pride. A pride that enables us to find our own beautiful and praiseworthy, an intense chauvinism that is content with its own types, that finds completeness within its own group; that loves its own as the French love their country, because it is their own.

Such a pride can accomplish the impossible."
He quoted:

> " It is not courage, no, nor hate
> That lets us do the things we do;
> It's pride that bids the heart be great,—"

He sat down to a surge of applause that shook
the building. Dark, drooping faces took on an
expression of ecstatic uplift, it was as though they
suddenly saw themselves, transformed by racial
pride as princes in a strange land in temporary
serfdom, princes whose children would know
freedom.

- Martha Burden and Ladislas went up to speak
to him; they were old friends. Angela, with Roger,
visibly impressed, stood on one side and waited.
Paulette and Hudson came pushing through the
crowd, the former flushed and excited. Little
groups of coloured people stood about, some deeply
content with a sort of vicarious pride, some arguing;
Angela caught sight of Virginia standing with three
young men and two girls. They were for the
most part gesticulating, lost in a great excitement.
But Jinny seemed listless and aloof; her childish
face looked thin and more forlornly young than
ever. Anthony Cross and a tall man of undeniably
Spanish type passed the little party and spoke to
one of the men, received introductions. Presently
Cross, swinging about, caught sight of Angela and
Roger. He bowed hastily, flushing; caught his
companion's arm and walked hurriedly from the
hall, his head very straight, his slender figure always
so upright, so *élancé*, more erect than ever.

Presently Martha's party was all out on the sidewalk; Roger in fine spirits invited Paulette and

Hudson to ride down town in his car. Paulette was bubbling over with excited admiration of Van Meièr. "He isn't a man, he's a god," she proclaimed. "Did you ever see such a superb personality? He's not a magnificent coloured man, he's not 'just as good as a white man'; he is a man, just that; colour, race, conditions in his case are pure accidents, he over-rides them all with his ego. Made me feel like a worm too; I gave him my prettiest smile, grand white lady making up to an 'exceptional Negro' and he simply didn't see me; took my hand,—I did my best to make my grasp a clinging one—and he passed me right along disengaging himself as cool as a cucumber and making room for a lady of colour." She finished reflectively, "I wonder what he would be like alone."

"None of your nonsense, Paulette," said Roger frowning.

Hudson smiled. "Paulette's a mighty attractive little piece, I'll admit, but I'd back Van Meier against her every time; she'd present no temptation to him; the man's not only a prophet and the son of a prophet; he's pride incarnate."

Roger said meditatively, "I wonder what proportion of white blood he has in his veins. Of course that's where he gets his ability."

"You make me tired," said Martha. "Of course he doesn't get it from his white blood; he gets it from all his bloods. It's the mixture that makes him what he is. Otherwise all white people would be gods. It's the mixture and the endurance which he has learned from being coloured in America and the determination to see life without bitterness,——"

" Oh help, help," exclaimed Roger. " No more lectures to-night. Look, you're boring Angèle to death."

" Nothing of the kind," said Angela, " on the contrary I never was more interested in my life." And reaching back she gave Martha's hand a hearty squeeze.

.   .   .   .   .

Sometimes as on that first day at the art class, the five of them, Miss Powell, Paulette, Cross, Martha and Angela met before hours. Miss Powell as always was silent—she came solely for her work—but the others enjoyed a little preliminary chat. A week or so after the Van Meier lecture all but Paulette were gathered thus on an afternoon when she too came rushing in, starry eyed, flushed, consumed with laughter.

" I've played the biggest joke on myself," she announced, " I've been to see Van Meier."

Martha was instant attention. " A joke on Van Meier? "

" No, on myself, I tell you."

It appeared that she had got Miss Powell to introduce her to one of the clerks in the great leader's office. Paulettte then with deliberate intention had asked the girl to lunch and afterwards had returned with her to the office expressing a desire to meet her employer. Van Meier had received her cordially enough but with the warning that he was very busy.

" So I told him that I wouldn't sit down, thinking of course he'd urge me to. But he just raised his eyebrows in the most quizzical way and said, ' Well '? "

" Of course I couldn't let matters rest like that so I sat down and began talking to him, nothing much you know, just telling him how wonderful he was and letting him see that I'd be glad to know him better. You should have seen him looking at me and not saying a word. Presently he reached out his hand and touched a bell and Miss Thing-um-bob came in,—your friend, you know, Miss Powell. He looked at her and nodding toward me said: ' Take her away '. I never felt such small potatoes in my life. I tell you he's a personage. Wasn't it great? "

Martha replied crossly that the whole thing seemed to her in dreadfully poor taste, while Miss Powell, after one incredulous stare at the first speaker, applied herself more sedulously to her work. Even Anthony, shocked out of his habitual moroseness pronounced the proceedings " a bit thick, Miss Lister ". Angela conscious of a swelling pride, stowed the incident away as a tit-bit for Virginia.

CHAPTER IV

LIFE had somehow come to a standstill; gone was its quality of high adventure and yet with the sense of tameness came no compensating note of assurance, of permanence. Angela pondered much about this; with her usual instinct for clarity, for a complete understanding of her own emotional life, she took to probing her inner consciousness. The fault, she decided, was bound up in her relationship with Roger. At present in a certain sense she might be said to be living for him; at least his was the figure about which her life resolved, revolved. Yet she no longer had the old, heady desire to feel herself completely his, to claim him as completely hers, neither for his wealth nor for the sense of security which he could afford nor for himself. For some reason he had lost his charm for her, much, she suspected, in the same way in which girls in the position which was hers, often lost their charm for their lovers.

And this realization instead of bringing to her a sense of relief, brought a certain real if somewhat fantastic shame. If there was to be no permanence in the relationship, if laying aside the question of marriage, it was to lack the dignity, the graciousness of an affair of long standing, of sympathy, of mutual need, then indeed according to the code of her childhood, according to every code of every phase of her development, she had allowed herself to drift into an inexcusably vulgar predicament. Even when her material safety and security were at stake and she had dreamed vaguely of yielding to Roger's entreaties to ensure that safety and security, there might have been some excuse. Life, she considered, came before creed or code or convention. Or if she had loved and there had been no other way she might have argued for this as the supreme experience of her life. But she was no longer conscious of striving for marriage with Roger; and as for love—she had known a feeling of gratitude, intense interest, even intense possessiveness for him but she did not believe she had ever known love.

But, because of this mingling of shame and re-proach she found herself consciously striving to keep their relations on the highest plane possible in the circumstances. She wished now not so much that she had never left Jinny and the security of their common home-life, as that the necessity for it had never arisen. Now suddenly she found herself lonely, she had been in New York nearly three years but not even yet had she struck down deep into the lode of genuine friendship. Paulette was kind and generous; she desired, she said, a close woman friend but Paulette was still the adventuress. She was as likely to change her voca-tion and her place of dwelling as she was to change her lover. Martha Burden, at once more stable and more comprehending in the conduct of a friendship once she had elected for it, was, on the other hand, much more conservative in the expenditure of that friendliness; besides she was by her very nature as reserved as Paulette was expansive, and her native intenseness made it difficult for her to dwell very long on the needs of anyone whose problems did not centre around her own extremely fixed ideas and principles.

As for Anthony Cross,—by some curious, utterly inexplicable revulsion of feeling, Angela could not bring herself to dwell long on the possibilities of a friendship with him. Somehow it seemed to her sacrilegious in her present condition to bring the memory of that far-off day in Van Cortlandt Park back to mind. As soon as his image arose she dismissed it, though there were moments when it was impossible for his vision to come before her without its instantly bringing to mind Rachel Salting's notions of love and self-sacrifice. Well, such dreams were not for her, she told herself impatiently. For her own soul's integrity she must make the most of this state in which she now found herself. Either she must effect through it a marriage whose excuse should be that of safety, assurance and a resulting usefulness; or she must resolve it by patience, steadfastness and affection into a very apotheosis of " free love." Of all possible *affaires du coeur* this must in semblance at any rate, be the ultimate desideratum, the finest flower of chivalry and devotion.

$$\bullet \qquad \bullet \qquad \bullet \qquad \bullet \qquad \bullet$$

To this end she began then devoting herself again to the renewal of that sense of possessiveness in Roger and his affairs which had once been so spontaneous within her. But to this Roger presented unexpected barriers; he grew restive under such manifestations; he who had once fought so bitterly against her indifference resented with equal bitterness any showing of possessive interest. He wanted no claims upon him, he acknowledged none. Gradually his absences, which at first were due to the business interests of his father, occurred for other reasons or for none at all. Angela could not grasp this all at once; it was impossible for her to conceive that kindness should create indifference; in spite of confirmatory stories which she had heard, of books which she had read, she could not make herself believe that devotion might sometimes beget ingratitude, loss of appreciation. For if that were so then a successful relationship between the sexes must depend wholly on the marriage tie without reference to compatibility of taste, training or ideals. This she could scarcely credit. In some way she must be at fault.

No young wife in the first ardour of marriage could have striven more than she to please Roger. She sought by reading and outside questions to inform herself along the lines of Roger's training —he was a mining engineer. His fondness for his father prompted her to numerous inquiries about the interest and pursuits of the older Fielding; she made suggestions for Roger's leisure hours. But no matter how disinterested her attitude and tone his response to all this was an increased sullenness, remoteness, wariness. Roger was experienced in the wiles of women; such interest could mean only one thing,—marriage. Well, Angela might just as well learn that he had no thought, had never had any thought, of marrying her or any other woman so far removed from his father's ideas and requirements.

Still Angela, intent on her ideals, could not comprehend. Things were not going well between them; affairs of this kind were often short-lived, that had been one of her first objections to the arrangement, but she had not dreamed that one withdrew when the other had committed no overt offence. She was as charming, as attractive, as pretty as she had ever been and far, far more kind and thoughtful. She had not changed, how could it be possible that he should be different?

A week had gone by and he had not dropped in to see her. Loneliness settled over her like a pall, frightening her seriously because she was realizing that this time she was not missing Roger so much as that a person for whom she had let slip the ideals engendered by her mother's early teaching, a man for whom she had betrayed and estranged her sister, was passing out of her ken. She had rarely called him on the telephone but suddenly she started to do so. For three days the suave voice of his man, Reynolds, told her that Mr. Fielding was " out, m'm."

" But did you give him my message? Did you ask him to call me as soon as he came in? "

" Yes, m'm."

" And did he? "

" That I couldn't tell you, m'm."

She could not carry on such a conversation with a servant.

On the fifth day Roger appeared. She sprang toward him. " Oh Roger, I'm so glad to see you. Did Reynolds tell you I called? Why have you been so long coming? "

" I'd have been still longer if you hadn't stopped 'phoning. Now see here, Angèle, this has got to stop. I can't have women calling me up all hours of the day, making me ridiculous in the eyes of my servants. I don't like it, it's got to stop. Do you understand me? "

Surprised, bewildered, she could only stammer: "But you call me whenever you feel like it."

"Of course I do, that's different. I'm a man." He added a cruel afterword. "Perhaps you notice that I don't call you up as often as I used."

● ● ● ● ●

Her pride was in arms. More than once she thought of writing him a brief note telling him that so far as she was concerned their " affair " was ended. But a great stubbornness possessed her; she was curious to see how this sort of thing could terminate; she was eager to learn if all the advice which older women pour into the ears of growing girls could be as true as it was trite. Was it a fact that the conventions were more important than the fundamental impulses of life, than generosity, kindness, unselfishness? For whatever her original motives, her actual relationship with Fielding had called out the most unselfish qualities in her. And she began to see the conventions, the rules that govern life, in a new light; she realized suddenly that for all their granite-like coldness and precision they also represented fundamental facts; a sort of concentrated compendium of the art of living and therefore as much to be observed and respected as warm, vital impulses.

Towards Roger she felt no rancour, only an apathy incapable of being dispersed. The conversation about the telephone left an effect all out of proportion to its actual importance; it represented for her the apparently unbridgeable difference between the sexes; everything was for men, but even the slightest privilege was to be denied to a woman unless the man chose to grant it. At least there were men who felt like that; not all men, she felt sure, could tolerate such an obviously unjust status. Without intent to punish, with no set purpose in her mind, simply because she was no longer interested, she began to neglect Roger. She no longer let other engagements go for him; she made no attempt to be punctual in keeping such engagements as they had already made; in his presence she was often absorbed, absentminded, lost in thought. She ceased asking him questions about his affairs.

Long before their quarrel they had accepted an invitation from Martha Burden to a small party. Angela was surprised that Roger should remember the occasion, but clearly he did; he was on hand at the correct date and hour and the two of them fared forth. During the brief journey he was courteous, even politely cordial, but the difference between his attitude and that of former days was very apparent. The party was of a more frivolous type than Martha usually sponsored, she was giving it for a young, fun-loving cousin of Ladislas; there was no general conversation, some singing, much dancing, much pairing off in couples. Carlotta Parks was present with Ralph Ashley, the slender, dark man who had appeared with Carlotta when Angela first met her. As soon as Roger appeared Carlotta came rushing toward him.

" I've been waiting for you! " She dragged at his hand and not unwillingly he suffered himself to be led to a small sofa. They chatted a few minutes; then danced; Roger simply must look at Martha's new etchings. The pair was inseparable for the evening. Try as she might Angela could discover no feeling of jealousy but her dignity was hurt. She could not have received less attention from her former lover if they had never met. At first she thought she would make up to Ashley but something malicious in Carlotta's glance deterred her. No, she was sick of men and their babyish, faithless ways; she did not care enough about Roger to play a game for him. So she sat quietly in a deep chair, smoking, dipping into the scattered piles of books which lent the apartment its air of cheerful disorder. Occasionally she chatted; Ladislas Starr perched on the arm of her chair and beguiled her with gay tales of his university days in pre-war Vienna.

But she would never endure such an indignity again. On the way home she was silent. Roger glanced at her curiously, raised his eyebrows when she asked him to come in. She began quietly: " Roger I'll never endure again the treatment——"

But he was ready, even eager for a quarrel. " It looks to me as though you were willing to endure anything. No woman with an ounce of pride would have stood for what you've been standing lately."

She said evenly: " You mean this is the end? We're through? "

" Well, what do you think about it? You certainly didn't expect it to last for ever.".

His tone was unbelievably insulting. Eyeing him speculatively she replied: " No, of course I didn't expect it to last for ever, but I didn't think it would end like this. I don't see yet why it should."

The knowledge of his unpardonable manner lay heavy upon him, drove him to fresh indignity. " I suppose you thought some day I'd kiss your hand and say ' You've been very nice to me; I'll always remember you with affection and gratitude. Good-bye.' "

" Well, why shouldn't you have said that? Certainly I'd expected that much sooner than a scene of this sort. I never dreamed of letting myself in for this kind of thing."

Some ugly devil held him in its grasp. " You knew perfectly well what you were letting yourself in for. Any woman would know it."

She could only stare at him, his words echoing in her ears: " You knew perfectly well what you were letting yourself in for."

The phrase had the quality of a cosmic echo; perhaps men had been saying it to women since the beginning of time. Doubtless their biblical equivalent were the last words uttered by Abraham to Hagar before she fared forth into the wilderness.

CHAPTER V

LONG after Roger had left her she sat staring into the dark shadows of the room. For a long time the end, she knew, had been imminent; she had been curious to see how it would arrive, but the thought had never crossed her mind that it would come with harsh words and with vulgarity. The departure of Roger himself—she shut her hand and opened it—meant nothing; she had never loved, never felt for him one-tenth of the devotion which her mother had known for her father, of the spontaneous affection which Virginia had offered Matthew Henson. Even in these latter weeks when she had consciously striven to show him every possible kindness and attention she had done so for the selfish preservation of her ideals. Now she looked back on those first days of delight when his emotions and her own had met at full tide; when she dreamed that she alone of all people in the world was exempt from ordinary law. How, she wondered futilely, could she ever have suffered herself to be persuaded to tamper with the sacred mysteries of life? If she had held in her hand the golden key,—love! But to throw aside the fundamental laws of civilization for passion, for the hot-headed wilfulness of youth and to have it end like this, drably, vulgarly, almost in a brawl! How could she endure herself? And Roger and his promises of esteem and golden memories!

For a moment she hated him for his fine words and phrases, hated him for tricking her. No matter what she had said, how she had acted, he should have let her go. Better a wound to her passion than later this terrible gash in her proud assurance, this hurt in the core of herself " God! " she said, raging in her tiny apartment as a tiger in a menagerie rages in its inadequate cage, " God, isn't there any place where man's responsibility to woman begins ? "

．　　．　　．　　．　　．

But she had grown too much into the habit of deliberately ordering her life, of hewing her own path, of removing the difficulties that beset that path, to let herself be sickened, utterly prostrated by what had befallen her. Roger, her companion, had gone; she had been caught up in an inexcusably needless affair without the pretext of love. Thank God she had taken nothing from Roger; she had not sold herself, only bestowed that self foolishly, unworthily. However upset and harassed her mind might be it could not dwell too long on this loss of a lover. There were other problems to consider; for Roger's passing meant the vanishing of the last hope of the successful marriage which once she had so greatly craved. And even though she had not actively considered this for some time, yet as a remote possibility it had afforded a sense of security. Now that mirage was dispelled; she was brought with a sudden shock back to reality. No longer was it enough for her to plan how she could win to a pleasant and happy means of existence, she must be on the *qui vive* for the maintenance of that very existence itself. New York had literally swallowed her original three thousand dollars; part of Virginia's gift was also dissipated. Less than a thousand dollars stood between her and absolute penury. She could not envisage turning to Jinny; life which had seemed so promising, so golden, had failed to supply her with a single friend to whom she could turn in an hour of extremity.

Such thoughts as these left her panic-stricken, cold with fear. The spectre of possible want filled her dreams, haunted her waking hours, thrust aside the devastating shame of her affair with Roger to replace it with dread and apprehension. In her despair she turned more ardently than ever to her painting; already she was capable of doing outstanding work in portraiture, but she lacked *cachet;* she was absolutely unknown.

This condition of her mind affected her appearance; she began to husband her clothes, sadly conscious that she could not tell where others would come from. Her face lost its roundness, the white warmness of her skin remained but there were violet shadows under her eyes; her forehead showed faint lines; she was slightly shabby. Gradually the triumphant vividness so characteristic of Angèle Mory left her, she was like any one of a thousand other pitiful, frightened girls thronging New York. Miss Powell glanced at her and thought: " she looks unhappy, but how can she be when she has a chance at everything in the world just because she's white? "

Anthony marked her fading brightness; he would have liked to question her, comfort her, but where this girl was concerned the rôle of comforter was not for him. Only the instructor, Mr. Paget guessed at her extremity. He had seen too many students not to recognize the signs of poverty, of disaster in love, of despair at the tardy flowering of dexterity that had been mistaken for talent. Once after class he stopped Angela and asked her if she knew of anyone willing to furnish designs for a well-known journal of fashion.

" Not very stimulating work, but the pay is good and the firm reliable. Their last artist was with them eight years. If you know of any-one,——"

She interrupted: " I know of myself. Do you think they'd take me on? "

" I could recommend you. They applied to me, you see. Doubtless they'd take my suggestions into account."

He was very kind; made all the necessary arrangements. The firm received Angela gladly, offering her a fair salary for work that was a trifle narrow, a bit stultifying. But it opened up possi-bilities; there were new people to be met; perhaps she would make new friends, form ties which might be lasting.

" Oh," she said hopefully to herself, " life is wonderful! It's giving me a new deal and I'll begin all over again. I'm young and now I'm sophisticated; the world is wide, somewhere there's happiness and peace and a place for me. I'll find it."

But her hope, her sanguineness, were a little forced, her superb self-confidence perceptibly diminished. The radiance which once had so bathed every moment of her existence was fading gently, inexorably into the " light of common day ".

HOME AGAIN

CHAPTER I

NEW YORK, it appeared, had two visages. It could offer an aspect radiant with promise or a countenance lowering and forbidding. With its flattering possibilities it could elevate to the seventh heaven, or lower to the depths of hell with its crushing negations. And loneliness! Loneliness such as that offered by the great, noisy city could never be imagined. To realize it one would have to experience it. Coming home from work Angela used to study the people on the trains, trying to divine what cause had engraved a given expression on their faces, particularly on the faces of young women. She picked out for herself four types, the happy, the indifferent, the preoccupied, the lonely. Doubtless her classification was imperfect, but she never failed, she thought, to recognize the signs of loneliness, a vacancy of expression, a listlessness, a faintly pervading despair. She remembered the people in Union Square on whom she had spied so blithely when she had first come to New York. Then she had thought of them as being " down and out ", mere idlers, good for nothing. It had not occurred to her that their chief disaster might be loneliness. Her office was on Twenty-third Street and often at the noon-hour she walked down to the dingy Square and looked again on the sprawling, half-recumbent, dejected figures. And between

them and herself she was able to detect a
terrifying relationship. She still carried her note-
book, made sketches, sitting watching them and
jotting down a line now and then when their
vacant, staring eyes were not fixed upon her.
Once she would not have cared if they had caught
her; she would have said with a shrug: " Oh they
wouldn't mind, they're too far gone for that."
But since then her sympathy and knowledge had
waxed. How fiercely she would have rebelled
had anyone from a superior social plane taken
her for copy!

In the evenings she worked at the idea of a picture which she intended for a masterpiece. It
was summer and the classes at Cooper Union
had been suspended. But she meant to return in
the fall, perhaps she would enter the scholarship
contest and if successful, go abroad. But the urge
to wander was no longer in the ascendant. The
prospect of Europe did not seem as alluring now
as the prospect of New York had appeared when
she lived in Philadelphia. It would be nice to
stay put, rooted; to have friends, experiences,
memories.

.   .   .   .   .

Paulette, triumphant to the last, had left with
Hudson for Russia. Martha and Ladislas were
spending the summer with Martha's people on
Long Island. Roger had dropped into the void,
but she could not make herself miss him; to her he
was the symbol of all that was most futile in her
existence, she could forgive neither him nor herself
for their year of madness. If the experience, she

told herself, had ended—so-beit—everything·ends.
If it had faded into a golden glow with a wealth
of memories, the promise of a friendship, she would
have had no qualms; but as matters had turned
out it was an offence in her nostrils, a great blot
on the escutcheon of her fastidiousness.

She wished that Martha had asked her to spend
week-ends with her but the idea had apparently
never crossed the latter's mind. " Good-bye until
fall," she had said gaily, " do you know, I'm
awfully glad to go home this time. I always have
my old room; it's like begining life all over again.
Of course I wouldn't give up New York but life
seems so much more real and durable down there.
After all it's where my roots are."

Her roots! Angela echoed the expression to
herself on a note that was wholly envious. How
marvellous to go back to parents, relatives, friends
with whom one had never lost touch! The peace,
the security, the companionableness of it! This
was a relationship which she had forfeited with
everyone, even with Jinny. And as for her other
acquaintances in Philadelphia, Henson, Butler,
Kate and Agnes Hallowell, so completely, so casually, without even a ripple had she dropped out
of their lives that it would have been impossible
for her to re-establish their old, easy footing even
had she so desired.

Virginia, without making an effort, seemed overwhelmed, almost swamped by friendships, pleasant
intimacies, a thousand charming interests. She
and Sara Penton, another teacher, had taken an
apartment together, a three room affair on the
top floor of a house on 139th Street, in " Striver's
Row ", explained Jinny. · Whether or not the nick-

name was deserved, it seemed to Angela well worth
an effort to live in this beautiful block with its
tree-bordered pavements, its spacious houses, its
gracious neighbourliness. A doctor and his wife
occupied the first two floors; they were elderly,
rather lonely people, for their two children had
married and gone to other cities. They had practically adopted Virginia and Sara; nursing them
when they had colds, indulgently advising them
as to their callers. Mrs. Bradley, the doctor's wife,
occasionally pressed a dress for them; on stormy
days the doctor drove them in his car around to
" Public School 89 " where they both taught.
Already the two girls were as full of intimacies,
joyous reminiscences, common plans as though
they had lived together for years. Secrets, nick-
names, allusions, filled the atmosphere. Angela
grew sick of the phrases: " Of course you don't
understand that; just some nonsense and it would
take too long to explain it. Besides you wouldn't
know any of the people." Even so, unwelcome as
the expression was, she did not hear it very often,
for Jinny did not encourage her visits to the apartment even as much as to the boarding house.

" Sara will think it strange if you come too often."

" We might tell her," Angela rejoined, " and ask
her to keep it a secret."

But Jinny opined coolly that that would never
do; it was bad to entrust people with one's secrets.
" If you can't keep them yourself, why should
they? " she asked sagely. Her attitude showed no
malice, only the complete acceptance of the stand
which her sister had adopted years ago.

.   .   .   .   .

In her sequestered rooms in the Village lying in the summer heat unkempt and shorn of its glamour Angela pondered long and often on her present mode of living. Her life, she was pretty sure, could not go on indefinitely as it did now. Even if she herself made no effort it was unlikely that the loneliness could persist. Jinny, she shrewdly suspected, had known something of this horrible condition when she, the older sister had left her so ruthlessly to go off and play at adventure. This loneliness and her unfortunate affair with Henson had doubtless proved too much for her, and she had deliberately sought change and distraction elsewhere. There were depths upon depths of strength in Jinny and as much purpose and resource as one might require. Now here she was established in New York with friends, occupation, security, leading an utterly open life, no secrets, no subterfuges, no goals to be reached by devious ways.

Jinny had changed her life and been successful. Angela had changed hers and had found pain and unhappiness. Where did the fault lie? Not, certainly, in her determination to pass from one race to another. Her native good sense assured her that it would have been silly for her to keep on living as she had in Philadelphia, constantly, through no fault of her own, being placed in impossible positions, eternally being accused and hounded because she had failed to placard herself, forfeiting old friendships, driven fearfully to the establishing of new ones. No, the fault was not there. Perhaps it lay in her attitude toward her friends. Had she been too coldly deliberate in her use of them? Certainly she had planned to utilize her connection with Roger, but on this point she had no qualms; he had been paid in full for any advantages which she had meant to gain. She had not always been kind to Miss Powell, " but," she murmured to herself, " I was always as kind to her as I dared be in the circumstances and far, far more attentive than any of the others." As for Anthony, Paulette, and Martha, her slate was clear on their score. She was struck at this point to realize that during her stay of nearly three years these five were the only people to whom she could apply the term friends. Of these Roger had dropped out; Miss Powell was negative; Paulette had gone to Russia. There remained only Martha and Anthony. Martha was too intensely interested in the conduct of her own life in connection with Ladislas to make a friend, a satisfying, comfortable, intimate friend such as Sara Penton seemed to be with Virginia. There remained then only Anthony—yes, and her new acquaintance, Rachel Salting.

· · · · ·

She began then in her loneliness to approach Rachel seeking for nothing other than those almost sisterly intimacies which spring up between solitary women cut off in big cities from their homes and from all the natural resources which add so much to the beauty and graciousness of young woman-hood. " If anything comes out of this friendship to advance me in any way," she told herself sol-emnly, " it will happen just because it happens but I shall go into this with clean hands and a pure heart—merely because I like Rachel."

After the fever and fret of her acquaintanceship with Roger, the slight unwholesomeness attendant on Paulette, the didactic quality lurking in Martha's household, it was charming, even delicious to enter on a friendship with this simple, intelligent, enthusiastic girl. Rachel, for all her native endowment, her wide reading and her broad scholastic contacts, had the straightforward utter sincerity and simplicity of a child; at times Angela felt quite sophisticated, even blasé beside her. But in reality they were two children together; Angela's brief episode with Roger had left no trace on her moral nature; she was ashamed now of the affair with a healthy shame at its unworthiness; but beyond that, she suffered from no morbidness. Her sum total of the knowledge of life had been increased; she saw men with a different eye, was able to differentiate between the attitudes underlying the pleasantries of the half dozen young men in her office; listening, laughing, weighing all their attentions, accepting none. In truth she had lost to a degree her taste for the current type of flirtations. She might marry some day but all that was still in the dim future. Meanwhile the present beckoned; materially she was once more secure, her itching ambition was temporarily lulled; she had a friend. It was just as well to let time slide by for a while.

The two girls spent their evenings together. Rachel's fiancé, John Adams, was a travelling salesman and nearly always out of town. When he was home Angela was careful to have an engagement, though Rachel assured her, laughing and sparkling, that the two were already so used to each other that a third person need not feel *de trop*. Occasionally the three of them went during the hot summer nights to Coney Island or Far Rockaway. But this jaunt took on the proportions more of an ordeal than a pleasure trip; so packed were the cars with helpless humanity, so crowded the beaches, so nightmarish the trip home. Fortunately Angela came face to face one day with Ralph Ashley, Carlotta's former friend. Low-spirited, lonely, distrait, he asked Angela eagerly to allow him to call occasionally. He seemed a rather bookish, serious young man who had failed to discover the possibilities of his inner resources. Without an acquaintance or a book he was helpless. Angela's self-reliance and cleverness seemed to offer a temporary harbour. Apparently with Carlotta out of town, he was at loose ends. By some tacit understanding he was taken into the little group and as he possessed a car which he was willing and eager to share the arrangement was a very happy one.

    •   •   •   •   •

These were pleasant days. Long afterwards, Angela, looking back recalled them as among the happiest she had known in New York. In particular she liked the hours when she and Rachel were together busied with domestic, homely affairs. They advised each other on the subject of dress; Angela tried out new recipes. In the late evenings she worked on the sketches, recalling them from her note-book while Rachel, sitting sidewise in the big chair, her legs dangling comfortably over its arm, offered comments and suggestions. She had had " courses in art ", and on a trip to France and Italy at the age of eighteen had visited the Louvre, the Pitti and Uffizi Galleries. All this lent a certain pithiness and authority to the criticisms which she poured forth for her friend's edification; her remarks rarely produced any effect on Angela, but both girls felt that Rachel's knowledge gave a certain effect of " atmosphere ".

Usually Rachel's talk was on John and their approaching marriage, their unparalleled courtship. Many years later Angela could have related all the details of that simple, almost sylvan wooing, the growing awareness of the two lovers, their mutual fears and hopes, their questionings, assurances and their blissful engagement. She knew to a penny what John made each week, how much he put by, the amount which thrifty Rachel felt must be in hand before they could marry. Once this recital, so unvarying, so persistent, would have bored her, but she was more sympathetic in these days; sometimes she found herself making suggestions, saving the house-wifely clippings culled from newspapers, proposing decorations for the interior of one of the ugly little houses on which Rachel had so inexplicably set her heart. She was a little older than her friend, she had had experience in keeping house and in shopping with her mother in those far-off days; she ventured occasionally to advise Rachel in her rare purchases very much as though the latter were her own sister instead of a chance acquaintance whom she had known less than a year.

It was a placid, almost ideal existence. Only one thread of worry ran through its fabric, the thought that Rachel and John would soon be marrying and again Angela would be left on the search for a new friend. With one of them in the Bronx and the other in Greenwich Village, frequent communication would be physically impossible. But, curiously enough, whenever Angela lamented over this to her friend, a deep sombreness would descend on the latter; she would remark gloomily: "Time enough to worry about that; after all we might not get married. You never can tell." This was too enigmatic for Angela and finally she grew to look on it as a jest, a rather poor one but still a jest.

CHAPTER II

INTO the midst of this serenity came a bolt from the blue. Rachel, a librarian, was offered the position of head librarian in a far suburb of Brooklyn. Furthermore a wealthy woman from Butte, Montana, desiring to stay in New York for a few months and taking a fancy to the dinginess of Jayne Street and to the inconveniences of Rachel's apartment found she must live there and not otherwhere. No other location in the whole great city would do; she was willing to sublet at any figure. Unwillingly Rachel named a price which she secretly considered in the nature of highway robbery, but none of this mattered to Mrs. Denver, who was used to paying for what she wanted. And Rachel could not refuse, for both offers meant a substantial increase in the nest-egg which was to furnish the little brown house in the Bronx. In reality it meant to her extraordinary, unhoped for luck whose only flaw consisted in the enforced separation from her new friend. But to Angela it brought the awfulness of a catastrophe, though not for one moment would she let her deep dismay be suspected. After her first involuntary exclamation of consternation she never faltered in her complete acquiesence in the plan. But at heart she was sick.

The sudden flitting entailed much work and bustle. Rachel was as untidy as Angela was neat; everything she possessed had to be collected separately; there were no stacks of carefully folded clothing to be lifted wholesale and placed in gaping trunks. To begin with the trunks themselves were filled with dubious odds and ends which required to be sorted, given or even thrown away. There was no question of abandoning the *débris*, for the apartment must be left habitable for Mrs. Denver.

A nightmare then of feverish packing ensued; hasty meals, general house-cleaning. In order to assuage the sinking of her heart Angela plunged into it with great ardour. But at night, weary as she would be from the extra activity of the day, she could not fight off the sick dismay which overflowed her in great, submerging waves. It seemed to her she could not again endure loneliness; she could never summon the strength to seek out new friends, to establish fresh intimacies. She was twenty-six years old and the fact that after having lived all those years she was still solitary appalled her. Perhaps some curse such as one reads of in mediæval legends had fallen upon her. " Perhaps I'm not meant to have friends," she told herself lying face downwards in her pillows on the sweltering June nights. And a great nostalgia for something real and permanent swept upon her; she wished she were either very, very young, safe and contented once more in the protection of her father's household or failing that, very, very old.

A nature as strong, as self-reliant as hers could not remain long submerged; she had seen too many bad beginnings convert themselves into good endings. One of her most valuable native endowments lay in her ability to set herself and her difficulties objectively before her own eyes; in this way she had solved more than one problem. On the long ride in the subway back from Brooklyn whither she had accompanied Rachel on the night of the latter's departure she resolved to pursue this course that very night. Mercifully the terrible heat had abated, a little breeze came sifting in her open windows, moving the white sash curtains, even agitating some papers on the table. Soberly she set about the business of getting supper. Once she thought of running up to Rachel's former apartment and proffering some hospitality to Mrs. Denver. Even if the rich new tenant should not accept she'd be pleased doubtless; sooner or later she would be offering a return of courtesies, a new friendship would spring up. Again there would be possibilities. But something in her rebelled against such a procedure; these intimacies based on the sliding foundation of chance sickened her; she would not lend herself to them—not ever again. From this day on she'd devote herself to the establishing of permanencies.

Supper over, the dishes cleared away, she sat down and prepared to think. Callers were unlikely; indeed there was no one to call, since Ashley was out of town for the week-end, but the pathos of this fact left her untouched. To-night she courted loneliness.

An oft heard remark of her mother's kept running through her mind: " You get so taken up with the

253

problem of living, with just life itself, that by and by being coloured or not is just one thing more or less that you have to contend with." It had been a long time since she had thought about colour; at one time it had seemed to complicate her life immensely, now it seemed to her that it might be of very little importance. But her thoughts skirted the subject warily for she knew how immensely difficult living could be made by this matter of race. But that should take a secondary place; at present life, a method of living was the main thing, she must get that problem adjusted and first she must see what she wanted. Companionship was her chief demand. No more loneliness, not even if that were the road that led to the fulfilment of vast ambition, to the realization of the loftiest hopes. And for this she was willing to make sacrifices, let go if need be of her cherished independence, lead a double life, move among two sets of acquaintances.

For deep in her heart she realized the longing to cast in her lot once more with Virginia, her little sister whom she should never have left. Virginia, it is true, showed no particular longing for her; indeed she seemed hardly cognizant of her existence; but this attitude might be a forced one. She thought, " I didn't want her, the darling, and so she just made herself put me out of her life." Angela was well aware of the pluck, the indomitableness that lay beneath Jinny's babyish exterior, but there was a still deeper stratum of tenderness and love and loyalty which was the real Virginia. To this Angela would make her appeal; she would acknowledge her foolishness, her selfishness; she would bare her heart and crave her sister's forgiveness. And then they would live together, Jinny and she and Sara Penton if need be; what a joke it would all be on Sara! And once again she would know the bliss and happiness of a home and the stabilities of friendships culled from a certain definite class of people, not friendships resulting from mere chance. There would be blessed Sunday mornings and breakfasts, long walks; lovely evenings in the autumn to be filled with reminiscences drawn from these days of separation. How Virginia would open her eyes at her tales of Paulette and Martha! She would never mention Roger. And as for colour; when it seemed best to be coloured she would be coloured; when it was best to be white she would be that. The main thing was, she would know once more the joys of ordinary living, home, companionship, loyalty, security, the bliss of possessing and being possessed. And to think it was all possible and waiting for her; it was only a matter of a few hours, a few miles.

A great sense of peace, of exaltation descended upon her. Almost she could have said: " I will arise and go unto my father ".

·   ·   ·   ·   ·

On Sunday accordingly she betook herself to her sister's apartment in 139th Street. Miss Penton, she thought, would be out; she had gathered from the girls' conversation many pointed references to Sara's great fondness, of late, for church, exceeded only by her interest in the choir. This interest in the choir was ardently encouraged by a member of that body who occasionally walked home with Sara in order more fully to discuss the art of music. Virginia no longer went to church; Sunday had become her " pick-up day ", the one period in the week which she devoted to her correspondence, her clothes and to such mysterious rites of beautifying and revitalizing as lay back of her healthy, blooming exquisiteness. This would be the first time in many months that the sisters would have been alone together and it was with high hopes that Angela, mounting the brown stone steps and ringing the bell, asked for Virginia.

Her sister was in, but so was Sara, so was a third girl, a Miss Louise Andrews. The room was full of the atmosphere of the lightness, of the badinage, of the laughter which belong to the condition either of youth or of extreme happiness. In the middle of the room stood a large trunk from whose yawning interior Jinny lifted a glowing, smiling face. Angela was almost startled at the bright ecstasy which radiated from it. Sara Penton was engaged rather negligently in folding clothes; Miss Andrews perched in magnificent ease on the daybed, struck an occasional tune from a ukelele and issued commands which nobody heeded.

" Hello," said Virginia carelessly. " Can you get in? I was thinking of writing to you."

" Oh," Angela's hopes fluttered, fell, perished. " You're not going away? " Her heart echoed Jinny's old cry: " And leave me—when I'm all ready to come back to you, when I need you so terribly ! "

But of all this Virginia was, of course, unaware. " Nothing different," she said briskly. " I'm going away this very afternoon to Philadelphia,

Merion, points south and west, going to stay with
Eda Brown."

Angela was aghast. " I wanted to see you about
something rather important, Virginia—at least,"
she added humbly, " important to me." Rather
impatiently she glanced at the two girls hoping they
would take the hint and leave them, but they had
not even heard her, so engrossed were they in dis-
cussing the relative merits of one- and two-piece
sports clothes.

Her sister was kind but not curious. " Unless
it's got something to do with your soul's salvation
I'm afraid it'll have to wait a bit," she said gaily.
" I'm getting a two o'clock train and I must finish
this trunk—Sara's such a poor packer or I'd leave
it for her. As it is she's going to send it after me.
Aren't you, darling? " Already Angela's request
was forgotten. " After I finish this," the gay voice
went on, " I've got some 'phoning to do and—oh
a million things."

" Let me help you," said Angela suddenly
inspired, " then we'll call a taxi and we can go
down to the station together and we'll have a long
talk so I can explain things."

Virginia was only half-attentive. " Miss Mory
wants to go to the station with me," she said throwing a droll look at her friends. " Shall I take
her along? " She vanished into the bedroom,
Louise Andrews at her heels, both of them overwhelmed with laughter bubbling from some secret
spring.

Cut and humiliated, Angela stood silent. Sara
Penton who had been looking after the vanishing
figures turned and caught her expression. " Don't
mind her craziness. She's not responsible to-day."

She came closer. "For heaven's sake don't let on I told you; she's engaged."

This was news. "Engaged? To whom?"

"Oh somebody she's always been crazy about." The inevitable phrase followed: "You wouldn't know who he was."

Not know who he was, not know Matthew! She began to say "Why I knew him before Virginia," but remembering her rôle, a stupid and silly one now, caught herself, stood expectantly.

"So you see," Sara went on mysteriously, one eye on the bedroom, "you mustn't insist on going to the station with her; he's going to take her down."

"Why, is he here?"

"Came yesterday. We've been threatening all morning to butt in. That's the reason she spoke as she did about your going down. She expressed herself to us, you bet, but she probably wouldn't feel like doing that to you."

"Probably not," said Angela, her heart cold. Her little sister was engaged and she was learning of it from strangers. It was all she could do to hold back the tears. "But you've only yourself to blame," she reminded herself valiantly.

The two girls came back; Virginia still laughing but underneath the merriment Angela was able to detect a flurry of nervousness. After all, Jinny was just a child. And she was so happy, it would never do to mar that happiness by the introduction of the slightest gloom or discomfort. Her caller rose to her feet. "I guess I'll be going."

Virginia made no effort to detain her, but the glance which she turned on her sister was suddenly very sweet and friendly. "Here, I'll run down to the door with you. Sara, be a darling and pick out the best of those stockings for me, put in lots. You know how hard I am on them."

Out in the hall she flung an impulsive arm about her sister. "Oh, Angela, I'm so happy, so happy. I'm going to write you about it right away, you'll be so surprised." Astonishingly she gave the older girl a great hug, kissed her again and again.

"Oh," said Angela, the tears welling from her eyes, "Oh Jinny, you do forgive me, you do, you do? I'm so sorry about it all. I've been wretched for a long time. I thought I had lost you, Virginia."

"I know," said Jinny, "I'm a hard-hearted little wretch." She giggled through her own tears, wiped them away with the back of her childish bronze hand. "I was just putting you through; I knew you'd get sick of Miss Anne's folks and come back to me. Oh Angela, I've wanted you so. But it's all right now. I won't be back for ten weeks, but then we will talk! I've got the most marvellous plans for both of us— for all of us." She looked like a wise baby. "You'll get a letter from me in a few days telling you all about it. Angela, I'm so happy, but I must fly. Good-bye, darling."

They clung for a moment in the cool, dim depths of the wide hall.

*   *   *   *   *

Angela could have danced in the street. As it was she walked gaily down Seventh Avenue to 110th Street and into the bosky reaches of the park. Jinny had forgiven her. Jinny longed for her, needed her; she had known all along that Angela was suffering, had deliberately punished her. Well, she was right, everything was right this glorious memorable day. She was to have a sister again, some one of her own, she would know the joy of sharing her little triumphs, her petty woes. Wise Jinny, wonderful Jinny!

And beautiful Jinny, too, she thought. How lovely, how dainty, how fresh and innocent her little sister seemed. This brought her mind to Matthew and his great good fortune. "I'd like to see him again," she mused, smiling mischievously. "Doubtless he's forgotten me. It would be great fun to make him remember." Only, of course, now he was Jinny's and she would never get in the way of that darling. "Not even if he were some one I really wanted with all my heart and soul. But I'd never want Matthew." It would be fun, she thought, to see him again. He would make a nice brother, so sturdy and kind and reliable. She must be careful never to presume on that old youthful admiration of his. Smiling and happy she reached her house, actually skipped up the steps to her rooms. Her apartment no longer seemed lonely; it was not beautiful and bright like Jinny's but it was snug and dainty. It would be fun to have Virginia and Sara down; yes, and that new girl, that Miss Andrews, too. She didn't care what the other people in the house thought. . And the girls . themselves, how astonished they would be to learn the true state of affairs! Suddenly remembering Mrs. Denver, she ran up to see her; that lady, in spite of her wealth and means for self-indulgence, was palpably lonely. Angela cheered her up with mirthful accounts of her own first days in New York; she'd been lonely too, she assured her despondent hostess, sparkling and fascinating.

"I don't see how anybody with a disposition like yours could ever be lonely," said Mrs. Denver enviously. She'd been perilously near tears all day.

Gone, gone was all the awful melancholy, the blueness that had hung about her like a palpable cloud. She was young, fascinating; she was going to be happy,—again. *Again!* She caught her breath at that. Oh, God was good! This feeling of lightness, of exaltation had been unknown to her so long; not since the days when she had first begun to go about with Roger had she felt so free, bird-like. In the evening Ralph Ashley came with his car and drove her halfway across Long Island, or so it seemed. They stopped at a gorgeous hotel and had a marvellous supper. Ashley was swept off his feet by her gay vitalness. In the doorway of the Jayne Street house she gave him her hand and a bewitching smile. "You can't imagine how much I've enjoyed myself. I'll always remember it." And she spoke sincerely, for soon this sort of thing would be far behind her.

"You're a witch," said Ashley, his voice shaking a little. "You can have this sort of thing whenever you want it and you know it. Be kind to me, Angèle. I'm not a bad fellow."

Frightened, she pushed him away, ran in and slammed the door. No, no, no, her heart pounded. Roger had taught her an unforgettable lesson. Soon she'd be with Jinny and Matthew, safe, sheltered.

CHAPTER III

IN the middle of the night she found herself sitting up in bed. A moment before she had been asleep, but a sudden thought had pierced her consciousness so sharply that the effect was that of an icy hand laid suddenly on her shoulder. Jinny and Matthew marry—why, that meant—why, of course it meant that they would have to live in Philadelphia. How stupid she had been! And she couldn't go back there—never, never. Not because of the difficulties which she had experienced as a child; she was perfectly willing to cast in her lot again with coloured people in New York. But that was different; there were signal injustices here, too—oh, many, many of them—but there were also signal opportunities. But Philadelphia with its traditions of liberty and its actual economic and social slavery, its iniquitous school system, its prejudiced theatres, its limited offering of occupation! A great, searing hatred arose in her for the huge, slumbering leviathan of a city which had hardly moved a muscle in the last fifty years. So hide-bound were its habits that deliberate insult could be offered to coloured people without causing the smallest ripple of condemnation or even consternation in the complacent commonwealth. Virginia in one of her expansive moments had told her of a letter received from Agnes

Hallowell, now a graduate of the Women's Medical College. Agnes was as fair as Angela, but she had talked frankly, even with pride, of her racial connections. "I had nothing to be ashamed of," Angela could imagine her saying, her cheeks flushing, her black eyes snapping. On her graduation she had applied for an interneship at a great hospital for the insane; a position greatly craved by ardent medical graduates because of the unusually large turnover of pathological cases. But the man in charge of such appointments, looking Agnes hard in the eye told her suavely that such a position would never be given to her "not if you passed ahead of a thousand white candidates."

As for Angela, here was the old problem of possible loneliness back on her hands. Virginia, it was true, would hardly marry at once, perhaps they would have a few happy months together. But afterwards. . . . She lay there, wide awake now, very still, very straight in her narrow bed, watching the thick blackness grow thinner, less opaque. And suddenly as on a former occasion, she thought of marriage. Well, why not? She had thought of it once before as a source of relief from poverty, as a final barrier between herself and the wolves of prejudice; why not now as a means of avoiding loneliness? "I must look around me," her thoughts sped on, and she blushed and smiled in the darkness at the cold-bloodedness of such an idea. But, after all, that was what men said—and did. How often had she heard the expression—"he's ready to settle down, so he's looking around for a wife". If that were the procedure of men it should certainly be much more so the procedure of women since their fate was so much more deeply involved. The room was growing lighter; she could see the pictures a deeper blur against the faint blur of the wall. Her passing shame suddenly spent itself, for, after all, she knew practically no men. There was Ashley—but she was through with men of his type. The men in her office were nearly all impossible, but there were three, she told herself, coldly, unenthusiastic, who were not such terrible pills.

" But no," she said out loud. " I'd rather stay single and lonely, too, all my life than worry along with one of them. There must be someone else." And at once she thought of Anthony Cross. Of course there was Anthony. " I believe I've always had him in the back of my mind," she spoke again to the glimmering greyness. And turning on her pillow she fell, smiling, asleep.

.   .   .   .   .

Monday was a busy day; copy must be prepared for the engraver; proofs of the current edition of the magazine had to be checked up; some important French fashion plates for which she was responsible had temporarily disappeared and must be unearthed. At four-thirty she was free to take tea with Mrs. Denver, who immediately thereafter bore her off to a " movie " and dinner. Not until nine o'clock was she able to pursue her new train of thought. And even when she was at liberty to indulge in her habit of introspection she found herself experiencing a certain reluctance, an unexpected shyness. Time was needed to brood on this secret with its promise of happiness; this means of salvation from the

265

problems of loneliness and weakness which beset her. For since the departure of Roger she frequently felt herself less assured; it would be a relief to have some one on whom to lean; some one who would be glad to shield and advise her,— and love her! This last thought seemed to her marvellous. She said to herself again and again: "Anthony loves me, I know it. Think of it, he loves me!" Her face and neck were covered with blushes; she was like a young girl on the eve of falling in love, and indeed she herself was entering on that experience for the first time. From the very beginning she had liked Anthony, liked him as she had never liked Roger—for himself, for his sincerity, for his fierce pride, for his poverty, for his honest, frantic love. "And now," she said solemnly, "I believe I'm going to love him; I believe I love him already."

There were many things to be considered. His poverty,—but she no longer cared about that; insensibly her association with Rachel Salting, her knowledge of Rachel's plans and her high flouting of poverty had worked their influence. It would be fun, fun to begin at the beginning, to save and scrape and mend. Like Rachel she would do no washing and ironing, she would keep herself dainty and unworn, but everything else, everything else she would do. Cook—and she could cook; she had her blessed mother to thank for that. For a moment she was home again on Opal Street, getting Monday dinner, laughing with Virginia about Mrs. Henrietta Jones. There they were at the table, her pretty mother, her father with his fine, black face—his black face, she had forgotten that.

266

Colour,—here the old problem came up again. Restlessly she paced the room, a smouldering cigarette in her fingers. She rarely smoked but sometimes the insensate little cylinder gave her a sense of companionship. Colour, colour, she had forgotten it. Now what should she do,—tell Anthony? He was Spanish, she remembered, or no,—since he came from Brazil he was probably Portuguese, a member of a race devoid, notoriously devoid of prejudice against black blood. But Anthony had lived in America long enough to become inoculated; had he ever spoken about coloured people, had the subject ever come up? Wait a minute, there was Miss Powell; she remembered now that his conduct towards the young coloured woman had always been conspicuously correct; he had placed chairs for her, opened doors, set up easels; once the three of them had walked out of Cooper Union together and Anthony had carefully helped Miss Powell on a car, removing his hat with that slightly foreign gesture which she admired so much. And so far as she knew he had never used any of Roger's cruelly slighting expressions; the terms " coon ", " nigger ", " darky " had never crossed his lips. Clearly he had no conscious feeling against her people—" my people " she repeated, smiling, and wondered herself which people she meant, for she belonged to two races, and to one far more conspicuously than the other. Why, Anthony had even attended the Van Meier lecture. And she wondered what Van Meier would say if she presented her problem to him. He had no brief, she knew, against intermarriage, though, because of the high social forfeit levied, he did not advocate its practice in America.

For a moment she considered going to him and asking his advice. But she was afraid that he would speak to her about racial pride and she did not want to think of that. Life, life was what she was struggling for, the right to live and be happy. And once more her mother's dictum flashed into her mind. " Life is more important than colour." This, she told herself, was an omen, her mother was watching over her, guiding her. And, burying her face in her hands, she fell on her knees and wept and prayed.

Virginia sent a gay missive: " As soon as you left that wretch of a Sara told me that she had let you in on the great news. I wish I'd known it, I'd have spoken to you about it there in the hall; only there was so much to explain. But now you know the main facts, and I can wait until I see you to tell you the rest. But isn't it all wonderful? Angela, I do believe I'm almost the happiest girl alive!

" It's too lovely here. Edna is very kind and you know I always did like Pennsylvania country. Matthew is out almost every day. He tells me it renews his youth to come and talk about old times, —anyone to hear us reminiscing, starting every other sentence with ' do you remember——? ' would think that we averaged at least ninety years apiece. It won't pique your vanity, will it, if I tell you that he seems to have recovered entirely from his old crush on you? Maybe he was just in love with the family and didn't know it.

" We go into Philadelphia every day or two. The city has changed amazingly. But after the hit or miss method of New York society there is something very restful and safe about this tight organization of ' old Philadelphians '. In the short time I've been here I've met loads of first families, people whose names we only knew when we were children. But they all seem to remember father and mother; they all begin: ' My dear, I remember when Junius Murray——' I meet all these people, old and young, through Matthew, who seems to have become quite the beau here and goes everywhere. He really is different. Even his hair in some mysterious way is changed. Not that I ever minded; only he's so awfully nice that I just would like all the nice things of the world added unto him. We were talking the other day about the wedding, and I was thinking what a really distinguished appearance he would make. Dear old Matt, I'm glad I put off marriage until he could cut a fine figure. Write me, darling, if you feel like it, but don't expect to hear much from me. I'm so happy I can't keep still long enough to write. The minute I get back to New York though we'll have such a talk as never was."

.   .   .   .   .

Mrs. Denver was growing happier; New York was redeeming itself and revealing all the riches which she had suspected lay hidden in its warehouses. Through one letter of introduction forced into her unwilling hands by an officious acquaintance on her departure from Butte she had gained an *entrée* into that kindest and happiest of

New York's varied groups, the band of writers,
columnists, publishers and critics. The lady from
the middle West had no literary pretensions herself, but she liked people who had them and lived
up to them; she kept abreast of literary gossip,
read *Vanity Fair*, the *New Yorker*, and *Mercury*.
As she was fairly young, dainty, wealthy and
generous and no grinder of axes, she was caught
up and whirled right along into the glaxy of
teas, luncheons, theatre parties and " barbecues "
which formed the relaxations of this joyous crowd.
Soon she was overwhelmed, with more invitations
than she could accept; to those which she did
consider she always couched her acceptance in
the same terms. " Yes I'll come if I may bring
my young friend, Angèle Mory, along with me.
She's a painter whom you'll all be glad to know.
some day." Angela's chance kindness to her in
her days of loneliness and boredom had not fallen
on barren ground.

Now indeed Angela was far removed from the
atmosphere which she had known in Greenwich
Village; the slight bohemianism which she had
there encountered was here replaced by a somewhat
bourgeois but satisfying sophistication. These
people saw the " Village " for what it was, a
network of badly laid off streets with, for the most
part, uncomfortable, not to say inconvenient
dwellings inhabited by a handful of artists in the
midst of a thousand *poseurs*. Her new friends were
frankly interested in the goods of this world. They
found money an imperative, the pre-eminent,
concomitant of life; once obtained, they spent it
on fine apartments, beautiful raiment, delicate
viands, and trips to Paris and Vienna. Conver-

sation with them was something more than an exchange of words; "quips and jests" passed among them, and, though flavoured with allusions to stage and book, so that Angela was at times hard put to it to follow the trend of the talk, she half suspected that she was in this company assisting more nearly at the restoration of a lost art than in any other circles in the world save in the corresponding society of London.

Once again her free hours could be filled to overflowing with attention, with gaiety, with intellectual excitement; it came to her one day that this was the atmosphere of which she once had dreamed. But she was not quite happy, her economic condition interfered here. Constantly she was receiving every conceivable manifestation of an uncalculating generosity at the hands not only of Mrs. Denver but of her new acquaintances. And she could make no adequate return; her little apartment had turned too shabby for her to have guests of this calibre, even in to tea. Her rich friend, making short shrift of such furniture as Rachel Salting had left behind, had transformed her dwelling into a marvel of luxury and elegance; tiny but beautiful. Mrs. Denver was the soul of real and delicate kindness but Angela could not accept favours indefinitely; besides she was afraid to become too used to this constant tide from a horn of plenty on which she had absolutely no claim. If there were any one thing which the harsh experiences of these last three years had taught her it was the impermanence of relationships; she must, she felt, lay down and follow a method of living for herself which could never betray her when the attention of the rich and great should be withdrawn. Gradually she ceased accepting Mrs. Denver's invitations; she pleaded the necessity of outside work along the lines of her employment; she was busy, too, on the portrait of her mother, stimulating her vivid memory with an old faded photograph. Her inten- tion was to have it as a surprise for Virginia upon the latter's return.

But before withdrawing completely she made the acquaintance of a young married woman and her husband, a couple so gifted, so genuine and sincere that she was unable to keep to the letter her spartan promise of cutting herself entirely adrift from this fascinating cross-section of New York society. The husband, Walter Sandburg, was a playwright; his name was a household word; the title of one or another of his dramas glittered on Broadway every night. His wife, Elizabeth, reviewed books for one of the great New York weeklies. Their charm- ing apartment in Fifty-fifth Street was the centre for many clever and captivating people. Between these two and Angela something of a real friendship awakened; she was not ashamed to have them see the shabbiness of her apartment. The luncheons to which she treated Elizabeth in the Village tea- rooms and in apartment stores brought as great satisfaction as the more elaborate meals at the Algonquin, the favourite rendezvous of many of these busy, happy, contented workers.

Ashley, too, had returned to a town still devoid of Carlotta, and in his loneliness was again con- stantly seeking Angela. His attitude was perfect; never by word or look did he revive the unpleasant impression which he had once made; indeed, in a sober, disillusioned sort of way, she was growing to like him very much. He was shy, sensitive, sympathetic and miserably lonely. It was not likely that his possessions were as fabulously great as Roger's but it was certain that he belonged to Roger's social group with all that such a ranking implies. But in spite of this he was curiously diffident; lacking in pep, the girls in his " set " coldly classified him, and let him alone. Outside his group ambitious Amazons daubed him " easy " and made a mad rush for him and his fabled millions. The two verdicts left him ashamed and frightened; annually he withdrew farther and farther into his shell, emerging only in response to Carlotta's careless and occasional beckoning or to Angela's genuine and pre-occupied indifference.

But this was not her world; for years she had craved such a *milieu*, only to find herself, when once launched into it, outwardly perfectly at ease, inwardly perturbed and dismayed. Although she rarely thought of colour still she was conscious of living in an atmosphere of falseness, of tangled implications. She spoke often of Martha Burden and her husband; Walter Sandburg the playwright, knew Ladislas Starr; Elizabeth had met Paulette Lister in some field of newspaper activity, and Ashley of course had seen Roger in Angela's company. Behind these three or four names and the background which familiarity with them implied, she did not dare venture and in her gayest moments she was aware of the constant stirring within of a longing for someone real and permanent with whom she could share her life. She would, of course make up with Jinny, but Jinny was going to live in Philadelphia, where she herself would never sojourn again. That aftermath was the real consideration.

Her thoughts went constantly winging to Anthony; her determination became static. Saving only this invisible mixture of dark blood· in her veins they, too, could meet on a par. They were both young, both gifted, ambitious, blessedly poor. Together they would climb to happier, sunnier heights. To be poor with Anthony; to struggle with him; to help him keep his secret vow; to win his surprised and generous approbation; finally to reach the point where she, too, could open her home to poor, unknown, struggling geniuses,—life could hold nothing more pleasing than these possibilities. And how kind she would be to these strangers! How much she hoped that among them there would be some girl struggling past the limitations of her heritage even as she herself had done. Through some secret, subtle bond of sympathy she would, she was sure, be able to recognize such a girl; and how she would help her and spur her on! To her communings she said humbly, " I am sure that this course will work out all right for me for see, I am planning chiefly for Anthony and for helpless, harassed people; hardly anything for myself but protection and love. I am willing to work for success and happiness." And even as she spoke she knew that the summit of her bliss would be reached in the days while she and Anthony were still poor and struggling and when she would be giving of her best to make things so.

Elizabeth Sandburg reminiscing about the early married days of herself and Walter gave a fillip to her thought. Said Elizabeth: " Walt and I were just as poor as we could be, we only made twenty dollars a week, and half of that went for a room in a cheap hotel. Meals even at the punkest places were awfully expensive, and half the time I used to cook things over the gas-jet. I didn't know much about cooking, and I imagine the stuff was atrocious, but we didn't mind. There were we with no one to interfere with us; we had each other and we didn't give a damn."

Smiling, glowing, she gave Angela a commission to paint hers and her Walter's portraits. " We'll leave the price to you and if you really put the job over I'll get you a lot of other sitters. No, don't thank me. What are friends for? That's what I always say."

CHAPTER IV

SOMETIMES this thought confronted her: "Perhaps Anthony no longer needs me; has forgotten me." And at the bare idea her heart would contract with an actual, palpable movement. For by now he was representing not only surcease from loneliness but peace and security; a place not merely in society but in the world at large. Marriage appeared, too, in a different light. Until she had met Roger she had not thought much about the institution except as an adventure in romance or as a means to an end; in her case the method of achieving the kind of existence which once had been her ideal. But now she saw it as an end in itself; for women certainly; the only, the most desirable and natural end. From this state a gifted, an ambitious woman might reach forth and acquit herself well in any activity. But marriage must be there first, the foundation, the substratum. Of course there were undoubtedly women who, like men, took love and marriage as the sauce of existence and their intellectual interests as the main dish. Witness for instance, Paulette. Now that she came to think of it, Paulette might vary her lovers but she never varied in the manifestation of her restless, clever mental energy. At no time did she allow her "love-life", as the psycho-analyst termed it, to interfere with her mental interests,

Indeed she made no scruple of furthering these same interests by her unusual and pervasive sex charm. But this was Paulette, a remarkable personage, a woman apart. But for most women there must be the safety, the assurance of relationship that marriage affords. Indeed, most women must be able to say as did men, " You are mine," not merely, " I am yours."

A certain scorching humility thrust itself upon her. In all her manifestations of human relationships, how selfish she had been! She had left Virginia, she had taken up with Roger to further her own interests. For a brief interval she had perhaps loved Roger with the tumultuous, heady passion of hot, untried youth. But again when, this subsiding, she had tried to introduce a note of idealism, it had been with the thought of saving her own soul. She thought of her day in the park with Anthony, his uncomplaining acceptance of her verdict; his wistfully grateful: " I almost touched happiness ". How easily she might have made him happy if she had turned her thoughts to his needs. But she had never thought of that; she had been too intent always on happiness for herself. Her father, her mother and Jinny had always given and she had always taken. Why was that? Jinny had sighed: " Perhaps you *have* more white blood than Negro in your veins." Perhaps · this selfishness was what the possession of white blood meant; the ultimate definition of Nordic Supremacy.

Then she remembered that Anthony was white and, bewildered; she ceased trying to cogitate, to unravel, decipher, evaluate. She was lonely, she loved. She meant to find a companion; she meant to be beloved.

She must act.

None of her new friends was acquainted with Anthony. Ralph Ashley in response to a tentative question could not recall ever having seen him. The time was August, consequently he could not be at the school. Telephone books revealed nothing. " Lost in a great city ! " she told herself and smiled at the cheap novel flavour of the phrase. She sent her thoughts fluttering back to the last time she had really seen Anthony, to their last intimate conversation. They had met that day after she had cut Jinny; she remembered, smiling now in her superior knowledge, the slight panic which she had experienced at his finding her in a 'bus in Harlem. There had been some chaffing about tea and he had given her his address and she had put it,—where? It was not in her address book. A feverish search through her little desk revealed it in the pages of her prayer book, the one which she had used as a child. This she considered a good omen. The bit of paper was crinkled and blurred but she was able to make out an address on One Hundred and Fourteenth Street. Suppose he were no longer there ! She could not brook the thought of another night of uncertainty; it was ten o'clock but she mounted a 'bus, rode up to One Hundred and Fourteenth and Seventh Avenue. Her heart beat so loudly as she turned the corner,— it seemed as though the inhabitants of the rather shabby block hearing that human dynamo would throng their windows. The street, like many others in New York, possessed the pseudo elegance and impressiveness which comes from an equipment of brown stone houses with their massive fronts, their ostentatious regularity and simplicity, but a second glance revealed its down-at-heel condition; gaping windows disclosed the pitiful smallness of the rooms that crouched behind the pretentious outsides. There was something faintly humorous, ironical, about being cooped up in these deceptive palaces; according to one's temperament one might laugh or weep at the thought of how these structures, the product of human energy could yet cramp, imprison, even ruin the very activity which had created them.

Angela found her number, mounted the steps, sought in the dim, square hall feverishly among the names in the bells. Sullivan, Brown, Hendrickson, Sanchez,—and underneath the name of Sanchez on the same card, five small, neat characters in Anthony's inimitably clear printing—Cross. She almost fainted with the relief of it. Her fingers stole to the bell,—perhaps her one-time fellow-student was up in his room now,—how strange that this bit of gutta percha and its attendant wires should bridge all the extent of time and space that had so long lain between them! But she could not push it; Anthony, she was sure, was real enough, close enough to the heart of living to refuse to be shocked by any mere breach of the conventionalities. Even so, however, to seek at eleven o'clock at night and without preliminary warning admission to the rooms of a man whom one has not noticed for a year, was, as he himself would have put it, " a bit thick ".

The little note which she sent was a model of demureness and propriety. " Dear Anthony," it read, " Do you remember my promising to ask you in for tea the next time I made a batch of cookies? Well, to-morrow at 5.30 will be the next time. Do come!"

He had changed; her interested, searching eyes descried it in a moment. Always grave, always austere, always responsible, there, was now in his manner an imponderable yet perceptible increment of each quality. But this was not all; his old familiar tortured look had left him; a peace, a quality of poise hovered about him, the composure which is achieved either by the attainment or by the relinquishment of the heart's desire. There is really very little difference, since each implies the cessation of effort.

All this passed rapidly through Angela's mind. Aloud she said: "How do, Anthony? you're really looking awfully well. It's nice to see you again."

"It's nice to see you," he replied. Certainly there was nothing remarkable about their conversation. After the bantering, the jests and allusions which she had been used to hearing at the Sandburgs,—compared with the snappy jargon of Mrs. Denver's "crowd" this was trivial, not to say banal. She burst out laughing. Anthony raised his eyebrows.

"What's so funny? Is it a secret joke?"

"No,—only I've been thinking hard about you for a long time." She made a daring stroke. "Presumably you've thought occasionally about me. Yet when we meet we sit up like a dandy and a dowager with white kid gloves on and exchange comments on our appearances. I suppose the next step in order would be to talk about the weather. Have you had much rain up in One Hundred and Fourteenth Street, Mr Cross?"

Some of his poise forsook him. The pervasive peacefulness that sat so palpably upon him deserted him like a rended veil. "You've been thinking about me for a long time? Just how long?"

"I couldn't tell you when it began." She ventured another bold stroke. "But you've been in the back of my mind,—oh for ages, ages."

The poise, the composure, the peace were all fled now. Hastily, recklessly he set down his glass of tea, came and towered over her. She bit her lips to hide their trembling. Oh he was dear, dearer than she had ever imagined, so transparent, so honest. Who was she to deserve him?

His face quivered. He should never have come near this girl! As suddenly as he had left his chair he returned to it, settled himself comfortably and picked up his glass. "I've been away from you so long I had forgotten."

"Forgotten what?"

"Forgotten how dangerous you are. Forgotten how a woman like you plays with poor fools like me. Why did you send for me? To set me dancing once more to your tune?"

His bitterness surprised and frightened her. "Anthony, Anthony don't talk like that! I sent for you because I wanted to see you, wanted to talk to my old friend."

Appeased, he lounged back in the famous and unique easy chair, lit a cigarette. She brought out some of her sketches, displayed her note-book. He was especially interested in the "Fourteenth Street Types", was pleased with the portrait of her mother. "She doesn't look like you, though I can see you probably have her hair and that pearly tint of her skin. But you must have got your nose from your father. You know all the rest of your face," he dwelt on her features dreamily, " your lips, your eyes, your curly lashes are so deliciously feminine. But that straight nose of yours betokens strength." The faded, yet striking photograph lay within reach. He picked it up, studying it thoughtfully. " What a beautiful woman;—all woman I should say. Did she have much effect on your life? "

" N-no, I can't say she did." She remembered those Saturday excursions and their adventures in " passing ", so harmless, yet so far-reaching. " Oh yes, in one respect she influenced me greatly, changed my whole life."

He nodded, gazing moodily at the picture. " My mother certainly affected me."

Angela started to say glibly; " She made you what you are to-day "; but a glance at his brooding countenance made her think better of it.

" What's this? " He had turned again to the sketch book and was poring upon a mass of lightly indicated figures passing apparently in review before the tall, cloaked form of a woman, thin to emaciation, her hands on her bony hips, slightly bent forward, laughing uproariously yet with a certain chilling malevolence. " I can't make it out."

With something shamefaced in her manner she took it from him. " I'm not sure yet whether I'll develop it. I,—it's an idea that has slowly taken possession of me since I've been in New York. The tall woman is Life and the idea is that she laughs at us; laughs at the poor people who fall into the traps which she sets for us."

Sorrow set its seal on his face as perceptibly as though it had been stamped there. He came closer. "You've found that out too? If I could have managed it you would never have known it. I wanted so to keep it from you." His manner suddenly changed. / "I must go. This afternoon has been perfect; I can't thank you enough,—but I'm not coming again."

"Not coming again! What nonsense! Why, why ever not? Now, Anthony, don't begin that vow business. To-day has been perfect, marvellous. You don't suppose I'm going to let my friend go when I'm really just discovering him!"

Weakly he murmured that it was foolish for them to take up each other's time; he was going away.

"All the more reason, then, why we should be seeing each other."

His glance fell on the formless sketch. "If I could only get one laugh on life. . . . When are you going to let me see you again? I'm my own man just now; my time is at your disposal."

The next afternoon they met outside her office building and dined together. On Friday they sailed to the Atlantic Highlands. Saturday, Sunday, Monday, Tuesday flashed by, meaning nothing to either except for the few hours which they spent in each other's company. Thursday was a slack day; she arranged her work so as to be free for the afternoon, and they passed the hurrying, glamorous hours in Van Cortlandt Park, laughing, jesting, relating old dreams, relapsing into silences more intimate than talk, blissfully aware of each other's presence, still more throbbingly aware of a conversation held in this very Park years ago   Back again in the little hall on Jayne Street he took her in his arms and kissed her slowly, with rapture, with adoration and she returned his kisses. For a long time he held her close against his pounding heart; she opened her languid eyes to meet his burning gaze which she could feel rather than see. Slowly he took her arms from his neck, let them drop.

"Angel, Angel, I shall love you always. Life cannot rob me of that. Good-bye, my sweetest."

He was lost in the shadowy night.

The next day passed and the next. A week sped. Absolute silence. No sign of him by either word or line.

.   .   .   .   .

At the end of ten days, on a never to be forgotten Sunday afternoon, she went to see him. Without conscious volition on her part she was one moment in her apartment on Jayne Street; and at the end of an hour she was pressing a button above the name Cross in a hall on One Hundred and Fourteenth Street, hearing the door click, mounting the black well of a stair-way, tapping on a door bearing the legend "Studio".

A listless voice said "Come in."

Presently the rather tall, slender young man sitting in his shirt sleeves, his back toward her, staring dejectedly but earnestly at a picture on the table before him asked: "What can I do for you?"

The long and narrow room boasted a rather good parquet floor and a clean plain wall paper covered with unframed pictures and sketches. In one corner stood an easel; the furniture for the

most part was plain but serviceable and comfortable, with the exception of an old-fashioned
horse-hair sofa which Angela thought she had
never seen equalled for its black shininess and its
promise of stark discomfort.

On entering the apartment she had felt perturbed, but as soon as she saw Anthony and
realized that the picture at which he was gazing
was an unfinished sketch of herself, her worry
fled. He had asked his question without turning,
so she addressed his back:

"You can tell me where you found that terrible
sofa; I had no idea there were any in existence.
Thought they had died out with the Dodo."

The sound of her voice brought him to her side.
"Angèle, tell me what are you doing here?"

She tried to keep the light touch: "Not until
you have told me about the sofa." But his dark,
tormented face and the strain under which she
had been suffering for the past week broke down
her defence. Swaying, she caught at his hand.
"Anthony, Anthony, how could you?"

He put his arm about her and led her to the
despised sofa; looked at her moodily. "Why did
you come to see me, Angèle?"

Ordinarily she would have fenced, indulged in
some fancy skirmishing; but this was no ordinary
occasion; indeed in ordinary circumstances she
would not have been here. She spoke gravely and
proudly.

"Because I love you. Because I think you love
me." A sudden terrible fear assailed her. "Oh,
Anthony, don't tell me you were only playing!"

"With you? So little was I playing that the
moment I began to suspect you cared,—and I

never dreamed of it until that last day in the park,
—I ran away from you. I knew you had so many
resources; men will always adore you, want you,
that I thought you'd soon forget; turn to someone
else just as you had turned for a sudden whim to
me from God knows how many admirers."

She shook her head, but she was frightened;
some nameless fear knocking at her heart. "I
turned to you from no one, Anthony. I've had
only one 'admirer' as you call it in New York
and I had long, long since ceased thinking of
him. No, Anthony, I came to you because I
needed you; you of all men in New York. I think
in the world. And I thought you needed me."

They sat in silence on the terrible sofa. He
seized her hand and covered it with kisses; started
to take her in his arms, then let them fall in a hopeless gesture.

"It's no good, Angel; there's no use trying
to buck fate. Life has caught us again. What
you're talking about is absolutely impossible."

"What do you mean, impossible?" The little
mute fear that had lain within her for a long time
as a result of an earlier confidence of his bestirred
itself, spoke.

"Anthony, those men, those enemies that killed
your father,—did you kill one of them?" She had
her arms about him. "You know it's nothing to
me. Don't even tell me about it. Your past
belongs to you; it's your future I'm interested in,
that I want."

He pushed her from him, finally, even roughly.
"No, I've never killed a man. Though I've
wanted to. But I was a little boy when it all
happened and afterwards I wouldn't go back

because of my mother." He went over to a drawer and took out a revolver, " I've half a mind to kill myself now, now before I go mad thinking how I've broken my promise, broken it after all these years." He looked at her wistfully, yet implacably. " I wish that I had died long before it was given to me to see that beautiful, loving look on your face change into one of hatred and dread and anger."

She thought he must be raving; she tried to sooth him. " Never mind, Anthony; I don't care a rap about what you've done. Only tell me why do you say everything's impossible for us? Why can't we mean everything to each other, be married——"

" Because I'm coloured." In her bewildered relief she fell away from him.

" Yes, that's right, you damned American! I'm not fit for you to touch now, am I? It was all right as long as you thought I was a murderer, a card sharp, a criminal, but the black blood in me is a bit too much, isn't it?" Beside himself he rushed to the windows, looked on the placid Sunday groups festooning the front steps of the brown stone houses. " What are you going to do, alarm the neighbourhood? Well, let me tell you, my girl, before they can get up here I'll be dead." His glance strayed to the revolver. " They'll never catch me as they did my father."

It was on the point of her tongue to tell him her great secret. Her heart within her bubbled with laughter to think how quickly she could put an end to this hysteria, how she could calm this black madness which so seethed within him, poisoning the very spring of his life. But his last words turned her thoughts to something else, to another need. How he must have suffered, loving a girl who he felt sure would betray him; yet scorning to keep up the subterfuge.

She said to him gently: " Anthony, did you think I would do that? "

His answer revealed the unspeakable depths of his acquaintance with prejudice; his incurable cynicism. " You're a white American. I know there's nothing too dastardly for them to attempt where colour is involved."

A fantastic notion seized her. Of course she would tell him that she was coloured, that she was willing to live with coloured people. And if he needed assurance of her love, how much more fully would he believe in her when he realized that not even for the sake of the conveniences to be had by passing would she keep her association with white people secret from him. But first she must try to restore his faith in human goodness. She said to him gently: " Tell me about it, Anthony."

And sitting there in the ugly, tidy room in the sunshot duskiness of the early summer evening, the half-subdued noises of the street mounting up to them, he told her his story. An old story it was, but in its new setting, coupled with the fact that Angela for years had closed her mind to the penalty which men sometimes pay for being " different ", it sounded like some unbelievable tale from the Inquisition.

His father, John Hall, of Georgia, had been a sailor and rover, but John's father was a well-known and capable farmer who had stayed in his little town and slowly amassed what seemed a fortune to the poor and mostly ignorant whites by whom he was surrounded. In the course of John's wanderings he had landed at Rio de Janeiro and he had met Maria Cruz, a Brazilian with the blood of many races in her veins. She herself was apparently white, but she looked with favour on the brown, stalwart sailor, thinking nothing of his colour, which was very much the same as that of her own father. The two married and went to many countries. But finally John, wearying of his aimless life, returned to his father, arriving a month before it was time to receive the old man's blessing and his property. Thence all his troubles. Certain white men in the neighbourhood had had their eyes turned greedily on old Anthony Hall's possessions. His son had been a wanderer for many years; doubtless he was dead. Certainly it was not expected that he would return after all these years to his native soil; most niggers leaving the South left for ever. They knew better than to return with their uppity ways.

Added to the signal injustice of John Hall's return and the disappointment caused thereby, was the iniquity of his marriage to a beautiful and apparently white wife. Little Anthony could remember his father's constant admonition to her never to leave the house; the latter had, in his sudden zeal for home, forgotten what a sojourn in Georgia could mean. But his memory was soon refreshed and he was already making every effort to dispose of his new possessions without total loss. This required time and patience, but he hoped that only a few months need elapse before they might shake off the dust of this cursed hole for ever.

"Just a little patience, Maria," he told his lovely wife.

But she could not understand. True, she never ventured into the town, but an infrequent visit to the little store was imperative and she did not mind an occasional admiring glance. Indeed she attributed her husband's admonitions to his not unwelcome jealousy. Anthony, always a grave child, constituted himself her constant guardian; his father, he knew, had to be away in neighbouring townships where he was trying to put through his deal, so the little boy accompanied his silly trusting mother everywhere. When they passed a group of staring, mouthing men he contrived to hurt his finger or stub his toe so as to divert his mother's attention. In spite of his childish subterfuges, indeed because of them, his mother attracted the notice of Tom Haley, son of the magistrate. Anthony apparently had injured his hand and his beautiful mother, bending over it with great solicitude, made a picture too charming, too challenging to be overlooked. Haley stepped forward, actually touched his cap. "Can I do anything to help you, ma'am?" She looked at him with her lovely, melting eyes, spoke in her foreign liquid voice. He was sure he had made a conquest. Afterwards, chagrined by the gibes of the bystanders who jeered at him for his courtesy to a nigger wench "for that's all she is, John Hall's wife", he ground his heel in the red dust; he would show her a thing or two.

In the hot afternoon, awakened from her siesta by a sudden knock, she came to the door, greeted her admirer of the early morning. She was not quite pleased with the look in his eyes, but she could not suspect evil. Haley, who had done some wandering on his own account and had picked up a few words of Spanish, let fall an insulting phrase or two. Amazed and angry she struck him across his face. The boy, Anthony, uneasily watching, screamed; there was a sudden tumult of voices and Haley fled, forgetting for the moment that these were Negro voices and so need not be dreaded. An old coloured man, mumbling and groaning " Gawd forgive you, Honey; we'se done fer now " guided the child and the panic-stricken mother into the swamp And lying there hidden at night they could see the sparks and flames rising from the house and buildings, which represented the labour of Anthony Hall's sixty years. In a sudden lull they caught the sounds of the pistol shots which riddled John Hall's body.

" Someone warned my father," said Anthony Cross wearily, " but he would go home. Besides, once back in town he would have been taken anyway, perhaps mobbed and burned in the public square. They let him get into his house; he washed and dressed himself for death. Before nightfall the mob came to teach this man their opinion of a nigger who hadn't taught his wife her duty toward white men. First they set fire to the house, then called him to the window. He stepped out on a little veranda; Haley opened fire. The body fell over the railing, dead before it could touch the ground, murdered by the bullets from twenty pistols. Souvenir hunters cut off fingers, toes, his ears,—a friend of my grandfather found the body at night and buried it. They said it was unlike anything they had ever seen before, totally dehumanized. After I heard that story I was unable to sleep for nights on end. As for my mother,——'"

Angela pressed his head close against her shoulder. There were no words for a thing like this, only warm human contact.

He went on wanly. "As for my mother, she was like a madwoman. She has gone all the rest of her life haunted by a terrible fear."

"Of white people," Angela supplemented softly. "Yes, I can see how she would."

He glanced at her sombrely. "No, of coloured people. She believes that we, particularly the dark ones, are cursed, otherwise why should we be so abused, so hounded. Two years after my father's death she married a white man, not an American—that was spared me,—but a German who, I believe, treats her very kindly. I was still a little boy but I begged and pleaded with her to leave the whole race alone; I told her she owed it to the memory of my father. But she only said women were poor, weak creatures; they must take protection where they could get it."

Horrified, mute with the tragedy of it all, she could only stare at him white-lipped.

"Don't ask me how I came up. Angèle, for a time I was nothing, worthless, only I have never denied my colour; I have always taken up with coloured causes. When I've had a special point to make I've allowed the world to think of me as it would but always before severing my connections I told of the black blood that was in my veins. And then it came to me that for my father's sake I would try to make something of myself. So I sloughed off my evil ways, they had been assumed

only in bravado,—and came to New York where
I've been living quietly, I hope usefully, keeping
my bitterness within myself where it could harm
no one but me.

"I made one vow and kept it,—never by any
chance to allow myself to become entangled with
white people; never to listen to their blandish-
ments; always to hate them with a perfect hate.
Then I met you and loved you and somehow
healing began. I thought, if she loves me she'll
be willing to hear me through. And if after she
hears me she is willing to take me, black blood
and all,—but mind," he interrupted himself
fiercely, " I'm not ashamed of my blood. Sometimes I think it's the leaven that will purify this
Nordic people of their cruelty and their savage
lust of power."

She ignored this. " So you were always going
to tell me."

" Tell you? Of course I would have told you.
Oh, I'm a man, Angel, with a man's record. When
I was a sailor,—there're some pages in my life' I
couldn't let your fingers touch. But *that* I'd have
told you, it was too vital, too important. Not that
I think it really means anything, this mixture of
blood, as life goes, as God meant the world to go.
But here in America it could make or mar life. Of
course I'd have told you."

Here was honour, here was a man! So would
her father have been. Having found this comparison her mind sought no further.

A deep silence descended upon them; in his
case the silence of exhaustion. But Angela was
thinking of his tragic life and of how completely,
how surprisingly she could change it. Smiling,

she spoke to him of happiness, of the glorious future. "I've something amazing to tell you, but I won't spring it on you all at once. Can't we go out to Van Cortlandt Park to-morrow evening?"

He caught her hand. "No matter what in the goodness of your heart you may be planning, there is no future, none, none, Angel, for you and me. Don't deceive yourself,—nor me. When I'm with you I forget sometimes. But this afternoon has brought it all back to me. I'll never forget myself and my vow again."

A bell shrilled three, four times.

He looked about frowning. "That's Sanchez; he's forgotten his key again. My dear girl, my Angel, you must go,—and you must not, must not come back. Hurry, hurry! I don't want him to see you here." He guided her towards the door, stemming her protestations. "I'll write you at once, but you must go. God bless and keep you."

In another moment she was out in the dim hall, passing a dark, hurrying figure on the stairs. The heavy door swung silently behind her, thrusting her inexorably out into the engulfing summer night; the shabby pretentious house was again between her and Anthony with his tragic, searing past.

CHAPTER V

ALL the next day and the next she dwelt on Anthony's story; she tried to put herself in his place, to force herself into a dim realization of the dark chamber of torture in which his mind and thoughts had dwelt for so many years. And she had added her modicum of pain, had been so unsympathetic, so unyielding; in the midst of the dull suffering, the sickness of life to which perhaps his nerves had become accustomed she had managed to inject an extra pinprick of poignancy. Oh, she would reward him for that; she would brim his loveless, cheated existence with joy and sweetness; she would cajole him into forgetting that terrible past. Some day he should say to her: "You have brought me not merely new life, but life itself." Those former years should mean no more to him than its pre-natal existence means to a baby.

Her fancy dwelt on, toyed with all the sweet offices of love; the delicate bondage that could knit together two persons absolutely *en rapport*. At the cost of every ambition which she had ever known she would make him happy. After the manner of most men his work would probably be the greatest thing in the world to him. And he should be the greatest thing in the world to her. He should be her task, her "job", the fulfilment of her ambition. A phrase from the writings of Anatole France came drifting into her mind. "There is a technique of love." She would discover it, employ it, not go drifting haphazardly, carelessly into this relationship. And suddenly she saw her affair with Roger in a new light; she could forgive him, she could forgive herself for that hitherto unpardonable union if through it she had come one iota nearer to the understanding and the need of Anthony.

His silence—for although the middle of the week had passed she had received no letter,—worried her not one whit. In the course of time he would come to her, remembering her perfect sympathy of the Sunday before and thinking that this woman was the atonement for what he considered her race. And then she would surprise him, she would tell him the truth, she would make herself inexpressibly dearer and nearer to him when he came to know that her sympathy and her tenderness were real, fixed and lasting, because they were based and rooted in the same blood, the same experiences, the same comprehension of this far-reaching, stupid, terrible race problem. How inexpressibly happy, relieved and overwhelmed he would be! She would live with him in Harlem, in Africa, anywhere, any place. She would label herself, if he asked it; she would tell every member of her little coterie of white friends about her mixed blood; she would help him keep his vow and would glory in that keeping. No sacrifice of the comforts which came to her from "passing", of the assurance, even of the safety which the mere physical fact of whiteness in America brings, would be too great for her. She would withdraw where he withdrew, hate where he hated.

.   .   .   .   .

His letter which came on Thursday interrupted her thoughts, her fine dreams of self-immolation which women so adore. It was brief and stern, and read:

> "Angèle, don't think for one moment that I do not thank you for Sunday. . . . My heart is at your feet for what you revealed to me then. But you and I have nothing in common, have never had, and now can never have. More than race divides us. I think I shall go away. Meanwhile you are to forget me; amuse yourself, beautiful, charming, magnetic Angel with the men of your own race and leave me to my own.
>
> "ANTHONY."

It was such a strange letter; its coldness and finality struck a chill to her heart. She looked at the lonely signature, "Anthony",—just that, no word of love or affection. And the phrase: "More than race divides us." Its hidden significance held a menace.

The letter was awaiting her on her return from work. She had come in all glowing with the promise of the future as she conceived it. And then here were these cold words killing her high hopes as an icy blast kills the too trusting blossoms of early spring. . . . Holding the letter she let her supper go untasted, unregarded, while she evolved some plan whereby she could see Anthony, talk to him. The tone of his letter did not sound as though he would yield to ordinary persuasion. And again in the midst of her bewilderment and suffering she was struck afresh with the difficulties inherent in womanhood in conducting the most ordinary and most vital affairs of life. She was still a little bruised in spirit that she had taken it upon herself to go to Anthony's rooms Sunday; it was a step she felt conventionally, whose justification lay only in its success. As long as she had considered it successful, she had been able to relegate it to the uttermost limbo of her self-consciousness. But now that it seemed to avail nothing it loomed up before her in all its social significance. She was that creature whom men, in their selfish fear, have contrived to paint as the least attractive of human kind,—" a girl who runs after men." It seemed to her that she could not stand the application of the phrase, no matter how unjustly, how inaptly used in her own case.

Looking for a word of encouragement she re-read the note. The expression " My heart is at your feet " brought some reassurance; she remembered, too, his very real emotion of Sunday, only a few days before. Men, real men, men like Anthony, do not change. No, she could not let him go without one last effort. She would go to Harlem once more to his house, she would see him, reassure him, allay his fears, quench his silly apprehensions of non-compatability. As soon as he knew that they were both coloured, he'd succumb. Now he was overwrought. It had never occurred to her before that she might be glad to be coloured. . . . She put on her hat, walked slowly out the door, said to herself with a strange foreboding: " When I see this room again, I'll either be very happy, or very, very sad. . . ." Her courage rose, braced her, but she was sick of being courageous, she wanted to be a beloved woman, dependent, fragile, sought for, feminine; after this last ordeal she would be " womanly " to the point of ineptitude. . . .

During the long ride her spirits rose a little. After all, his attitude was almost inevitable. He thought she belonged to a race which to him stood for treachery and cruelty; he had seen her with Roger, Roger, the rich, the gay; he saw her as caring only for wealth and pleasure. Of course in his eyes she was separated from him by race and by more than race.

For long years she was unable to reconstruct that scene; her mind was always too tired, too sore to re-enact it.

As in a dream she saw Anthony's set, stern face, heard his firm, stern voice: " Angel-girl,— Angèle I told you not to come back. I told you it was all impossible."

She found herself clutching at his arm, blurting out the truth, forgetting all her elaborate plans, her carefully pre-concerted drama. " But, Anthony, Anthony, listen, everything's all right. I'm coloured; I've suffered too; nothing has to come between us."

For a moment off his guard he wavered. " Angèle, I didn't think you'd lie to me."

She was in tears, desperate. " I'm not lying, Anthony. It's perfectly true."

" I saw that picture of your mother, a white woman if I ever saw one,——"

"Yes, but a white coloured woman. My father was black, perfectly black and I have a sister, she's brown. My mother and I used to 'pass' sometimes just for the fun of it; she didn't mind being coloured. But I minded it terribly,—until very recently. So I left my home,—in Philadelphia,—and came here to live,—oh, going for white makes life so much easier. You know it, Anthony." His face wan and terrible frightened her. "It doesn't make you angry, does it? You've passed yourself, you told me you had. Oh Anthony, Anthony, don't look at me like that! What is it?"

She caught at his hand, following him as he withdrew to the shiny couch where they both sat breathless for a moment. "God!" he said suddenly; he raised his arms, beating the void like a madman. "You in your foolishness, I in my carelessness, 'passing, passing' and life sitting back laughing, splitting her sides at the joke of it. Oh, it was all right for you,—but I didn't care whether people thought I was white or coloured,—if we'd only known,——"

"What on earth are you talking about? It's all right now."

"It isn't all right; it's worse than ever." He caught her wrist. "Angel, you're sure you're not fooling me?"

"Of course I'm not. I have proof, I've a sister right here in New York; she's away just now. But when she comes back, I'll have you meet her. She is brown and lovely,—you'll want to paint her . . . don't you believe me, Anthony?"

"Oh yes, I believe you," he raised his arms again in a beautiful, fluid gesture, let them fall. "Oh,

damn life, damn it, I say . . . isn't there any
end to pain!"

Frightened, she got on her knees beside him.
"Anthony, what's the matter? Everything's going
to be all right; we're going to be happy."

"You may be. I'll never be happy. You were
the woman I wanted,—I thought you were white.
For my father's sake I couldn't marry a white girl.
So I gave you up."

"And I wouldn't stay given up. See, here I
am back again. You'll never be able to send me
away." Laughing but shamefaced, she tried to
thrust herself into his arms.

"No, Angel, no! You don't understand
There's, there's somebody else——"

She couldn't take it in. "Somebody else.
You mean,—you're married? Oh Anthony, you
don't mean you're married!"

"No, of course not, of course not! But I'm
engaged."

"Engaged, engaged and not to me,—to another
girl? And you kissed me, went around with me?
I knew other men did that, but I never thought
that of you! I thought you were like my father!"
And she began to cry like a little girl.

Shame-faced, he looked on, jamming his hands
tightly into his pockets. "I never meant to harm
you; I never thought until that day in the park
that you would care. And I cared so terribly!
Think, I had given you up, Angèle,—I suppose
that isn't your name really, is it?—and all of a
sudden, you came walking back into my life and
I said, ' I'll have the laugh on this damned mess
after all. I'll spend a few days with her, love her
a little, just a little. She'll never know, and I'll

have a golden memory! Oh, I had it coming to me, Angel! But the minute I saw you were beginning to care I broke off short."

. A line from an old text was running through her head, rendering her speechless, inattentive. She was a little girl back in the church again in Philadelphia; the minister was intoning " All we like sheep have gone astray ". He used to put the emphasis on the first word and Jinny and she would look at each other and exchange meaning smiles; he was a West Indian and West Indians had a way of misplacing the emphasis. The line sounded so funny: " *All* we like sheep,——" but perhaps it wasn't so funny after all; perhaps he had read it like that not because he was a West Indian but because he knew life and human nature. Certainly *she* had gone astray,—with Roger. And now here was Anthony, Anthony who had always loved her so well. Yet in his background there was a girl and he was engaged.

This brought her to a consideration of the unknown fiancée,—her rival. Deliberately she chose the word, for she was not through yet. This unknown, unguessed at woman who had stolen in like a thief in the night. . . .

" Have you known her long? " she asked him sharply.

" Who? Oh my,—my friend. No, not as long as I've known you."

A newcomer, an upstart. Well at least she, Angela, had the advantage of precedence.

" She's coloured, of course? "

" Of course."

They sat in a weary silence. Suddenly he caught her in his arms and buried his head in her neck.

A quick pang penetrated to the very core of her being. He must have been an adorable baby.
. . . Anthony and babies!

"Now God, Life, whatever it is that has power, this time you must help me!" cried her heart. She spoke to him gently.

"Anthony, you know I love you. Do you still love me?"

"Always, always, Angel."

"Do you—Oh, Anthony, I don't deserve it, but do you by any chance worship me?"

"Yes, that's it, that's just it, I worship you. I adore you. You are God to me. Oh, Angèle, if you'd only let me know. But it's too late now."

"No, no don't say that, perhaps it isn't too late. It all depends on this. Do you worship *her*, Anthony?" He lifted his haggard face.

"No—but she worships *me*. I'm God to *her* do you see? If I fail her she won't say anything, she'll just fall back like a little weak kitten, like a lost sheep, like a baby. She'll die." He said as though unaware of his listener. "She's such a little thing. And sweet."

Angela said gently: "Tell me about her. Isn't it all very sudden? You said you hadn't known her long."

He began obediently. "It was not long after I—I lost you. She came to me out of nowhere, came walking to me into my room by mistake; she didn't see me. And she put her head down on her hands and began to cry terribly. I had been crying too—in my heart, you understand, —and for a moment I thought she might be the echo of that cry, might be the cry itself. You see,

I'd been drinking a little,—you were so far removed, white and all that sort of thing. I couldn't marry a white woman, you know, not a white American. I owed that to my father.

" But at last I saw it was a girl, a real girl and I went over to her and put my hand on her shoulder and said: 'Little girl, what's the matter?'

" And she lifted her head, still hidden in the crook of her arm, you know the way a child does and said: 'I've lost my sister'. At first I thought she meant lost in the street and I said 'Well, come with me to the police station, I'll go with you, we'll give them a description and you'll find her again. People don't stay lost in this day and time'. ' I got her head on my shoulder, I almost took her on my knee, Angèle, she was so simple and forlorn. And presently she said: 'No, I don't mean lost that way; I mean she's left me, she doesn't want me any more. She wants other people'. And I've never been able to get anything else out of her. The next morning I called her up and somehow I got to seeing her, for her sake, you know. But afterwards when she grew happier,—she was so blithe, so lovely, so healing and blessed like the sun or a flower,—then I saw she was getting fond of me and I stayed away.

" Well, I ran across you and that Fielding fellow that night at the Van Meier lecture. And you were so happy and radiant, and Fielding so possessive,—damn him!—damn him!—he—you didn't let him hurt you, Angèle? "

As though anything that had ever happened in her life could hurt her like this! She had never known what pain was before. White-lipped, she shook her head. " No, he didn't hurt me."

304

"Well, I went to see her the next day. She came into the room like a shadow,—I realized she was getting thin. She was kind and sweet and far-off; impalpable, tenuous and yet there. I could see she was dying for me. And all of a sudden it came to me how wonderful it would be to have someone care like that. I went to her; I took her in my arms and I said: 'Child, child, I'm not bringing you a whole heart but could you love me?' You see I couldn't let her go after that."

"No," Angela's voice was dull, lifeless. "You couldn't. She'd die."

"Yes, that's it; that's just it. And I know you won't die, Angel."

"No, you're quite right. I won't die."

An icy hand was on her heart. At his first words: "She came walking into my room,——" an icy echo stirred a memory deep, deep within her inner consciousness. She heard Jinny saying: "I went walking into his room,——"

Something stricken, mortally stricken in her face fixed his attention. "Don't look like that, my girl, my dear Angel. . . . There are three of us in this terrible plight,—if I had only known. . . . I don't deserve the love of either of you but if one of you two must suffer it might as well be she as you. Come, we'll go away; even unhappiness, even remorse will mean something to us as long as we're together."

She shook her head. "No, that's impossible,— if it were someone else, I don't know, perhaps —I'm so sick of unhappiness,—maybe I'd take a chance. But in her case it's impossible."

He looked at her curiously. "What do you mean 'in her case'?"

"Isn't her name Virginia Murray?" ˹ ˹˹ ˹˹

"Yes, yes! How did you guess it? Do you know her?"

"She's my sister. Angèle Mory,—Angela Murray, don't you see. It's the same name. And it's all my fault. I pushed her, sent her deliberately into your arms."

He could only stare.

"I'm the unkind sister who didn't want her. Oh, can't you understand? That night she came walking into your room by mistake it was because I had gone to the station to meet her and Roger Fielding came along. I didn't want him to know that I was coloured and I,—I didn't acknowledge her, I cut her."

"Oh," he said surprised and inadequate. "I don't see how you could have done that to a little girl like Virginia. Did she know New York?"

"No." She drooped visibly. Even the loss of him was nothing compared to this rebuke. There seemed nothing further to be said.

Presently he put his arm about her. "Poor Angèle. As though you could foresee! It's what life does to us, leads us into pitfalls apparently so shallow, so harmless and when we turn around there we are, caught, fettered,——"

Her miserable eyes sought his. "I was sorry right away, Anthony. I tried my best to get in touch with her that very evening. But I couldn't find her,—already you see, life was getting even with me, she had strayed into your room."

He nodded. "Yes, I remember it all so plainly. I was getting ready to go out, was all prepared as a matter of fact. Indeed I moved that very night. But I loitered on and on, thinking of you.

" The worst of it is I'll always be thinking of you.
Oh Angèle, what does it matter, what does anything matter if we just have each other? This
damned business of colour, is it going to ruin all
chances of happiness? I've known trouble, pain,
terrible devastating pain all my life. You've
suffered too. Together perhaps we could find
peace. We'd go to your sister and explain. She
is kind and sweet; surely she'd understand."

He put his arms about her and the two clung
to each other, solemnly, desperately, like children.

" I'm sick of pain, too, Anthony, sick of longing
and loneliness. You can't imagine how I've
suffered from loneliness."

" Yes, yes I can. I guessed it. I used to watch
you. I thought you were probably lonely inside,
you were so different from Miss Lister and Mrs.
Starr. Come away with me and we'll share our
loneliness together, somewhere where we'll forget,——"

" And Virginia? You said yourself she'd
die,——"

" She's so young, she—she could get over it."
But his tone was doubtful, wavering.

She tore herself from him. " No, I took her
sister away from her; I won't take her lover. Kiss
me good-bye, Anthony."

They sat on the hard sofa. " To think we should
find one another only to lose each other ! To think
that everything, every single thing was all right
for us but that we were kept apart by the stupidity
of fate. I'd almost rather we'd never learned the
truth. Put your dear arms about me closer,
Angel, Angel. I want the warmth, the sweetness
of you to penetrate into my heart. I want to

keep it there forever. Darling; how can I let you go? ”

·She clung to him weeping, weeping with the heart-broken abandonment of a child.

A bell shrilled four times.

He jumped up. “ It’s Sanchez, he’s forgotten his key; thank God he did forget it. My darling, you must go. But wait for me. I’ll meet you,— we’ll go to your house, we’ll find a way. We can’t part like this ! ” His breath was coming in short gasps; she could see little white lines deepening about his mouth, his nostrils. Fearfully she caught at her hat.

“ God bless you; good-bye Anthony. I won’t see you again.”

Halfway down the black staircase she met the heedless Sanchez, tall, sallow, thin, glancing at her curiously with a slightly amused smile. Politely he stood aside to let her pass, one hand resting lightly against his hip. Something in his attitude made her think of her unfinished sketch of Life. Hysterical, beside herself, she rushed down the remaining steps afraid to look around lest she should see the thin dark figure in pursuit, lest her ears should catch the expansion of that faint meaning smile into a guffaw, uproarious, menacing.

CHAPTER VI

ONCE long ago in the old days in the house on Opal Street she had been taken mysteriously ill. As a matter of fact she had been coming down with that inglorious disease, the mumps. The expense of having a doctor was a consideration, and so for twenty-four hours she was the object of anxious solicitude for the whole house. Her mother had watched over her all night; her father came home twice in the day to see how she felt; Jinny had with some reluctance bestowed on her an oft-coveted, oft-refused doll. In the midst of all her childish pain and suffering she had realized that at least her agony was shared, that her tribulation was understood. But now she was ill with a sickness of the soul and there was no one with whom she could share her anguish.

For two days she lay in her little room; Mrs. Denver, happening in, showered upon her every attention. There was nothing, nothing that Angela could suggest, the little fluttering lady said sincerely, which she might not have. Angela wished that she would go away and leave her alone, but her experiences had rendered her highly sensitive to the needs of others; Mrs. Denver, for all her money, her lack of responsibility, her almost childish appetite for pleasure, was lonely, too; waiting on the younger, less fortunate woman gave her a sense of being needed; she was pathetically glad when the girl expressed a desire for anything no matter how expensive or how trivial. Angela could not deprive her entirely of those doubtful pleasures. Still there were moments, of course, when even Mrs. Denver for all her kindly officiousness had to betake herself elsewhere and leave her willing patient to herself and her thoughts.

Minutely, bit by bit, in the long forty-eight hours she went over her life; was there, anything, any over tact, any crime which she had committed and for which she might atone? She had been selfish, yes; but, said her reasoning and unwearied mind, " Everybody who survives at all is selfish, it is one of the pre-requisites of survival." In " passing " from one race to the other she had done no harm to anyone. Indeed she had been forced to take this action. But she should not have forsaken Virginia. Here at this point her brain, so clear and active along all other lines, invariably failed her. She could not tell what stand to take; so far as leaving Philadelphia was concerned she had left it to seek her fortune under more agreeable circumstances; if she had been a boy and had left home no one would have had a word of blame, it would have been the proper thing, to be expected and condoned. There remained then only the particular incident of her cutting Jinny on that memorable night in the station. That was the one really cruel and unjust action of her whole life.

" Granted," said something within her rooted either in extreme hard common sense or else in a vast sophistry, " granted, but does that carry with it as penalty the shattering of a whole life, or even the suffering of years? Certainly the punishment is far in excess of the crime." And it was then that she would lie back exhausted, hopeless, bewildered, unable to cope further with the myterious and apparently meaningless ferocity of life. For if this were a just penalty for one serious misdemeanour, what compensation should there not be for the years in which she had been a dutiful daughter, a loving sister? And suddenly she found herself envying people possessed of a blind religious faith, of the people who could bow the head submissively and whisper: "Thy will be done." For herself she could see how beaten and harried, one might subside into a sort of blind passivity, an acceptance of things as they are, but she would never be able to understand a force which gave one the imagination to paint a great desire, the tenacity to cling to it, the emotionalism to spend on its possible realization but which would then with a careless sweep of the hand wipe out the picture which the creature of its own endowment had created.

More than once the thought came to her of dying. But she hated to give up; something innate, something of the spirit stronger than her bodily will, set up a dogged fight, and she was too bruised and sore to combat it. "All right," she said to herself wearily, "I'll keep on living." She thought then of black people, of the race of her parents and of all the odds against living which a cruel, relentless fate had called on them to endure. And she saw them as a people powerfully, almost overwhelmingly endowed with the essence of life. They had to persist, had to survive because they did not know how to die.

' Not because she felt like it, but because some day she must begin once more to take up the motions of life, she moved on the third day, from her bed to the easy chair, sat there listless and motionless. To-morrow she would return to work,—to work and the sick agony of forcing her mind back from its dolorous, painful, vital thoughts to some consideration of the dull, uninteresting task in hand. God, how she hated that! She remembered studying her lessons as a girl; the intense absorption with which she used to concentrate. Sometimes she used to wonder: " Oh what will it be like when I am grown up; when I won't be studying lessons . . . " Well, this was what it was like. Or no, she was still studying with the same old absorption,—an absorption terribly, painfully concentrated,—the lessons set down by life. It was useless to revolve in her head the causes for her suffering, they were so trivial, so silly. She said to herself, " There is no sorrow in the world like my sorrow ", and knew even as she said it that some one else, perhaps only in the next block, in the next house, was saying the same thing.

Mrs. Denver tapped lightly, opened the door, came in closing it mysteriously behind her.

" I've a great surprise for you.' She went on with an old childish formula: " Will you have it now, or wait till you get it? "

Angela's features twisted into a wan smile. " I believe I'd better have it now. I'm beginning to think I don't care for surprises." ·

" You'll like this one." She went to the door and ushered in Rachel Salting.

" I know you two want to talk," Mrs. Denver called over her shoulder. · " Cheer her up, Rachel, and I'll bring you both a fine spread in an hour or so." She closed the door carefully behind her.

Angela said, " What's the matter, Rachel? " She almost added, " I hardly knew you." For her friend's face was white and wan with grief and hopelessness; gone was all her dainty freshness, her pretty colour; indeed her eyes, dark, sunken, set in great pools of blackness, were the only note,—a terrible note,—of relief against that awful whiteness.

Angela felt her strength leaving her; she rose and tottered back to the grateful security of her bed, lay down with an overwhelming sense of thankfulness for the asylum afforded her sudden faintness. In a moment, partly recovered, she motioned to Rachel to sit beside her.'

" Oh," said Rachel, " you've been ill,—Mrs. Denver told me. I ought not to come bothering you with my worries. Oh, Angèle, I'm so wretched! Whatever shall I do? "

Her friend, watching her, was very gentle. " There're lots of awful things that can happen. I know that, Rachel. Maybe your trouble isn't so bad that it can't be helped. Have you told John about it? " But even as she spoke she sensed that the difficulty in some way concerned John. Her heart contracted at the thought of the pain and suffering to be endured.

" Yes, John knows,—it's about him. Angèle, we can't marry."

" Can't marry. Why, is he,—it can't be that he's—involved with some one else! " ·

A momentary indignation flashed into Rachel's face bringing back life and colour. For a small space she was the Rachel Salting of the old happy days. "Involved with some one else!" The indignation was replaced by utter despair. "How I wish he were! That at least could be arranged. But this can never be altered. He,—I, our parents are dead set against it. Hadn't you ever noticed, Angèle? He's a Gentile and I'm a Jew."

"But lots of Jews and Gentiles marry."

"Yes, I know. Only—he's a Catholic. But my parents are orthodox—they will never consent to my marriage. My father says he'd rather see me dead and my mother just sits and moans. I kept it from her as long as I could,—I used to pray about it, I thought God must let it turn out all right, John and I love each other so. But I went up to Utica the other day, John went with me, and we told them. My father drove him out of the house; he said if I married him he'd curse me. I am afraid of that curse. I can't go against them. Oh, Angèle, I wish I'd never been born."

It was a delicate situation; Angela had to feel her way; she could think of nothing but the trite and obvious. "After all, Rachel, your parents have lived their lives; they have no business trying to live yours. Personally I think all this pother about race and creed and colour, tommyrot. In your place I should certainly follow my own wishes; John seems to be the man for you."

But Rachel weeping, imbued with the spirit of filial piety, thought it would be selfish.

"Certainly no more selfish than their attempt to regulate your life for you."

"But I'm afraid," said Rachel shivering, "of my father's curse." It was difficult for Angela to sympathize with an attitude so archaic; she was surprised to find it lurking at the bottom of her friend's well-trained intelligence.

" Love," she said musing to herself rather than to her friend, " is supposed to be the greatest thing in the world but look how we smother and confine it. Jews mustn't marry Catholics; white people mustn't marry coloured——"

" Oh well, of course not," Rachel interrupted in innocent-surprise. . " I wouldn't marry a nigger in any circumstances. Why, would you? "

But Angela's only answer was to turn and, burying her head in her pillow, to burst into unrestrained and bitter laughter. Rachel went flying to call Mrs. Denver.

" Oh come quick, come quick! Angèle's in hyterics. I haven't the ghost of an idea what to do for her! "

Once more the period of readjustment. Once more the determination to take life as she found it; bitter dose after sweet, bitter after sweet. But it seemed to her now that both sweetness and bitterness together with her high spirit for adventure lay behind her. How now was she to pass through the tepid, tasteless days of her future? She was not quite twenty-seven, and she found herself wondering what life would be like in ten, five, even one years' time. Changes did flow in upon one, she knew, but in her own case she had been so used herself to give the impetus to these·changes. Now she could not envisage herself as making a move in any direction. With the new sullenness which seemed to be creeping upon her daily, she said " Whatever move I make is always wrong. Let life take care of itself." And she saw life, even her own life, as an entity quite outside her own ken and her own directing. She did not care greatly what happened; she would not, it was true, take her own life, but she would not care if she should die. Once if her mind had harboured such thoughts she 'would have felt an instant self-pity. " What a shame that I so young, so gifted, with spirits so high should meet with death!" But now her senses were blunting; so much pain and confusion had brought about their inevitable attrition. " I might just as well be unhappy, or meet death as anyone else," she told herself still with that mounting sullenness.

Mrs. Denver, the Sandburgs and Ashley were the only people who saw her. It did seem to Mrs. Denver that the girl's ready, merry manner was a little dimmed; if her own happy, sunny, vocabulary had known the term she would have daubed her cynical. The quasi-intellectual atmosphere at the Sandburgs suited her to perfection; the faint bitterness which so constantly marred her speech was taken for sophistication, her frequent silences for profoundness; in a small way, aided by her extraordinary good looks and the slight mystery which always hung about her, she became quite a personage in their entourage; the Sandburgs considered her a splendid find and plumed themselves on having " brought her out ".

.   .   .   .   .

The long golden summer, so beautiful with its promise of happiness, so sickening with its actuality of pain ripened into early, exquisite September. Virginia was home again; slightly more golden, very, very faintly plumper, like a ripening fruit perfected; brimming with happiness, excitement and the most complete content, Angela thought, that she had ever seen in her life.

Jinny sent for the older girl and the two sat on a Sunday morning, away from Sara Penton and the other too insistent friends, over on Riverside Drive looking out at the river winding purple and alluring in the soft autumn haze.

" Weren't you surprised? " asked Jinny. Laconically, Angela admitted to no slight amazement. She still loved her sister but more humbly, less achingly than before. Their lives, she thought now would never, could never touch and she was quite reconciled. Moreover, in some of Virginia's remarks there was the hint of the acceptance of such a condition. Something had brought an irrevocable separation. They would always view each other from the two sides of an abyss, narrow but deep, deep.

The younger girl prattled on. " I don't know whether Sara told you his name,—Anthony Cross? Isn't it a dear name? "

" Yes, it's a nice name, a beautiful name," said Angela heartily; when she had learned it was of no consequence. She added without enthusiasm that she knew him already; he had been a member of her class at Cooper Union.

" You don't talk as though you were very much taken with him," said Jinny, making a face. " But never mind, he suits me, no matter whom he doesn't suit." There was that in her countenance which made Angela realize and marvel again at the resoluteness of that firm young mind. No curse of parents could have kept Virginia from Anthony's arms. As long as Anthony loved her, was satisfied to have her love, no one could come between them. Only if he should fail her would she shrivel up and die.

On the heels of this thought Virginia made an astounding remark: "You know it's just perfect that I met Anthony; he's really been a rock in a weary land. Next to Matthew Henson he will, I'm sure, make me happier than any man in the world." Dreamily she added an afterthought: "And I'll make him happy too, but, oh, Angela, Angela, I always wanted to marry Matthew!"

The irony of that sent Angela home. Virginia wanting Matthew and marrying Anthony; Anthony wanting Angela and marrying Virginia. Herself wanting Anthony and marrying, wanting, no other; unable to think of, even to dream of another lover. The irony of it was so palpable, so ridiculously palpable that it put her in a better mood; life was bitter but it was amusingly bitter; if she could laugh at it she might be able to outwit it yet. The thought brought Anthony to mind: "If I could only get a laugh on life, Angèle!"

Sobered, she walked from the 'bus stop to Jayne Street. Halfway up the narrow, tortuous staircase she caught sight of a man climbing, climbing. He stopped outside her door. "Anthony?" she said to herself while her heart twisted with pain. "If it is Anthony,——" she breathed, and stopped. But something within her, vital, cruel, persistent, completed her thought. "If it is Anthony,—after what Virginia said this morning,—if he knew that he was not the first, that even as there had been one other there might still be others; that Virginia in her bright, hard, shallow youthfulness would not die any more than she had died over Matthew,—would console herself for the loss of Anthony even as she had consoled herself for the loss of Matthew!" But no, what Jinny had told her was in confidence, a confidence from sister to sister. She would never break faith with Jinny again; nor with herself,

"But Anthony," she said to herself in the few remaining seconds left on the staircase, "you were my first love and I think I was yours."

However, the man at the door was not Anthony; on the contrary he was, she thought, a complete stranger. But as he turned at her footsteps, she found herself looking into the blue eyes of Roger. Completely astounded, she greeted him, "You don't mean it's you, Roger?"

"Yes," he said humbly, shamefacedly, "aren't you going to let me in, Angèle?"

"Oh yes, of course, of course"; she found herself hoping that he would not stay long. She wanted to think and she would like to paint; that idea must have been in the back of her head ever since she had left Jinny. Hard on this thought came another. "Here's Roger. I never expected to see him in these rooms again; perhaps some day Anthony will come back. Oh, God, be kind!"

But she must tear her thoughts away from Anthony. She looked at Roger curiously, searchingly; in books the man who had treated his sweetheart unkindly often returned beaten, de-jected, even poverty-stricken, but Roger, except for a slight hesitation in his manner, seemed as jaunty, as fortunate, as handsome as ever. He was even a trifle stouter.

Contrasting him with Anthony's hard-bitten leanness, she addressed him half absently. " I believe you're actually getting fat! "

His quick high flush revealed his instant sensi-tiveness to her criticism. But he was humble. " That's all right, Angèle. I deserve anything you choose to say if you'll just say it."

She was impervious to his mood, utterly indiffer-ent, so indifferent that she was herself unaware of her manner. " Heavens, I've sort of forgotten, but I don't remember your ever having been so eager for criticism heretofore! "

He caught at one phrase. " Forgotten! You don't mean to say you've forgotten the past and all that was once so dear to us? "

Impatience overwhelmed her. She wished he would go and leave her to her thoughts and to her picture; such a splendid idea had come to her; it was the first time for weeks that she had felt like working. Aware of the blessed narcotic value of interesting occupation, she looked forward to his departure with a sense of relief; even hoped with her next words to pre-cipitate it.

" Roger, you don't mean to say that you called on me on a hot September Sunday just to talk to me in that theatrical manner? I don't mind telling you I've a million things to do this after-noon; let's get down to bed rock so we can both be up and doing."

She had been sitting, almost lolling at ease
in the big chair, not regarding him, absently
twisting a scarf in her fingers. Now she glanced
up and something in the hot blueness of his eyes
brought her to an upright position, alert, attentive.

"Angèle, you've got to take me back."

"Back! I don't know what you're talking
about. Between you and me there is no past, so
don't mention it. If you've nothing better to say
than that, you might as well get out."

He tried to possess himself of her hands but
she shook him off, impatiently, angrily, with no
pretence at feeling. "Go away, Roger. I don't
want to be bothered with you!" This pinchbeck
emotionalism after the reality of her feeling for
Anthony, the sincerity of his feeling for her! "I
won't have this sort of thing; if you won't go
I will." She started for the door but he barred
her way, suddenly straight and serious.

"No listen, Angèle, you must listen. I'm in
earnest this time. You must forgive me for the
past, for the things I said. Oh, I was unspeakable!
But I had it in my head,—you don't know the
things a man has borne in on him about designing
women,—if he's got anything, family, money,——"
she could see him striving to hide his knowledge of
his vast eligibility. "I thought you were trying
to 'get' me, it made me suspicious, angry. I knew
you were poor,——"

"And nobody! Oh say it, say it!"

"Well, I will say it. According to my father's
standards, nobody. And when you began to
take an interest in me, in my affairs,——"

"You thought I was trying to marry you. Well,
at first I was. I was poor, I was nobody! I

wanted to be rich, to be able to see the world, to help people. And then when you and I came so near to each other I didn't care about marriage at all—just about living! Oh, I suppose my attitude was perfectly pagan. I hadn't meant to drift into such a life, all my training was against it, you can't imagine how completely my training was against it. And then for a time I was happy. I'm afraid I didn't love you really, Roger, indeed I know now that in a sense I didn't love you, but somehow life seemed to focus into an absolute perfection. Then you became petulant, ugly, suspicious, afraid of my interest, of my tenderness. And I thought, ' I can't let this all end in a flame of ugliness; it must be possible for people to have been lovers and yet remain friends.' I tried so hard to keep things so that it would at least remain a pleasant memory. But you resented my efforts. What I can't understand is—why shouldn't I, if I wanted to, either try to marry you or to make an ideal thing of our relationship? Why is it that men like you resent an effort on our part to make our commerce decent? Well, it's all over now. . . . Theoretically ' free love ' or whatever you choose to call it, is all right. Actually, it's all wrong. I don't want any such relationship with you or with any other man in this world. Marriage was good enough for my mother, it's good enough for me."

" There's nothing good enough for you, Angèle; but marriage is the best thing that I have to offer and I'm offering you just that. And it's precisely because you were honest and frank and decent and tried to keep our former relationship from deteriorating into sordidness that I am back."

Clearly she was staggered. Marriage with Roger meant protection, position, untold wealth, unlimited opportunities for doing good. Once how she would have leapt to such an offer!

" What's become of Carlotta? " she asked bluntly.

" She's on the eve of marrying Tom Estes, a fellow who was in college with me. He has heaps more money than I. Carlotta thought she'd better take him on."

"" I see." She looked at him thoughtfully, then the remembrance of her great secret came to her, a secret which she could never share with Roger. No! No more complications and their consequent disaster! " No, no, we won't talk about it any more. What you want is impossible; you can't guess how completely impossible."

He strode toward her, seized her hands. " I'm in earnest, Angèle; you've no idea how tired I am of loneliness and uncertainty and,—and of seeking women; I want someone whom I can love and trust, whom I can teach to love me,—we could get married to-morrow. There's not an obstacle in our way."

His sincerity left her unmoved. " What would your father say? "

" Oh, we wouldn't be able to tell him yet; he'd never consent! Of course we'd have to keep things quiet, just ourselves and one or two friends, Martha and Ladislas perhaps, would be in the know."

More secrets! She pulled her hands away from him. " Oh Roger, Roger! I wouldn't consider it. No, when I marry I want a man, a man, a real one, someone not afraid to go on his own! " She actually pushed him toward the door. "Some people might revive dead ashes, but not you and I. . . . I'd never be able to trust you again and I'm sick of secrets and playing games with human relationships. I'm going to take my friendships straight hereafter. Please go. I've had a hard summer and I'm very tired. Besides I want to work."

Baffled, he looked at her, surprise and indignation struggling in his face. "Angèle, are you sure you know what you're doing? I've no intention of coming back, so you'd better take me now."

"Of course you're not coming back! I'm sure I wouldn't want you to; my decision is final." Not unsympathetically she laughed up into his doleful face, actually touched his cheek. "If you only knew how much you look like a cross baby!"

.   .   .   .   .

Her newly developed sympathy and understanding made her think of Ashley. Doubtless Carlotta's defection would hit him very hard. Her conjecture was correct although the effect of the blow was different from what she had anticipated. Ashley was not so perturbed over the actual loss of the girl as confirmed in his opinion that he was never going to be able to form and keep a lasting friendship. In spite of his wealth, his native timidity had always made him distrustful of himself with women of his own class; a veritable Tony Hardcastle, he spent a great deal of time with women whom he did not actually admire, whom indeed he disliked, because, he said to Angela wistfully, they were the only ones who took him seriously.

" No one but you and Carlotta have ever given me any consideration, have ever liked me for myself, Angèle."

They were seeing a great deal of each other; in a quiet, unemotional way they were developing a real friendship. Angela had taken up her painting again. She had re-entered the classes at Cooper Union and was working with great zest and absorption on a subject which she meant to enter in the competition for scholarships at the school at Fontainebleau. Ashley, who wrote some good verse in the recondite, falsely free style of the present day, fell into the habit of bringing his work down to her little living room, and in the long tender autumn evenings the two worked seriously, with concentration. Ashley had travelled widely and had seen a great deal of life, though usually from the side-lines; Angela for all her lack of wandering, " had lived deeply ", he used to tell her, pondering on some bit of philosophy which she let fall based on the experiences of her difficult life.

" You know, in your way you're quite a wonder, Angèle; there's a mystery hanging about you; for all your good spirits, your sense of humour, you're like the Duse, you seem to move in an aura of suffering, of the pain which comes from too great sensitivity. And yet how can that be so? You're not old enough, you've had too few contacts to know how unspeakable life can be, how damnably she can get you in wrong,——"

An enigmatic smile settled on her face. " I don't know about life, Ralph? How do you think

I got the idea for this masterpiece of mine? " She pointed to the painting on which she was then engaged.

" That's true, that's true. I've wondered often about that composition; lots of times I've meant to ask you how you came to evolve it. But keep your mystery to yourself, child; it adds to your charm."

About this she had her own ideas. Mystery might add to the charm of personality but it certainly could not be said to add to the charm of living. Once she thought that stolen waters were sweetest, but now it was the unwinding road and the open book that most intrigued.

Ashley, she found, for all his shyness, possessed very definite ideas and convictions of his own, was absolutely unfettered in his mode of thought, and quite unmoved by social traditions and standards. An aristocrat if ever there were one, he believed none the less in the essential quality of man and deplored the economic conditions which so often tended to set up superficial and unreal barriers which make as well as separate the classes.

With some trepidation Angela got him on the subject of colour. He considered prejudice the greatest blot on America's shield. " We're wrong, all wrong about those people; after all they did to make America habitable! Some day we're going to wake up to our shame. I hope it won't be too late."

" But you wouldn't want your sister to marry a nigger ! "

" I'm amazed, Angèle, at your using such a word as an exclusive term. I've known some fine coloured people. There're hardly any of unmixed blood in the United States, so the term Negro is usually a misnomer. I haven't a sister; if I had I'd advise her against marriage with an American coloured man because the social pressure here would probably be too great, but that would be absolutely the only ground on which I'd object to it. And I can tell you this; I wouldn't care to marry a woman from the Congo but if I met a coloured woman of my own nationality, well-bred, beautiful, sympathetic, I wouldn't let the fact of her mixed blood stand in my way, I can tell you."

.   .   .   .   .

A sort of secondary interest in living was creeping into her perspective. The high lights, the high peaks had faded from her sight. She would never, she suspected, know such spontaneity of feeling and attitude again as she had felt toward both Roger and Anthony. Nor would she again approach the experiences of existence with the same naïve expectation, the same desire to see how things would turn out. Young as she was she felt like a battle-scarred veteran who, worn out from his own strenuous activities, was quite content to sit on the side-lines gazing at all phases of warfare with an equal eye.

Although she no longer intended to cast in her lot with Virginia, she made no further effort to set up barriers between herself and coloured people. Let the world take her as it would. If she were in Harlem, in company with Virginia and Sara Penton she went out to dinner, to the noisy, crowded, friendly " Y " dining-room, to " Gert's " tea-room, to the clean, inviting drug-store for rich "sundaes". Often, too, she went shopping with her sister and to the theatre; she had her meet Ashley and Martha. But she was careful in this company to avoid contact with people whose attitude on the race question was unknown, or definitely antagonistic.

Harlem intrigued her; it was a wonderful city; it represented, she felt, the last word in racial pride, integrity and even self-sacrifice. Here were people of a very high intellectual type, exponents of the realest and most essential refinement living cheek by jowl with coarse or ill-bred or even criminal, certainly indifferent, members of their race. Of course some of this propinquity was due to outer pressure, but there was present, too, a hidden consciousness of race-duty, a something which if translated said: "Perhaps you do pull me down a little from the height to which I have climbed. But on the other hand, perhaps, I'm helping you to rise."

There was a hair-dresser's establishment on 136th Street where Virginia used to have her beautiful hair treated; where Sara Penton, whose locks were of the same variety as Matthew's, used to repair to have their unruliness "pressed". Here on Saturdays Angela would accompany the girls and sit through the long process just to overhear the conversations, grave and gallant and gay, of these people whose blood she shared but whose disabilities by a lucky fluke she had been able to avoid. For, while she had been willing for the sake of Anthony to re-enlist in the struggles of this life, she had never closed her eyes to its disadvantages; to its limitedness! What a wealth of courage it took for these people to live! What

high degree of humour, determination, steadfastness, undauntedness were not needed,—and poured
forth! Maude, the proprietress of the business,
for whom the establishment was laconically called
" Maude's ", was a slight, sweet-faced woman
with a velvety seal-brown skin, a charming voice
and an air of real refinement. She was from Texas,
but had come to New York to seek her fortune, had
travelled as ladies' maid in London and Paris, and
was as thoroughly conversant with the arts of her
calling as any hairdresser in the vicinity of the Rue
de la Paix or on Fifth Avenue. A rare quality of
hospitality emanated from her presence; her little
shop was always full not only of patrons but of
callers, visitors from " down home ", actresses from
the current coloured " show ", flitting in like radiant
birds of paradise with their rich brown skins,
their exotic eyes and the gaily coloured clothing
which an unconscious style had evolved just for
them.

In this atmosphere, while there was no coarse-
ness, there was no restriction; life in busy Harlem
stopped here and yawned for a delicious moment
before going on with its pressure and problems.
A girl from Texas, visiting " the big town " for a
few weeks took one last glance at her shapely,
marvellously " treated " head, poised for a second
before the glass and said simply, " Well, good-bye,
Maude; I'm off for the backwoods, but I'll never
forget Harlem." She passed out with the sinuous
elegant carriage acquired in her few week's sojourn
on Seventh Avenue.

A dark girl, immaculate in white from head to
foot, asked: " What's she going back South for?
Ain't she had enough of Texas _yet ? "

Maude replied that she had gone back there because of her property. " Her daddy owns most of the little town where they live."

" Child, ain't you learned that you don't *never* own no property in Texas as long as those white folks are down there too? Just let those Ku Kluxers get it into their heads that you've got something they want. She might just as well leave there first as last; she's bound to have to some day. I know it's more'n a notion to pull up stakes and start all over again in a strange town and a strange climate, but it's the difference between life and death. I know I done it and I don't expect ever to go back."

She was a frail woman, daintily dressed and shod. Her voice was soft and drawling. But Angela saw her sharply as the epitome of the iron and blood in a race which did not know how to let go of life.

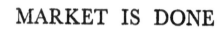

MARKET IS DONE

CHAPTER I.

THE eternal routine of life went on,—meals, slumber, talk, work—and all of it meaning nothing; a void starting nowhere and leading nowhither; a "getting through" with the days. Gradually however two points fixed themselves in her horizon, and about these her life revolved. One was her work,—her art. Every week found her spending three or four of its nights at her easel. She was feverishly anxious to win one of the prizes in the contest which would be held in May; if successful she would send in her application for registration in the Fountainebleau School of Fine Arts which was financed by Americans and established, so read the circular, " as a summer school for American architects, painters and sculptors ". If she were successful in winning this, she would leave the United States for a year or two, thus assuring herself beyond question of a new deal of the cards. The tenacity with which she held to this plan frightened her a little until she found out that there were also possible funds from which she could, with the proper recommendation, borrow enough money to enable her to go abroad with the understanding that the refund was to be made by slow and easy payments. Ashley discovered this saving information, thus relieving her of the almost paralyzing fear which beset her from time to time. It both amused and saddened her to realize that her talent which she had once used as a blind to shield her real motives for breaking loose and coming to New York had now become the greatest, most real force in her life.

Miss Powell, with whom Angela in her new mood had arranged a successful truce, knew of her ambition, indeed shared it. If she herself should win a prize, that money, combined with some small savings of her own and used in connection with the special terms offered by the American Committee, would mean the fruition of her dearest dreams. All this she confided to Angela on two Sunday mornings which the latter spent with her in her rather compressed quarters up in 134th Street. A dwelling house nearby had been converted into a place of worship for one of the special divisions of religious creed so dear to coloured people's hearts. Most of the service seemed to consist of singing, and so the several hours spent by the two girls in earnest talk were punctuated by the outbursts of song issuing from the brazen-coated throats of the faithful.

The other point about which her thoughts centred was her anomalous position. Yet that clear mind of hers warned her again and again that there was nothing inherently wrong or mean or shameful in the stand which she had taken. The method thereof might come in perhaps for a little censure. But otherwise her harshest critics, if unbiased, could only say that instead of sharing the burdens of her own group she had elected to stray along a path where she personally could find the greatest ease, comfort and expansion. She had long since given up the search for happiness.

But there were moments when a chance discussion about coloured people couched in the peculiarly brutal terms which white America affects in the discussion of this problem made her blood boil, and she longed to confound her *vis-à-vis* and his tacit assumption that she, being presumbably a white woman, would hold the same views as he, with the remark: " I'm one of them,—do you find me worthless or dishonest or offensive in any way? " Such a *dénouement* would have, she felt, been a fine gesture. But life she knew had a way of allowing grand gestures to go unremarked and unrewarded. Would it be worth while to throw away the benefits of casual whiteness in America when no great issue was at stake? Would it indeed be worth while to forfeit them when a great issue was involved? Remembering the material age in which she lived and the material nation of which she was a member, she was doubtful. Her mother's old dictum recurred: " Life is more important than colour."

.   .   .   .   .

The years slipped by. Virginia seemed in no haste to marry. Anthony whom Angela saw occasionally at the Art School shared apparently in this cool deliberateness. Yet there was nothing in his action or manner to make her feel that he was anticipating a change. Rather, if she judged him correctly he, like herself, tired of the snarl into which the three of them had been drawn, had settled down to a resigned acceptance of fate. If conceivable, he was quieter, more reserved than ever, yet radiating a strange restfulness and the peace which comes from surrender.

In May the prizes for the contest were announced. Angela received the John T. Stewart Prize for her " Fourteenth Street Types "; her extreme satisfaction was doubled by the knowledge that the Nehemiah Sloan Prize, of equal value, had been awarded Miss Powell for her picture entitled " A Street in Harlem ". The coloured girl was still difficult and reserved, but under Angela's persistent efforts at friendship her frank and sympathetic interest and comprehension of her class-mate's difficulties, the latter had finally begun to thaw a little. They were not planning to live together in France, their tastes were not sufficiently common for that closeness, but both were looking forward to a year of pleasure, of inspiring work, to a life that would be " different ". Angela was relieved, but Miss Powell was triumphant; not unpleasantly, she gave the impression of having justified not only her calling but herself and, in a lesser degree, her race. The self-consciousness of colour, racial responsibility, lay, Angela had discovered, deep upon her.

The passage money to France was paid. Through the terms offered by the committee of the School for Americans at Fontainebleau, an appreciable saving had been effected. The girls were to sail in June. As the time drew nearer Angela felt herself becoming more and more enthusiastic. She had at first looked upon her sojourn abroad as a heaven-sent break in the montony and difficulties of her own personal problems, but lately, with the involuntary reaction of youth, she was beginning to recover her sense of embarking on a great adventure. Her spirits mounted steadily.

One evening she went around to Martha Burden's to discuss the trip; she wanted information about money, clothes, possible tips.

" Everything you can think of, Martha," she said with something of her former vital manner. " This is an old story to you,—you've been abroad so many times you ought to write an encyclopædia on ' What to take to Europe '. I mean to follow your advice blindly and the next time I see Miss Powell I'll pass it along to her."

" No need to," said Martha laconically and sombrely. " She isn't going."

" Not going! Why she was going two weeks ago."

" Yes, but she's not going this week nor any other week I'm afraid; at least not through the good offices of the American Committee for the Fontainebleau School of Fine Arts. They've returned her passage money. Didn't you know it? I thought everybody had heard of it."

Angela fought against a momentary nausea. " No, I didn't know it. I haven't seen her for ages. I'm so busy getting myself together. Martha, what's it all about? Is it because she's coloured? You don't mean it's because she's coloured? "

" Well, it is. They said they themselves were without prejudice, but that they were sure the enforced contact on the boat would be unpleasant to many of the students, garnered as they would be from all parts of the United States. Furthermore they couldn't help but think that such contact would be embarrassing to Miss Powell too. Oh, there's no end to the ridiculous piffle which they've written and said. I've had a little committee of students and instructors going about, trying to stir up public sentiment. Mr. Cross has been helping and Paget too. I wish Paulette were here; she'd get some yellow journal publicity. Van Meier has come out with some biting editorials; he's shown up a lot of their silly old letters. I shouldn't be surprised but what if we kept at it long enough we'd get somewhere."

She reflected a moment. "Funny thing is we're having such a hard time in making Miss Powell show any fight. I don't understand that girl."

Angela murmured that perhaps she had no hope of making an impression on prejudice. "It's so unreasonable and far-reaching. Maybe she doesn't want to sacrifice her peace of mind for what she considers a futile struggle."

"That's what Mr. Cross said. He's been wonderful to her and an indefatigable worker. Of course you'll be leaving soon since none of this touches you, but come into a committee meeting or two, won't you? We're meeting here. I'll give you a ring."

"Well," said Angela to herself that night after she had regained her room. "I wonder what I ought to do now?" Even yet she was receiving an occasional reporter; the pleasant little stir of publicity attendant on her prize had not yet died away. Suppose she sent for one of them and announced her unwillingness to accept the terms of the American Committee inasmuch as they had withdrawn their aid from Miss Powell. Suppose she should finish calmly: "I, too, am a Negro". What would happen? The withdrawal of the assistance without which her trip abroad, its hoped for healing, its broadening horizons would be impossible. Evidently, there was no end to the problems into which this matter of colour could involve one, some of them merely superficial, as in this instance, some of them gravely physical. Her head ached with the futility of trying to find a solution to these interminable puzzles.

As a child she and Jinny had been forbidden to read the five and ten cent literature of their day. But somehow a copy of a mystery story entitled " Who killed Dr. Cronlin? " found its way into their hands, a gruesome story all full of bearded men, hands preserved in alcohol, shadows on window curtains. Shivering with fascination, they had devoured it after midnight or early in the morning while their trusting parents still slumbered. Every page they hoped would disclose the mystery. But their patience went unrewarded for the last sentence of the last page still read: " Who killed Dr. Cronlin? "

Angela thought of it now, and smiled and sighed. " Just what is or is not ethical in this matter of colour? " she asked herself. And indeed it was a nice question. Study at Fontainebleau would have undoubtedly changed Miss Powell's attitude toward life forever. If she had received the just reward for her painstaking study, she would have reasoned that right does triumph in essentials. Moreover the inspiration might have brought out latent talent, new possibilities. Furthermore, granted that Miss Powell had lost out by a stroke of ill-fortune, did that necessarily call for Angela's loss? If so, to what end?

Unable to answer she fell asleep.

Absorbed in preparations she allowed two weeks to pass by, then, remembering Martha's invitation, she went again to the Starr household on an evening when the self-appointed committee was expected to meet. She found Anthony, Mr. Paget, Ladislas and Martha present. The last was more perturbed than ever. Indeed an air of sombre discouragement lay over the whole company.

"Well," asked the newcomer, determined to appear at ease in spite of Anthony's propinquity, "how are things progressing?"

"Not at all," replied Mr. Paget. "Indeed we're about to give up the whole fight."

Ladislas with a sort of provoked amusement explained then that Miss Powell herself had thrown up the sponge. "She's not only withdrawn but she sends us word to-night that while she appreciates the fight we're making she'd rather we'd leave her name out of it."

"Did you ever hear anything to equal that?" snapped Martha crossly. "I wonder if coloured people aren't natural born quitters. Sometimes I think I'll never raise another finger for them."

"You don't know what you're talking about," said Anthony hotly. "If you knew the ceaseless warfare which most coloured people wage, you'd understand that sometimes they have to stop their fight for the trimmings of life in order to hang on to the essentials which they've got to have and for which they must contend too every day just as hard as they did the first day. No, they're not quitters, they've merely learned to let go so they can conserve their strength for another bad day. I'm coloured and I know."

There was a moment's tense silence while the

three white people stared speechless with surprise. Then Martha said in a still shocked voice:
" Coloured! Why, I can't believe it. Why, you
never told us you were coloured."

" Which is precisely why I'm telling you
now," said Anthony, coldly rude. " So you won't
be making off-hand judgments about us." He
started toward the door. " Since the object for
which this meeting has been called has become
null and void I take it that we are automatically
dismissed. Good-night."

Martha hastened after him. " Oh, Mr. Cross,
don't go like that. As though it made any difference! Why should this affect our very real regard
for each other? "

" Why should it indeed? " he asked a trifle
enigmatically. " I'm sure I hope it won't. But I
must go." He left the room, Paget and Ladislas
both hastening on his heels.

Martha stared helplessly after him. " I suppose
I haven't said the right thing. But what could I
do? I was so surprised! " She turned to Angela:
" And I really can't get over his being coloured,
can you? "

" No," said Angela solemnly, " I can't . . ."
and surprised herself and Martha by bursting into
a flood of tears.

.   .   .   .   .

For some reason the incident steadied her determination. Perhaps Anthony was the vicarious
sacrifice, she told herself and knew even as she said
it that the supposition was pure bunk. Anthony
did not consider that he was making a sacrifice;

341

his confession or rather his statement with regard to his blood had the significance of the action of a person who clears his room of rubbish. Anthony did not want his mental chamber strewn with the chaff of deception and confusion. He did not label himself, but on the other hand he indulged every now and then in a general house-cleaning because he would not have the actions of his life bemused and befuddled.

As for Angela she asked for nothing better than to put all the problems of colour and their attendant difficulties behind her. She could not meet those problems in their present form in Europe; literally in every sense she would begin life all over. In France or Italy she would speak of her strain of Negro blood and abide by whatever consequences such exposition would entail. But the consequences could not engender the pain and difficulties attendant upon them here.

Somewhat diffidently she began to consider the idea of going to see Miss Powell. The horns of her dilemma resolved themselves into an unwillingness to parade her own good fortune before her disappointed classmate and an equal unwillingness to depart for France, leaving behind only the cold sympathy of words on paper. And, too, something stronger, more insistent than the mere consideration of courtesy urged her on. After all, this girl was one of her own. A whim of fate had set their paths far apart but just the same they were more than " sisters under the skin." They were really closely connected in blood, in racial condition, in common suffering. Once again she thought of herself as she had years ago when she had seen the coloured girl refused service in the restaurant: "It might so easily have been Virginia."

Without announcement then she betook herself up town to Harlem and found herself asking at the door of the girl's apartment if she might see Miss Powell. The mother whom Angela had last seen so proud and happy received her with a note of sullen bafflement which to the white girl's consciousness connoted: "Easy enough for you, all safe and sound, high and dry, to come and sympathize with my poor child." There was no trace of gratitude or of appreciation of the spirit which had inspired Angela to pay the visit.

To her inquiry Mrs. Powell rejoined: "Yes, I guess you c'n see her. There're three or four other people in there now pesterin' her to death. I guess one mo' won't make no diffunce."

Down a long narrow hall she led her, past two rooms whose dark interiors seemed Stygian in contrast with the bright sunlight which the visitor had just left. But the end of the hall opened into a rather large, light, plain but comfortable dining-room where Miss Powell sat entertaining, to Angela's astonishment, three or four people, all of them white. Her astonishment, however, lessened when she perceived among them John Banky, one of the reporters who had come rather often to interview herself and her plans for France. All of them, she judged angrily, were of his profession, hoping to wring their half column out of Miss Powell's disappointment and embarrassment.

Angela thought she had never seen the girl one half so attractive and exotic. She was wearing a thin silk dress, plainly made but of a flaming red from which the satin blackness of her neck rose, a straight column topped by her squarish, somewhat massive head. Her thin, rather flat dark lips brought into sharp contrast the dazzling perfection of her teeth; her high cheek bones showed a touch of red. To anyone whose ideals of beauty were not already set and sharply limited, she must have made a breathtaking appeal. As long as she sat quiescent in her rather sulky reticence she made a marvellous figure of repose; focussing all the attention of the little assemblage even as her dark skin and hair drew into themselves and retained the brightness which the sun, streaming through three windows, showered upon her.

As soon as she spoke she lost, however, a little of this perfection. For though a quiet dignity persisted, there were pain and bewilderment in her voice and the flat sombreness of utter despair. Clearly she did not know how to get rid of the intruders, but she managed to maintain a poise and aloofness which kept them at their distance. Surely, Angela thought, listening to the stupid, almost impertinent questions put, these things can mean nothing to them. But they kept on with their baiting rather as a small boy keeps on tormenting a lonely and dispirited animal at the Zoo.

" We were having something of an academic discussion with Miss Powell here," said Banky, turning to Angela. " This," he informed his co-workers, " is Miss Mory, one of the prize-winners of the Art Exhibit and a classmate of Miss Powell. I believe Miss Powell was to cross with you,—as—er—your room-mate did you say? "

" No," said Angela, flushing a little for Miss Powell, for she thought she understood the double

meaning of the question, " we weren't intending
to be room-mates. Though so far as I am concerned," she heard herself, to her great surprise,
saying: " I'd have been very glad to share Miss
Powell's state-room if she had been willing." She
wanted to get away from this aspect. " What's
this about an academic discussion? "

Miss Powell's husky, rather mutinous voice
interrupted: " There isn't any discussion, Miss
Mory, academic or otherwise. It seems Mr. Paget
told these gentlemen and Miss Tilden here, that
I had withdrawn definitely from the fight to induce
the Committee for the American Art School
abroad to allow me to take advantage of their
arrangements. So they came up here to get me
to make a statement and I said I had none to
make other than that I was sick and tired of the
whole business and I'd be glad to let it drop.":

" And I," said Miss Tilden, a rangy young lady
wearing an unbecoming grey dress and a peculiarly straight and hideous bob, " asked her if she
weren't really giving up the matter because in her
heart she knew she hadn't a leg to stand on."

Angela felt herself growing hot. Something
within her urged caution, but she answered
defiantly: " What do you mean she hasn't a leg
to stand on? "

" Well, of course, this is awfully plain speaking
and I hope Miss Powell won't be offended,"
resumed Miss Tilden, showing only too plainly
that she didn't care whether Miss Powell were
offended or not, " but after all we do know that
a great many people find the—er—Negroes
objectionable and so of course no self-respecting
one of them would go where she wasn't wanted."

Miss Powell's mother hovering indefinitely in the background, addressing no one in particular, opined that she did not know that "that there committee owned the boat. If her daughter could only afford it she'd show them how quickly she'd go where she wanted and not ask no one no favours either."

"Ah, but," said Miss Tilden judicially, "there's the fallacy. Something else is involved here. There's a social side to this matter, inherent if not expressed. And that *is* the question." She shook a thin bloodless finger at Miss Powell. "Back of most of the efforts which you people make to get into schools and clubs and restaurants and so on, isn't there really this desire for social equality? Come now, Miss Powell, be frank and tell me."

With such sharpness as to draw the attention of everyone in the room Angela said: "Come, Miss Tilden, that's unpardonable and you know it. Miss Powell hadn't a thought in mind about social equality. All she wanted was to get to France and to get there as cheaply as possible."

Banky, talking in a rather affected drawl, confirmed the last speaker. "I think, too, that's a bit too much, Miss Tilden. We've no right to interpret Miss Powell's ideas for her."

A short, red-faced young man intervened: "But just the same *isn't* that the question involved? Doesn't the whole matter resolve itself into this: Has Miss Powell or any other young coloured woman knowing conditions in America the right to thrust her company on a group of people with whom she could have nothing in common except her art? If she stops to think she must realize that not one of the prospective group of students who would be accompanying her on that ship would really welcome her presence. Here's Miss Mory, for instance, a fellow student. What more natural under other circumstances than that she should have made arrangements to travel with Miss Powell? She knows she has to share her cabin with some one. But no; such a thought apparently never entered her head. Why? The answer is obvious. Very well then. If she, knowing Miss Powell, feels this way, how much more would it be the feeling of total strangers?"

A sort of shocked silence fell upon the room. It was an impossible situation. How, thought Angela desperately, knowing the two sides, could she ever explain to these smug, complacent people Miss Powell's ambition, her chilly pride, the remoteness with which she had treated her fellow-students, her only too obvious endeavour to share their training and not their friendship? Hastily, almost crudely, she tried to get something of this over, ashamed for herself ashamed for Miss Powell whose anguished gaze begged for her silence.

At last the coloured girl spoke. " It's wonderful of you to take my part in this way, Miss Mory. I had no idea you understood so perfectly. But don't you see there's no use in trying to explain it? It's a thing which one either does see or doesn't see." She left her soft, full, dark gaze rest for a second on her auditors. "I'm afraid it is not in the power of these persons to grasp what you mean."

The stocky young man grew a little redder. " I think we do understand, Miss Powell. All that Miss Mory says simply confirms my first idea. For otherwise, understanding and sympathizing with you as she does, why has she, for instance, never made any very noticeable attempt to become your friend? Why shouldn't she have asked you to be her side-partner on this trip which I understand you're taking together? There would have been an unanswerable refutation for the committee's arguments. But no, she does nothing even though it means the thwarting for you of a life-time's ambition. Mind, I'm not blaming you, Miss Mory. You are acting in accordance with a natural law. I'm just trying to show Miss Powell here how inevitable the workings of such a law are."

It was foolish reasoning and fallacious, yet containing enough truth to make it sting. Some icy crust which had formed over Angela's heart shifted, wavered, broke and melted. Suddenly it seemed as though nothing in the world were so important as to allay the poignancy of Miss Powell's situation; for this, she determined quixotically, no price would be too dear. She said icily in tones which she had never heard herself use before: "It's true I've never taken any stand hitherto for Miss Powell for I never thought she needed it. But now that the question has come up I want to say that I'd be perfectly willing to share my state-room with her and to give her as much of my company as she could stand. However, that's all out of the question now because Miss Powell isn't going to France on the American Committee Fund and I'm not going either." She stopped a second and added quietly: "And for the same reason."

Someone said in bewilderment: "What do you mean when you say you're not going? And for the same reason?"

"I mean that if Miss Powell isn't wanted, I'm not wanted either. You imply that she's not wanted because she's coloured. Well, I'm coloured too."

One of the men said under his breath, "God, what a scoop!" and reached for his hat. But Banky, his face set and white, held him back.

"I don't believe you know what you're saying, Miss Mory. But anyway, whether it's true or untrue, for God's sake take it back!"

His tone of horror added the last touch. Angela laughed in his face. "Take it back!" She could hardly contain herself. "Do you really think that being coloured is as awful as all that? Can't you see that to my way of thinking it's a great deal better to be coloured and to miss—oh—scholarships and honours and preferments, than to be the contemptible things which you've all shown yourselves to be this morning? Coming here baiting this poor girl and her mother, thrusting your self-assurance down their throats, branding yourselves literally dogs in the manger?" She turned to the coloured girl's mother. "Mrs. Powell, you surely don't want these people here any longer. Have I your permission to show them out?" Crossing the room superbly she opened the door. "This way, please, and don't come back any more. You can rest assured we'll find a way to keep you out."

Silently the little line filed out. Only Miss Tilden, laying her hand on Angela's arm paused to say avidly: "You'll let me come to see you, surely? I can give you some fine publicity, only I must have more data. How about an exclusive interview?"

Angela said stonily: " Mrs. Powell will show you the front door." Then she and her former class-mate stood regarding each other. The dark girl crossed the room and caught her hands and kissed them. " Oh," she said, " it was magnificent —I never guessed it,—but you shouldn't have done it. It's all so unjust, so—silly—and so tiresome. You, of course, only get it when you bring it upon youreslf. But I'm black and I've had it all my life. You don't know the prizes within my grasp that have been snatched away from me again because of colour." She turned as her mother entered the room. " Mother, wasn't she magnificent? "

" She was a fool," Mrs. Powell replied shortly.

Her words brought the exalted Angela back to earth. " Yes," she said, smiling whimsically, " I am just that, a fool. I don't know what possessed me. I'm poor, I was in distress; I wanted a new deal. Now I don't know which way to turn for it. That story will be all over New York by to-morrow morning." She burst out laughing. " Think of my choosing four reporters before whom to make my great confession! " Her hand sought Miss Powell's. " Good-bye, both of you. Don't worry about me. I never dreamed that anything like this could happen, but the mere fact that is has shows that the truth was likely to come out any day. So don't blame yourselves for it. Good-bye."

.　　.　　.　　.　　.

Banky was waiting for her in the vestibule downstairs. " I'm so sorry about the whole damned business, Miss Mory," he said decently. " It's

a damned shame. If there's anything I can
do——"

Rather shortly she said there was nothing.
"And you don't need to worry. As I told you
upstairs, being coloured isn't as awful as all that.
I'll get along." Ignoring his hand she passed by
him into the street. It was Saturday afternoon
so there was a chance of her finding Jinny at
home.

"And if she isn't there I can wait," she told
herself, and thanked God in her heart for the
stability implied in sisterhood.

Jinny was home, mulling happily over the small
affairs which kept her a little girl. Her sister,
looking at the serene loveliness of her face, said
irrelevantly: "You make me feel like an old
woman."

"Well," replied Jinny, "you certainly have the
art of concealing time's ravages, for you not only
look young but you have the manner of someone
who's just found a million dollars. Come in and
tell me about it."

"Found a million dollars! H'm, lost it I
should say!" But a sudden wave of relief and
contentment broke over her. "Oh, Jinny, tell
me, have I been an utter fool! I've thrown away
every chance I've ever had in the world,—just
for a whim." Suddenly close in the full tide of
sisterliness, they sat facing each other on the comfortable couch while Angela told her story. "I
hadn't the faintest idea in the world of telling it.
I was thinking only the other day how lucky I was
compared to Miss Powell, and the first thing I
knew there it all came tripping off my tongue.
But I had to do it. If you could just have seen

those pigs of reporters and Miss Powell's face
under their relentless probing. And old Mrs.
Powell, helpless and grunting and sweating and
thinking me a fool; she told me so, you know.
. . . Why, Jinny, darling, you're not ever crying! Darling, there's nothing to cry about;
what's the matter, Honey!"

"It's because you *are* a fool that I am crying,"
said Jinny sobbing and sniffling, her fingers in her
eyes. "You're a fool and the darlingest girl that
ever lived, and my own precious, lovely, wonderful sister back again. Oh, Angela, I'm so happy.
Tell them to send you your passage money back;
say you don't want anything from them that they
don't want to give; let them go, let them all go
except the ones who like you for yourself. And
dearest, if you don't mind having to skimp a bit for
a year or two and not spreading yourself as you
planned, we'll get you off to Europe after all.
You know I've got all my money from the house.
I've never touched it. You can have as much of
that as you want and pay me back later or not
at all."

Laughing and crying, Angela told her that she
couldn't think of it. "Keep your money for your
marriage, Jinny. It'll be some time before—
Anthony will make any real money, I imagine.
But I will take your advice and go to Europe after
all. All this stuff will be in the paper to-morrow,
I suppose, so I'll write the American Committee
people to-night. As for the prize money, if they
want that back they can have it. But I don't
think they will; nothing was said about Miss
Powell's. That's a thousand dollars. I'll take
that and go to Paris and live as long as I can. If

I can't have the thousand I'll use the few hundreds that I have left and go anyway. And when I come back I'll go back to my old job or—go into the schools. But all that's a long way off and we don't know what might turn up."

There were one or two matters for immediate consideration. The encounter with the reporters had left Angela a little more shaken than was at first apparent. "I don't want to run into them again," she said ruefully. Her lease on the little apartment in Jayne Street had still a month to run. She would go down this very evening, get together her things, and return to Jinny, with whom she would live quietly until it was time for her to sail. Her mail she could leave with the janitor to be called for. Fortunately the furniture was not hers; there were only a few pictures to be removed. After all, she had very few friends to consider,— just the Sandburgs, Martha Burden, Mrs. Denver, Ralph Ashley and Rachel Salting.

"And I don't know what to do about them," she said, pondering. "After all, you can't write to people and say: ' Dear friend:—You've always thought I was white. But I'm not really. I'm coloured and I'm going back to my own folks to live.' Now can you? Oh, Jinny, Jinny, isn't it a great old world? "

In the end, after the story appeared, as it assuredly did, in the next morning's paper, she cut out and sent to each of her former friends copies of Miss Tilden's story whose headlines read: " Socially Ambitious Negress Confesses to Long Hoax."

With the exception of Banky's all the accounts took the unkindest attitude possible. The young Hungarian played up the element of self-sacrifice and the theory that blood after all was thicker than water. Angela guessed rightly that if he could have he would have preferred omitting it, and that he had only written it up to offset as far as possible the other accounts. Of the three other meanly insinuating stories Miss Tilden's was the silliest and most dangerous. She spoke of mixed blood as the curse of the country, a curse whose "insidiously concealed influence constantly threatens the wells of national race purity. Such incidents as these make one halt before he condemns the efforts of the Ku Klux Klan and its unceasing fight for 100 per cent. Americanism."

The immediate effect of this publicity was one which neither of the sisters had foreseen. When Angela reported for work on the following Monday morning she found a note on her desk asking her immediate appearance in the office. The president returning her good-morning with scant courtesy, showed her a clipping and asked if she were the Miss Mory of the story. Upon her assurance that she was none other, he handed her a month's salary in lieu of notice and asked her to consider her connection with the firm at an end.

"We have no place for deceit in an institution such as this," he said augustly.

The incident shook both girls to a degree. Virginia particularly was rendered breathless by its cruel immediacy. Never before had she come so close to the special variation of prejudice manifested to people in Angela's position. That the president of the concern should attribute the girl's reticence on this subject to deceit seemed to her the last ounce of injustice. Angela herself was far less perturbed.

" I've seen too much of this sort of thing to feel it as you do, Virginia. Of course, as you see, there are all kinds of absurdities involved. In your case, showing colour as you do, you'd have been refused the job at the very outset. Perhaps they would have said that they had found coloured people incompetent or that other girls had a strong natural aversion toward working beside one of us. Now here I land the position, hold it long enough to prove ability and the girls work beside me and remain untainted. So evidently there's no blind inherent disgust to be overcome. Looking just the same as I've ever looked I let the fact of my Negro ancestry be known. Mind, I haven't changed the least bit, but immediately there's all this holding up of hands and the cry of deceit is raised. Some logic, that! It really would be awfully funny, you see, Jinny, if it couldn't be fraught with such disastrous consequences for people like, say, Miss Powell."

" Don't mention her," said Jinny vehemently. " If it hadn't been for her you wouldn't have been in all this trouble."

Angela smiled. " If it hadn't been for her, you and I probably never would have really found each other again. But you mustn't blame her. Sooner or later I'd have been admitting,—' confessing ', as the papers say,—my black blood. Not that I myself think it of such tremendous importance; in spite of my efforts to break away I really don't, Virginia. But because this country of ours makes it so important, against my own conviction

I was beginning to feel as though I were laden down with a great secret. Yet when I begin to delve into it, the matter of blood seems nothing compared with individuality, character, living. The truth of the matter is, the whole business was just making me fagged to death."

She sat lost intently in thought. " All of the complications of these last few years,—and you can't guess what complications there have been, darling child,—have been based on this business of ' passing '. I understand why Miss Powell gave up the uneven fight about her passage. Of course, in a way it would have been a fine thing if she could have held on, but she was perfectly justified in letting go so she could avoid still greater bitterness and disappointment and so she could have something left in her to devote to her art. You can't fight and create at the same time. And I understand, too, why your Anthony bestirs himself every little while and makes *his* confession; simply so he won't have to be bothered with the trappings of pretence and watchfulness. I suppose he told you about that night down at Martha Burden's? "

" Yes," said Jinny, sighing, " he has terrible ideals. There's something awfully lofty about Anthony. I wish he were more like Matthew, comfortable and homey. Matt's got some ideals, too, but he doesn't work them overtime. Anthony's a darling, two darlings, but he's awfully, awfully what-do-you-call-it, ascetic. I shouldn't be at all surprised but what he had a secret canker eating at his heart."

Angela said rather sternly, " Look here, Jinny, I don't believe you love him after all, do you? "

" Well now, when I get right down to it sometimes I think I do. Sometimes I think I don't. Of
course the truth of the matter is, I'd hardly have
thought about Anthony or marriage either just
now, if I hadn't been so darn lonely. You know
I'm not like you, Angela. When we were children
I was the one who was going to have a career,
and you were always going to have a good time.
Actually it's the other way round; you're the
one who's bound to have a career. You just
gravitate to adventure. There's something so
forceful and so strong about you that you can't
keep out of the battle. But, Angela, I want a
home,—with you if you could just stand still long
enough, or failing that, a home with husband and
children and all that goes with it. Of course I
don't mind admitting that at any time I'd have
given up even you for Matthew. But next to being
his wife I'd rather live with you, and next to that
I'd like to marry Anthony. I don't like to be
alone; for though I can fend for myself I don't
want to."

Angela felt herself paling with the necessity of
hiding her emotion. " So poor Anthony's only
third in your life? "

" Yes, I'm afraid he is . . . Darling, what do
you say to scallops for dinner? I feel like cooking
to-day. Guess I'll hie me to market."

She left the room, and her sister turned to the large
photograph of Cross which Virginia kept on the
mantel. She put her fingers on the slight youthful
hollows of his pictured cheeks, touched his pictured
brow. " Oh Anthony, Anthony, is Life cheating
you again? You'll always be first in my life,
dearest."

357

Perhaps Virginia's diagnosis of her character was correct. At any rate she welcomed the present combination of difficulties through which she was now passing. Otherwise this last confession of Jinny's would have plunged her into fresh unhappiness. But she had many adjustments to make and to face. First of all there was her new status in the tiny circle in which she had moved. When at the end of two weeks she went down to her old apartment in Jayne Street to ask for her mail, she was, in spite of herself amazed and hurt to discover a chilled bewilderment, an aloofness, in the manner of Mrs. Denver, with whom she had a brief encounter. On the other hand there were a note and a calling card from Martha Burden, and some half dozen letters from Elizabeth and Walter Sandburg.

Martha's note ran: " Undoubtedly you and Mr. Cross are very fine people. But I don't believe I could stand another such shock very soon. Of course it was magnificent of you to act as you did. But oh, my dear, how quixotic. And after all *à quoi bon?* Will you come to see me as soon as you get this, or send me word how I may see you? And Angèle, if you let all this nonsense interfere with your going to Europe I'll never forgive you. Ladislas and I have several thousand dollars stored away just begging to be put out at interest."

Elizabeth Sandburg said nothing about the matter, but Angela was able to read her knowledge between the lines. The kind-hearted couple could not sufficiently urge upon her their unchanging regard and friendship. " Why on earth don't you come and see us? " Elizabeth queried in her immense, wandering chirography, five words to a page. " You can't imagine how we miss you. Walter's actually getting off his feed. Do take a moment from whatever masterpiece you're composing and give us a week-end."

But from Rachel Salting and from Ashley not one single word !

CHAPTER II

MORE than ever her determination to sail became
fixed. "Some people," she said to Jinny, "might
think it the thing to stay here and fight things out.
Martha, for instance, is keenly disappointed
because I won't let the committee which had been
working for Miss Powell take up my case. I suspect she thinks we're all quitters. But I know
when I've had enough. I told her I wanted to
spend my life doing something besides fighting.
Moreover, the Committee, like myself, is pretty
sick of the whole affair, though not for the same
reason, and I think there'd be even less chance
for a readjustment in my case than there was in
Miss Powell's."

An interview with Clarke Otter, Chairman of
the Advisory Board of the American Committee,
had given her this impression. Mr. Otter's
attitude betokened a curious admixture of resentment at what he seemed to consider her
deceit in "passing" and exasperation at her
having been quixotic enough to give the show
away. "We think you are quite right in expressing your determination not to take advantage
of the Committee's arrangements. It evidences
a delicacy of feeling quite unusual in the circumstances." Angela was boiling with anger when
she left.

A letter to the donor of the prize brought back the laconic answer that the writer was interested "not in Ethnology but in Art."

"I'd like to see that party," said Angela, reverting to the jargon of her youth. "I'll bet he's nowhere near as stodgy as he sounds. I shouldn't wonder but what he was just bubbling over with mirth at the silliness of it all."

Certainly she herself was bubbling over with mirth or with what served for that quality. Virginia could not remember ever having seen her in such high spirits, not since the days when they used to serve Monday's dinner for their mother and play at the *rôles* in which Mrs. Henrietta Jones had figured so largely. But Angela herself knew the shallowness of that mirth whose reality, Anthony, unable to remain for any length of time in her presence and yet somehow unable to stay away, sometimes suspected.

Her savings, alas! including the prize money, amounted roughly to 1,400 dollars. Anthony had urged her to make the passage second class on one of the large, comfortable boats. Then, if she proved herself a good sailor, she might come back third class.

"And anyway don't put by any more than enough for that," said Jinny maternally, "and if you need any extra money write to me and I'll send you all you want."

From stories told by former foreign students who had sometimes visited the Union it seemed as though she might stretch her remaining hundreds over a period of eight or nine months. "And by that time I'll have learned enough to know whether

I'm to be an honest-to-God artist or a plain drawing teacher."

" I almost hope it will be the latter," said Jinny
with a touching selfishness, " so you'll have to
come back and live with us. Don't you hope so,
Anthony? "

Angela could see him wince under the strain
of her sister's artlessness. " Eight or nine months
abroad ought to make a great difference in her
life," he said with no particular relevance. " Indeed in the lives of all of us." Both he and Angela
had only one thought these days, that the time for
departure would have to arrive. Neither of them
had envisaged the awfulness of this pull on their
self-control.

．　　　　．　　　　．　　　　．　　　　．

Now there were only five days before her
departure on Monday. She divided them among
the Sandburgs, Anthony and Jinny who was
coming down with a summer cold. On Saturday
the thought came to her that she would like to
see Philadelphia again; it was a thought so persistent that by nine o'clock she was in the train
and by 11.15 she was preparing for bed in a
small side-room in the Hotel Walton in the city
of her birth. Smiling, she fell asleep vaguely
soothed by the thought of being so close to all
that had been once the scene of her steady, un-
checked life.

The propinquity was to shake her more than she
could dream.

In the morning she breakfasted in her room,
then coming downstairs stood in the portico of

the hotel drawing on her gloves as she had done so many years before when she had been a girl shopping with her mother. A flood of memories rushed over her, among them the memory of that day when her father and Virginia had passed them on the street and they had not spoken. How trivial the reason for not speaking seemed now! In later years she had cut Jinny for a reason equally trivial.

She walked up toward Sixteenth Street. It was Sunday and the beautiful melancholy of the day was settling on the quiet city. There was a freshness and a solemnity in the air as though even the atmosphere had been rarified and soothed. A sense of loneliness invaded her; this was the city of her birth, of her childhood and of most of her life. Yet there was no one, she felt, to whom she could turn this beautiful day for a welcome; old acquaintances might be mildly pleased, faintly curious at seeing her, but none of them would show any heart-warming gladness. She had left them so abruptly, so completely. Well, she must not think on these things. After all, in New York she had been lonely too.

The Sixteenth Street car set her down at Jefferson Street and slowly she traversed the three long blocks. Always quiet, always respectable, they were doubly so in the sanctity of Sunday morning. What a terrible day Sunday could be without friends, ties, home, family. Only five years ago, less than five years, she had had all the simple, stable fixtures of family life, the appetizing breakfast, the music, the church with its interesting, paintable types, long afternoons and evenings with visitors and discussions beating in the void.

And Matthew Henson, would he, she wondered, give her welcome? But she thought that still she did not want to see him. She was not happy, but she was not through adventuring, through tasting life. And she knew that a life spent with Matthew Henson would mean a cessation of that. After all, was he, with his steadiness, his uprightness, his gift for responsibility any happier than she? She doubted it.

Oh, she hoped Sundays in Paris would be gay!

Opal Street came into her vision, a line, a mere shadow of a street falling upon the steadfastness of Jefferson. Her heart quickened, tears came into her eyes as she turned that corner which she had turned so often, that corner which she had once left behind her forever in order to taste and know life. In the hot July sun the street lay almost deserted. A young coloured man, immaculate in white shirt sleeves, slim and straight, bending in his doorway to pick up the bulky Sunday paper, straightened up to watch her advancing toward him. Just this side of him stood her former home,—how tiny it was and yet how full of secrets, of knowledge of joy, despair, suffering, futility—in brief Life! She stood a few moments in front of it, just gazing, but presently she went up and put her hand on the red brick, wondering blindly if in some way the insensate thing might not communicate with her through touch. A coloured woman sitting in the window watching her rather sharply, came out then and asked her suspiciously what she wanted.

"Nothing," Angela replied dully. "I just wanted to look at the house."

" It isn't for sale, you know."

" No, no, of course not. I just wanted to look at it again. I used to live here, you see. I wondered——" Even if she did get permission to go inside, could she endure it? If she could just stand once in that little back room and cry and cry—perhaps her tears would flood away all that mass of regret and confusion and futile memories, and she could begin life all over with a blank page. Thank God she was young! Suddenly it seemed to her that entering the house once more, standing in that room would be a complete panacea. Raising her eyes expectantly to the woman's face she began: " Would you be so kind——? "

But the woman, throwing her a last suspicious look and muttering that she was " nothing with poor white trash," turned and, slamming the door behind her, entered the little square parlour and pulled down the blinds.

•   •   •   •   •

The slim young man came running down the street toward her. Closer inspection revealed his ownership of a pleasant brown freckled face topped by thick, soft, rather closely cropped dark-red hair.

" Angela," he said timidly, and then with more assurance: " It *is* Angela Murray."

She turned her stricken face toward him. " She wouldn't let me in, Matthew. I'm going to France to-morrow and I thought I'd like to see the old house. But she wouldn't let me look at it. She called me,"—her voice broke with the injustice of it,—" poor white trash."

365

"I know," he nodded gravely. "She'd do that kind of thing; she doesn't understand, you see." He was leading her gently toward his house. "I think you'd better come inside and rest a moment. My father and mother have gone off for their annual trip to Bridgeton; mother was born there, you know. But you won't mind coming into the house of an old and tried friend."

"No," she said, conscious of an overwhelming fatigue and general sense of let-downness, "I should say I wouldn't." As they crossed the threshold she tried faintly to smile but the effort was too much for her and she burst into a flood of choking, strangling, noisy tears.

Matthew removed her hat and fanned her; brought her ice-water and a large soft handkerchief to replace her own sodden wisp. Through her tears she smiled at him, understanding as she did so, the reason for Virginia's insistence on his general niceness. He was still Matthew Henson, still freckled and brown, still·capped·with that thatch of thick bad hair. But care and hair-dressings and improved toilet methods and above all the emanation of a fine and generous spirit had metamorphosed him into someone still the old Matthew Henson and yet someone somehow translated into a quintessence of kindliness and gravity and comprehending.

She drank the water gratefully, took out her powder puff.

"I don't need to ask you how you are," he said, uttering a prayer of thanks for averted hysterics. "When a lady begins to powder her nose, she's bucking up all right. Want to tell me all about it?"

366

" There's nothing to tell. Only I wanted to see the house and suddenly found myself unexpectedly homesick, lonely, misunderstood. And when that woman refused me so cruelly, it was just too much." Her gaze wavered, her eyes filled again.

" Oh," he said in terror, " for God's sake don't cry again! I'll go over and give her a piece of my mind; I'll make her turn the whole house over to you. I'll bring you her head on a charger. Only 'dry those tears'." He took her handkerchief and dried them himself very, very gently.

She caught his hand. " Matthew, you're a dear."

He shrugged negligently, " You haven't always thought that."

This turn of affairs would never do. " What were you planning to do when I barged in? Getting ready to read your paper and be all homey and comfortable? "

" Yes, but I don't want to do that now. Tell you what, Angela, Let's have a lark. Suppose we have dinner here? you get it. Remember how it used to make me happy as a king in the old days if you'd just hand me a glass of water? You said you were sailing to-morrow; you must be all packed. What time do you have to be back? I'll put you on the train."

The idea enchanted her. " I'd love it! Matthew, what fun! " They found an apron of his mother's, and in the ice-box, cold roast beef, lettuce which Philadelphians call salad, beets and corn. " I'll make muffins," said Angela joyously, " and you take a dish after dinner and go out and get some ice-cream. Oh, Matthew, how it's all coming back to me! Do you still shop up here in the market?"

They ate the meal in the little dark cool dining-room, the counterpart of the dining-room in Junius Murray's one-time house across the way. But somehow its smallness was no longer irksome; rather it seemed a tiny island of protection reared out of and against an encroaching sea of troubles. In fancy she saw her father and mother almost a quarter of a century ago coming proudly to such a home, their little redoubt of refuge against the world. How beautiful such a life could be, shared with some one beloved,—with Anthony! Involuntarily she sighed.

Matthew studying her thoughtfully said: "You're dreaming, Angela. Tell me what it's all about."

"I was thinking what a little haven a house like this could be; what it must have meant to my mother. Funny how I almost pounded down the walls once upon a time trying to get away. Now I can't think of anything more marvellous than having such a place as this, here, there, anywhere, to return to."

Startled, he told her of his surprise at hearing such words from her. "If Virginia had said them I should think it perfectly natural; but I hadn't thought of you as being interested in home. How, by the way, is Virginia?"

"Perfect."

With a wistfulness which barely registered with her absorption, he queried: "I suppose she's tremendously happy?"

"Happy enough."

" A great girl, little Virginia." In his turn
he fell to musing, roused himself. " You haven't
told me of your adventures and your flight into
the great world."

" There's not much to tell, Matthew. All I've
seen and experienced has been the common fate
of most people, a little sharpened, perhaps, a
little vivified. Briefly, I've had a lot of fun and a
measure of trouble. I've been stimulated by
adventure; I've known suffering and love and
pain."

" You're still surprising me. I didn't suppose a
girl like you could know the meaning of pain."
He gave her a twisted smile. " Though you certainly know how to cause it. Even yet I can get
a pang which no other thought produces if I let
my mind go back to those first few desperate
days after you left me. Heavens, can't you suffer
when you're young ! "

She nodded, laid her hand on his. " Terribly. Remember, I was suffering too, Matthew,
though for different causes. I was so pushed, so
goaded . . . well, we won't talk about that any
more. . . . I hope you've got over all that
feeling. Indeed, indeed I wasn't worth it. Do
tell me you haven't let it harass you all these
years."

His hand clasped hers lightly, then withdrew.
" No I haven't. . . . The suddenness, the in-
evitableness of your departure checked me, pulled
me up short. I suffered, oh damnably, but it was
suffering with my eyes open. I knew then you
weren't for me; that fundamentally we were too
far apart. And eventually I got over it. Those
days ! " He smiled again wryly, recalling a

memory. "But I went on suffering just the same, only in another way. I fell in love with Jinny."

Her heart in her breast stopped beating. "Matthew, you didn't! Why on earth didn't you ever say so?"

"I couldn't. She was such a child, you see; she made it so plain all the time that she looked on me as her sister's beau and therefore a kind of dependable brother. After you went I used to go to see her, take her about. Why she'd swing on my arm and hold up her face for a good-night kiss! Once, I remember, we had been out and she became car-sick,—poor little weak thing! She was so ashamed! Like a baby, you know, playing at being grown-up and then ashamed for reverting to babyhood. I went to see her the next day and she was so little and frail and confiding! I stayed away then for a long time and the next thing I knew she, was going to New York. I misjudged you awfully then, Angela. You must forgive me. I thought you had pulled her away. I learned later that I was wrong, that you and she rarely saw each other in New York. Do you know why she left?"

There was her sister's pride to shield but her own need to succour; who could have dreamed of such a dilemma? "I can't betray Jinny," she said to herself and told him that while she personally had not influenced her sister the latter had had a very good reason for leaving Philadelphia.

"I suppose so. Certainly she left. But she'd write me, occasionally, letters just like her dear self, so frank and girlish and ingenuous and making it so damnably plain that any demonstration of love on my part was out of the question. I said to myself: ' I'm not going to wreck my whole life over those Murray girls '. And I let our friendship drift off into a nothingness. . . . Then she came to visit Edna Brown this summer. I fairly leaped out to Merion to see her. The moment I laid eyes on her I realized that she had developed, had become a woman. She was as always, kind and sweet, prettier, more alluring than ever. I thought I'd try my luck . . . . and Edna told me she was engaged. What's the fellow like, Angela? "

" Very nice, very fine."

" Wild about her, I suppose? "

Desperately she looked at him. "He's a rather undemonstrative sort. I suppose he's wild enough. Only,—well they talk as though they had no intention of marrying for years and years and they both seem perfectly content with that arrangement."

He frowned incredulously. " What! If I thought they weren't in earnest! "

Impulsively she broke out: " Oh, Matthew, don't you know,—there's so much pain, such suffering in the world,—a man should never leave any stone unturned to achieve his ultimate happiness. Why don't you—write to Jinny, go to New York to see her? "

Under his freckles his brown skin paled. " You think there's a chance? "

" My dear, I wouldn't dare say. I know she likes you very, very much. And I don't think she regards you as a brother."

" Angela, you wouldn't fool me? "

" Why should I do that? And remember after all I'm giving you no assurance. I'm merely saying it's worth taking a chance. Now let's see, we'll straighten up this place and then we must fly."

At the station she kissed him good-bye. " Anyway you're always a brother to me. Think of what I've told you, Matthew; act on it."

" I shall. Oh, Angela, suppose it should be that God sent you down here to-day? "

" Perhaps He did." They parted solemnly.

Three hours later found her entering her sister's apartment. Jinny, her cold raging, her eyes inflamed and weeping, greeted her plaintively. " Look at me, Angela. And you leaving to-morrow! I'll never be able to make that boat!" The telephone rang. " It's been ringing steadily for the last hour, somebody calling for you. Do answer it."

The message was from Ashley. He had been away in New Orleans. " And I came back and found that clipping. I knew you sent it. Girl, the way I've pursued you this day! Finally I caught up with Martha Burden, she told me where you were staying. May I come up? Be there in half an hour."

" Not to-night, Ralph. Would you like to come to the boat to-morrow? "

" So you're going anyhow? Bully! But not before I've seen you! Suppose I take you to the boat? "

" Awfully nice of you, but I'm going with my sister,"

Here Jinny in a voice full of misplaced consonants told her she was going to do nothing of the sort. " With this cold! "

Angela spoke into the receiver again. " My sister says she isn't going, so I will fall back on you if I may." She hung up.

Virginia wanted to hear of the trip. The two sisters sat talking far into the night, but Angela said no word about Matthew.

.   .   .   .   .

Monday was a day of surprises. Martha and Ladislas Starr, unable to be on hand for the sailing of the boat, came up to the house to drive down town with the departing traveller. Secretly Angela was delighted with this arrangement, but it brought a scowl to Ashley's face.

Virginia, miserable with the wretchedness attendant on a summer cold, bore up bravely. " I don't mind letting you go like this from the house; but I couldn't stand the ship! Angela, you're not to worry about me one bit. Only come back to me,—happy. I know you will. Oh how different this is from that parting years ago in Philadelphia! "

" Yes," said Angela soberly. " Then I was to be physically ninety miles away from you, but we were really seas apart. Now—darling, three thousand miles are nothing when there is love and trust and understanding. And Jinny, listen! Life is full of surprises. If a chance for real happiness comes your way don't be afraid to grasp at it."

" Cryptic," wheezed Jinny, laughing. " I don't know what you're talking about, but I'll do my best to land any happiness that comes drifting toward me." They kissed each other gravely, almost coldly, without tears. But neither could trust herself to say the actual good-bye.

Angela was silent almost all the way down to the dock, answering her friends only in mono-syllables. There, another surprise awaited her in the shape of Mrs. Denver, who remained, how-ever, only for a few moments. " I couldn't stand having you go," she said pitifully, "without seeing you for one last time." And, folding the girl in a close embrace, she broke down and murmured sadly of a lost daughter who would have been " perhaps like you, dear, had she lived."

Elizabeth Sandburg, the gay, the complacent, the beloved of life, clung to her, weeping, " I can't bear to lose you, Angèle." Walter put his arm about her. " Kiss me, old girl. And mind, if you need anything, *anything*, you're to call on us. If you get sick we'll come over after you,—am I right, Lizzie? "

" Yes, of course, of course . . . and don't call me Lizzie. . . . Come away, can't you, and leave them a moment together. Don't you see Ashley glaring at you? "

They withdrew to a good point of vantage on the dock.

Angela, surprised and weeping, remembering both Mrs. Denver's words and the manifestations of kindness in her stateroom said: " They really did love me after all, didn't they? "

" Yes," said Ashley earnestly, " we all love you. I'm coming over to see you by and by, Angèle, may I? You know we've a lot of things to talk about, some things which you perhaps think mean a great deal to me but which in reality mean nothing. Then on the other hand there are some matters which actually do mean something to me but whose value to you I'm not sure of."

"Oh," she said, wiping her eyes and remembering her former secret. "You aren't coming over to ask me to marry you, are you? You don't have to do that. And anyway ' it is not now as it hath been before'. There's no longer a mystery about me, you know. So the real attraction's gone. Remember, I'm not expecting a thing of you, so please, please don't ask it. Ralph, I can't placard myself, and I suppose there will be lots of times when in spite of myself I'll be ' passing '. But I want you to know that from now on, so far as sides are concerned, I am on the coloured side. And I don't want you to come over on that side." She shook her head finally. "Too many complications even for you."

For though she knew he believed in his brave words, she was too sadly experienced to ask an American to put them to the test.

"All right," he said, smiling at her naïve assumptions. "I won't ask you to marry me,— at least not yet. But I'm coming over just the same. I don't suppose you've got a lien on Paris."

"Of course I haven't," she giggled a little. "You know perfectly well I want you to come." Her face suddenly became grave. "But if you do come you won't come to make love without meaning anything either, will you? I'd hate that between you and me."

" No," he said gently, instantly comprehending.
" I won't do that either."

" You'll come as a friend? "

" Yes, as a friend."

A deck hand came up then and said civilly that
in a few minutes they would be casting off and all
visitors must go ashore.

CHAPTER III

AMONG her steamer-letters was a brief note from Anthony:

" Angela, my angel, my dear girl, good-bye. These last few weeks have been heaven and hell. I couldn't bear to see you go,—so I've taken myself off for a few hours . . . don't think I'll neglect Jinny. I'll never do that. Am I right in supposing that you still care a little? Oh Angela, try to forget me,—but don't do it! I shall never forget you! "

There were letters and flowers from the Burdens, gifts of all sorts from Ashley and Mrs. Denver, a set of notes for each day out from Virginia. She read letters, examined her gifts and laid them aside. But all day long Anthony's note reposed on her heart; it lay at night beneath her head.

.   .   .   .   .   .

Paris at first charmed and wooed her. For a while it seemed to her that her old sense of joy in living for living's sake had returned to her. It was like those first few days which she had spent in exploring New York. She rode delightedly in the motor-buses on and on to the unknown, unpredictable terminus; she followed the winding Seine; crossing and re-crossing the bridges each

377

with its distinctive characteristics. Back of the Panthéon, near the church of St. Geneviève she discovered a Russian restaurant where strange, exotic dishes were served by tall blond waiters in white, stiff Russian blouses. One day, wandering up the Boulevard du Mont Parnasse, she found at its juncture with the Boulevard Raspail the Café Dome, a student restaurant of which many returned students had spoken in the Art School in New York. On entering she was recognized almost immediately by Edith Martin, a girl who had studied with her in Philadelphia.

Miss Martin had lived in Paris two years; knew all the gossip and the characters of the Quarter; could give Angela points on pensions, cafés, tips and the Gallic disposition. On all these topics she poured out perpetually a flood of information, presented her friends, summoned the new comer constantly to her studio or camped uninvited in the other girl's tiny quarters at the Pension Franciana. There was no chance for actual physical loneliness, yet Angela thought after a few weeks of persistent comradeship that she had never felt so lonely in her life. For the first time in her adventuresome existence she was caught up in a tide of homesickness. ·

Then this passed too with the summer, and she found herself by the end of September engrossed in her work. She went to the Academy twice a day, immersed herself in the atmosphere of the Louvre and the gallery of the Luxembourg. It was hard work, but gradually she schooled herself to remember that this was her life, and that her aim, her one ambition, was to become an acknow-ledged, a significant painter of portraits. The instructor, renowned son of a still more renowned father, almost invariably praised her efforts.

With the coming of the fall the sense of adventure left her. Paris, so beautiful in the summer, so gay with its thronging thousands, its hosts bent on pleasure, took on another garb in the sullen greyness of late autumn. The tourists disappeared and the hard steady grind of labour, the intent application to the business of living, so noticeable in the French, took the place of a transient, careless freedom. Angela felt herself falling into line; but it was good discipline as she herself realized. Once or twice, in periods of utter loneliness or boredom, she let her mind dwell on her curiously thwarted and twisted life. But the ability for self-pity had vanished. She had known too many others whose lives lay equally remote from goals which had at first seemed so certain. For a period she had watched feverishly for the incoming of foreign mail, sure that some word must come from Virginia about Matthew, but the months crept sullenly by and Jinny's letters remained the same artless missives prattling of school-work, Anthony, Sara Penton, the Movies and visits to Maude the inimitable.

"Of course not everything can come right," she told herself. Matthew evidently had, on second thought, deemed it wisest to consult the evidence of his own senses rather than be guided by the hints which in the nature of things she could offer only vaguely.

Within those six months she lost forever the blind optimism of youth. She did not write Anthony nor did she hear from him.

Christmas Eve day dawned or rather drifted greyly into the beholder's perception out of the black mistiness of the murky night. In spite of herself her spirits sank steadily. Virginia had promised her a present,—" I've looked all over this whole town," she wrote, " to find you something good enough, something absolutely perfect. Anthony's been helping me. And at last I've found it. We've taken every possible precaution against the interference of wind or rain or weather, and unless something absolutely unpredictable intervenes, it will be there for you Christmas Eve or possibly the day before. But remember, don't open it until Christmas."

But it was now six o'clock on Christmas Eve and no present had come, no letter, no remembrance of any kind. " Oh," she said to herself, " what a fool I was to come so far away from home!" For a moment she envisaged the possibility of throwing herself on the bed and sobbing her heart out. Instead she remembered Edith Martin's invitation to make a night of it over at her place, a night which was to include dancing and chaffing, a trip just before midnight to hear Mass at St. Sulpice, and a return to the studio for doubtless more dancing and jesting and laughter, and possibly drunkenness on the part of the American male.

At ten o'clock as she stood in her tiny room rather sullenly putting the last touches to her costume, the maid, Héloise, brought her a cable. It was a long message from Ashley wishing her health, happiness and offering to come over at a week's notice. Somehow the bit of blue paper cheered her, easing her taut nerves.

"Of course they're thinking about me. I'll hear from Jinny any moment; it's not her fault that the delivery is late. I wonder what she sent me."

Returning at three o'clock Christmas morning from the party she put her hand cautiously in the door to switch on the light for fear that a package lay near the threshold, but there was no package there. "Well, even if it were there I couldn't open it," she murmured, "for I'm too sleepy." And indeed she had drugged herself with dancing and gaiety into an overwhelming drowsiness. Barely able to toss aside her pretty dress, she tumbled luxuriously into bed, grateful in the midst of her somnolence for the fatigue which would make her forget. . . . In what seemed to her less than an hour, she heard a tremendous knocking at the door.

"*Entrez,*" she called sleepily and relapsed immediately into slumber. The door, as it happened, was unlocked; she had been too fatigued to think of it the night before. Héloise stuck in a tousled head. "My God," she told the cook afterwards, "such a time as I had to wake her! There she was asleep on both ears and the gentleman downstairs waiting!"

Angela finally opened bewildered eyes. "A gentleman," reiterated Héloise in her staccato tongue. "He awaits you below. He says he has a present which he must put into your own hands. Will Mademoiselle then descend or shall I tell him to come back?"

"Tell him to come back," she murmured, then opened her heavy eyes. "Is it really Christmas, Héloise? Where is the gentleman?"

" As though I had him there in my pocket," said Héloise later in her faithful report to the cook.

But finally the message penetrated. Grasping a robe and slippers, she half leaped, half fell down the little staircase and plunged into the five foot square drawing-room. Anthony sitting on the tremendously disproportionate tan and maroon sofa rose to meet her.

His eyes on her astonished countenance, he began searching about in his pockets, slapping his vest, pulling out keys and handkerchiefs. " There ought to be a tag on me somewhere," he remarked apologetically, " but anyhow Virginia and Matthew sent me with their love."

THE END

ImTheStory.com

Personalized Classic Books in many genre's

Unique gift for kids, partners, friends, colleagues

Customize:

- Character Names
- Upload your own front/back cover images (optional)
- Inscribe a personal message/dedication on the inside page (optional)

Customize many titles Including

- Alice in Wonderland
- Romeo and Juliet
- The Wizard of Oz
- A Christmas Carol
- Dracula
- Dr. Jekyll & Mr. Hyde
- And more...